Praise for
THE OTHER SIDE OF THE RIVER

Evocative and beautifully written.

**Craig Chalquist, author *Terrapsychology* and
Professor in Ecopsychology**

This book is an instant classic for the new paradigm.

**Lucia Chivola Birnbaum, award-winning author
and Professor Emeritus in Women's Spirituality**

*Beautiful, important, wise work! This is fluid writing . . . Eila
deftly transitions between matters of family, culture, race, geography,
mind and body. The river is a wonderful metaphor.*

Carolyn Cooke, author *Amor and Psycho*

*Eila's words flow as water, and these stories quench the thirsty soul
like a much-needed walk to the river.*

**Viviane Dzyak, PhD,
Professor in Women's Spirituality**

What you hold in your hands is not just a book, but a mytho-poetic portal. A portal into the humble truths and sacred ecstasies of one woman's journey into the elemental, eternal and everyday mysteries of Life. It is also a vast and wise articulation of all of humanity's great work in this raw and potent time on the Earth.

We are living in a crucial epoch, a time of radical culture change and evolution. We need to prioritize the feminine values of poetry and beauty, of magic and soul. Eila's book shows us the way, her words weaving a watery and wonderful spell. Her affinity for water as the great primal connector and conductor of life force seeps out of every page and you will find yourself remembering ancient truths of belonging and destiny.

If you are one who has come to re-imagine and create the world anew, you will find your own journey and soul illuminated and inspired with each page you turn. The world is aching for a new paradigm and this book is a delicious, intelligent and elegant feast for our hungering hearts.

**Holly Hamilton, PhD, Teacher, Priestess,
Founder, Awakening Avalon School of Earth
Wisdom**

The Other Side of the River

Stories of Women, Water and the World

ALSO FROM WOMANCRAFT PUBLISHING

The Heart of the Labyrinth—Nicole Schwab

Moods of Motherhood: the inner journey of mothering—Lucy H. Pearce

Moon Time: harness the ever-changing energy of your menstrual cycle—Lucy H. Pearce

Reaching for the Moon—Lucy H. Pearce

The Other Side of the River

Stories of Women,
Water and the World

Eila Kundrie Carrico

Womancraft
PUBLISHING

Life-changing, paradigm-shifting books
by women, for women

The Other Side of the River

© Eila Kundrie Carrico 2015

Cover art © Leah Dorion
Cover design by LucentWord.com

Extended quotations used with the express permission of their authors. If you feel a permission has not been sought, we will be happy to rectify this.

Some names and identifying characteristics have been changed to protect the privacy of the individuals involved.

Published by Womancraft Publishing, 2015
www.womancraftpublishing.com

ISBN: 978-1910559-109 (paperback)
ISBN: 978-1910559-116 (Kindle)

A percentage of Womancraft Publishing profits are invested back into the environment reforesting the tropics (via TreeSisters) and forward into the community: providing books for girls in developing countries, and affordable libraries for red tents and women's groups around the world.

Womancraft Publishing is committed to sharing powerful new women's voices, through a collaborative publishing process. We are proud to midwife this work, however the story, the experiences and the words are the author's alone.

For the fresh waters of the world: that every spring, creek, marsh, pond, lake and river may flow freely in abundance and grace.

For my mother, who gifted me with her love of stories, her devotion to truth, and the unwavering heart of a mystic.

ACKNOWLEDGEMENTS

My FIRST THANK YOU is for my family. This book is meant to bring healing to my mom, dad, sister and brother—each of whom have taught me the many shapes and colors of love. I humbly ask again and again for their grace in lending themselves as characters so I can tell a story larger than ourselves. Thank you. I want to express deep gratitude to my beloved, my husband—thank you for your patience, your inspiration, and your warmth. To our little son: thank you for teaching me from the inside out about weaving spirit into matter—I would not have written this book without you.

I want to express endless gratitude and love for my heart teacher, Holly Hamilton, whose words and wisdom have inspired and echoed so many of the themes that follow. And I want to say thank you for the many, many blessings Sianna Sherman's teachings and storytelling talents have brought to my life. Thank you sisters!

I have a grand thank you for Pireeni Sundaralingam, whose thoughtful editing helped guide a trickling stream of untamed poetry into a full flowing prose manuscript. So much gratitude for your countless readings, invaluable guidance and constant support from the very start. Thank you to Susan Griffin, who read a very early version of this story and inspired me with the courage to take the space I needed in order to tell the whole tale. I also want to say thank you to Carolyn Cooke, who helped at a crucial point in the manuscript to bring some much-needed, stronger banks to this wild river of a book. Thank you!

I want to offer gratitude and appreciation for the women of the California Institute of Integral Studies' Women's Spirituality program who bring strength, presence and grace to difficult questions. I am especially blessed to have learned from Alka Arora, Mara Keller, Lucia Chivola Birnbaum and Arisika Razak. Thank you all for your work in the world. And thank you Lucia Chivola Birnbaum for your scholarship, support and encouragement with this project in particular.

I am so delighted and happy to have found Lucy Pearce and Womancraft Publishing. This is a powerful press with a beautiful mission. Thank you Lucy for *getting* this book, and for the rich language you use to help articulate its purpose. I am honored to be part of your community of women writers.

I have been continuously blessed by many extraordinary teachers over the years, thank you from the bottom of my heart to: Luisah Teish, Anna Dorian, Starhawk, Hareesh Wallis, Douglas Brooks, Jennifer Welwood, Don Humberto and Dona Elena, Ty and Sarah Powers, Thanissara and Kittissaro, Suzanne Marlow, the words of John O'Donohue, and the stories of Joan Didion—may the seeds of wisdom I've received from each of you continue to sprout in the world through these stories.

STORY WATER

A story is like water
that you heat for your bath.
It takes messages between the fire
and your skin.

The body itself is a screen
to shield and partially reveal
the light that's blazing
inside your presence.

Beauty is everywhere,
but we usually need to be walking
in a garden to notice it.

Water, stories, the body,
all the things we do, are mediums
that hide and show what's hidden.

Study them,
and enjoy this being washed
with a secret we sometimes know,
and then not.

Rumi

CONTENTS

SWIMMING IN THE DARK

The quality of light by which we scrutinize our lives has direct bearing on the product which we live, and upon the changes which we hope to bring about through those lives. It is within this light that we pursue our magic and make it realized.

Audre Lorde

Drops of water float suspended in the air. Mist forms a veil of hazy light and palpable shadow, and bubbles hurry from the depths to the surface.

I see my skin through the water, pale and naked as the day I was born. I am alone except for the thick green of the forest and the delicate clarity of the hot spring next to Mt. Kurama in Japan. A circle of ancient cedars surrounds me. They hold me in their passive gaze, and I stare back transfixed.

Today is the darkest day of 2012: the winter solstice. Earth has completed a massive exhale, ending an era, and she stays empty in this sacred pause before she inhales, beginning a new world era. I watch as a golden sun melts into the horizon, and darkness thickens. It's been too long since I stopped moving long enough to feel this deeply. I too am emptied, washed clean. I am born again to myself.

I feel the age of the trees. Their strong, tangled roots exposed from centuries of erosion, like the finger bones on an old woman's hands. I feel a profound steadiness, a basic acceptance, and a deep calm that moves from the bones of my pelvis to my low belly and warms my center. I remember that I am small, and my life is fleeting. As the water holds me, the constant droning fear that resides in my shoulders and lungs turns to a quiet curiosity. I wonder what of my character is strong enough to persist in one place as these trees have. I want to learn to endure, to put down roots, to belong somewhere. I realize I spend most of my time wishing I was elsewhere, feeling something different, resisting reality. It is exhausting. I let out a deep exhale and fill myself with mountain air—I am fully here. The faint aroma of an ancient promise rises like mist from the earth's center, and I expand.

Life gifts us each with at least one moment when resistance is pointless. We spend years in comfort on the shore, fooling ourselves with elaborate illusions of control and consistency. We find routine and false security in jobs, sidewalks, air conditioning, bills, and bank accounts, and this life feels more real (and more convenient) than the wild of the rich green forest full of insects that bite, rolling thunderstorms that ruin our picnics, bitter cold nights that make us shiver, and prowling panthers that cause us to question our strength.

When the monotony of predictability penetrates all the way into our bones, we hear the wild calling, and we drive down to the ocean, but we sit in the car and watch the sun set through the windshield. We flock to the lake, but we sunbathe on a chair and cover our skin with sunscreen. We walk to the river, but we stay affixed to our smartphones to capture the memories.

We are called by the wild, but we resist full engagement.

We have an innate sense that the place where land meets water is a liminal space, a space with a personality and an agenda of her own. She acts as a gatekeeper between the surface layers of awareness and the less traversed depths of our individual psyches. It is she who chooses when and how and why to open that carefully guarded threshold. If we spend enough time at the edge of the water, she will consider this an invitation to splay open our souls, and we will eventually have to confront the unseen depths of our watery past.

There may be any number of strange, alien looking creatures down there in our subconscious, but how can we know what is there if we've never left the safety of the shore? We fool ourselves into believing the sand, the surface, and the sunshine are all there is, while hidden beliefs, lies we keep from ourselves, ancient memories of churning oceans, lightless caves and moonless skies are suppressed and pushed deeper and deeper into the subconscious.

But life promises this: that moment when resistance is futile will come. The fluid parts of our souls pull us into chaos, pushing us to look at all we've avoided, tossing us unwilling into waves of uncertainty and currents of dramatic change. Life keeps her promises. And when she calls you, you must learn to swim in the dark mystery of possibility.

Later I would look back at my time with the cedar trees and say I was visited by the mythical crone—the old woman of the crossroads who allows travelers to ask her one question, which she is bound by the laws of nature to answer in truth. My question might well have been: *where do I belong?* And her answer, with a gesture to the wild forests, sprawling meadows and dark waters of the earth, would have been: *here.*

I've come to several crossroads in my life, and each time I have been blessed with a gentle nudge from the natural world that shows me the next direction. At the tail end of 2012, it was the old woman of the trees, but water has guided me through most other transitions. I wonder, what would it mean to follow the teachings of water?

While the trees are manifest, tangible and structured, water is pure fluid potential rising from the depths of the earth; water contains secrets from the dark unseen. One of the mysteries water holds is in her ability to connect seemingly disparate objects and invite them into relationship. My life, too, is full of disjointed moments that, in time, reveal an unexpected synchronicity—I excavate meaning from these moments like an archaeologist reassembling broken bits of ancient sculpture. Following this inquiry, I know there is an intangible, intuitive relationship between rivers and stories, which are two of my great fascinations.

Stories lay the outline for individual understanding, for human dynamics, and for culture to arise. We learn how to interact with one another through listening to and living these stories. We recognize ourselves and our relationships reflected in the situations of the story, and then we find a way to solve the problems that arise in our lives based on what the characters in our favorite stories have done. At our best, we learn to take different paths than those that cause imbalance and suffering because we learned to recognize these patterns in narrative.

But there's more to story time than simple entertainment or morality: through the language of symbols it is possible to re-wire our physiology. Picture this: a tire forms a groove in a muddy road. The next car that comes down that path then falls into the same groove. This groove deepens each time a car's tires pass through it. Similar to tires in a muddy road, the memory that is embedded in an energetic groove along our neurological pathways from past moments informs all future moments. In this way, we become what we repeatedly think and act on. We are fundamentally wired by the stories we tell ourselves.

Rivers remember in the same way. The water carves grooves

in the landscape that show future water droplets where to descend and rise and splash back toward the sand, over rocks, eventually weaving a pattern that knows how to make its way to the ocean. A river creates her own patterns. She starts with a few drops of curiosity in one direction, followed by a trickle of play in another, and eventually the route is engraved for greater surges of creativity and streams of delight to follow. Serpents of currents form over the land in patterns that may seem random, but the currents follow the law of their own hidden memories. The river feels her way along the earth's surface, finding the way of least resistance, of acquiescent texture, and in this way a river actualizes herself into the landscape as a sculptor, a painter, and a storyteller. The banks of a river provide a constant structure that allows water the freedom to flow and bounce and sparkle in a chaotic dance of balance and beauty.

In humans, it is partly our DNA that provides the structure of memory that acts as river banks. Each time our cells divide, they make a copy with instructions to help them keep to a roughly similar pattern of creation, over and over. But the cells do not always make an exact copy. Just as one cell begins to split into two there is a sacred pause, a moment pregnant with possibility, when the cell may choose to add a little play into the code. This is technically known as a mutation, but it is in effect a transformation that allows for adaptability, and it holds the key to all successful species' survival on this planet.

Zooming out a bit, our friends, our families, and our own notions about ourselves also act as banks to the rivers of ourselves, providing a reliable structure that creates a pattern based on history. The people close to us continue to create us in roughly the same style and caricature as they knew us the moment before, for the most part: because of natural variations in memory and perception, we evolve ourselves, our stories, and our cultures. The stored memories and stories our village holds for us provide a guiding structure that shapes our lives.

This constant co-creation among our community is part of why travel is so exhilarating—no one knows our story in a foreign land, and so we are free to be more emergent (which may feel like an emergency.) We appear solid, but are in fact quite fluid. I am curious about those moments that steer us off structured courses into wild, fluid possibility.

A new feeling is born with each inhale and dies with each exhale. In this way, we may have several incarnations (as the one who is happy, the one who is mad, sad, tired, bored, etc.) before breakfast. If we are present to the moment at hand, and if we can only remember our simple, basic fluidity, we can re-create ourselves in any image with every breath. And that could cause a collective mutation that would radically change our world.

~

What is my story today? Hardly a year after I sat with the cedar trees in Japan, I find myself unexpectedly pregnant. I'm twenty-nine years old and about to be a mother. I stand at the end of life as I know it and look out into the vast night sky. I hold a heavy story in my heart and a great fear of what it means to be a mother. My great-grandmother Maria, known as the river gypsy, had seven children and then disappeared down the road she came from. I feel a cloying archetype trying to capture me, and the netting closes in around me. Is this how my great-grandmother felt before she disappeared? Trapped. Caged. Dammed. Was she also afraid of the rushing river moving through her? Did she experience the same lack of understanding in her culture and hide from her deepest nature until she felt so small she had no choice but to run?

I will not choose when or how; one day my body will

decidedly flip the switch and begin the irreversible process of labor that will bring a new person into the world. I will have to learn to feel my way across a fluid and changing situation that I cannot plan or control, and that is foreign to me.

Maureen Murdock, author of *The Heroine's Journey*, says that women find their way back to themselves differently than men do. Men move up and out into the lights of the world, but women's challenge is to move down into the depths of their own ground of being. Water moves that way too, downhill and inward.

I move toward motherhood like a river runs toward the sea. I stand hesitantly on the shore of the known and unknown, seen and unseen. I am in between, and I wonder what on earth to do with myself while I'm here. I stand at the edge of the continent I've known and look across a dark purple, infinite ocean that merges into a blackening sky.

Berkeley, California. June 2014.

Stars hang low in the moonless sky. A river parts the tall, looming trees on either side of her wide banks. I stand at the edge and watch as the water laps gently closer to me, and then further from me, and back again. Without meaning to do so, my feet move into the surprisingly warm water. I relax. I walk in a straight line into the river until my feet no longer feel the safety of earth beneath them—I hesitate and resist floating before I swim.

I stop with my eyes just over the water line, like an alligator. From this perspective, the land appears to float like an island moving toward me. Water droplets decorate my lashes like jewels of light, and the water's surface glistens like moonlight on an eerie luminous black snow. It is surreal; it is beautiful.

But the joy is short-lived as I feel the immensity of the liquid surround me. I clench my fists at the thought of the various vicious creatures that may lurk below. I feel a flash of a scaly tail brush past my calf beneath. I'm cold and tightening, but before I can turn back to the shore the water pulls me toward her center. My feet leave the sand, and I have to swim or drown. This is my death. I'm merging with a shapeless form of darkness.

As I prepare to meet my end, a panther appears in front of me. She looks back at me over her shoulder and swims ahead. I try to breathe and follow between the little waves she makes behind her, like lines on the edge of a page of parchment paper. The current resists me. I'm heavy and struggling, I lose sight of the panther and then find her again. Water jumps into my eyes and floods my nostrils, stinging. I look up and notice the stars dim as the sky lightens.

And then I am awake.

At home in the dry warmth of my bed, I consider this dream. It's one I've had more than once, so it must be worth my attention. I have always had a curiously ambivalent attachment to water. I find sublime peace at the edges of land and water, but my only phobias as a little girl were bridges and boats. I used to crouch on the floor of the old Toyota van and cover my ears when we crossed bridges, and I refused to go aboard any boat bigger than a canoe.

I begin my morning yoga routine with the flavor of this dream saturating my psyche. I still feel partially under water. I think of the mythic Greek river, the Styx, that separates the world of the living from the world of spirits. Relatives of the deceased used to leave coins on the eyes of corpses, to pay the ferryman who would take their loved ones to the land of the dead. What is it about rivers that causes humans to associate them with death? Mara Freeman writes that: *The crossing of water is an esoteric reference to the change of consciousness from the sensory world to the astral plane in which only the inner sense can be our guide.* I have a felt sense of this shift, and I know my world is about to change beyond recognition.

I sit still, cross-legged on the floor and open my central channel from the crown of my head down to my perineum. I feel a gentle flow from top to bottom, like a sleepy creek reluctantly waking up at my center. I'm just a few weeks pregnant, and most people don't even know yet. I've even questioned myself. Am I making this up? I have no evidence but my own knowing. I feel a new empathy for salmon; I am aware of a strong instinct that is something like I imagine a salmon might feel before she begins her long journey back to the place she was born in order to reproduce. I need to go back over the inner landscapes of home before I give birth.

I've spent a large portion of my life searching for a definitive home, a place I finally belong. I know that home is supposed to be a feeling of inner peace you carry around with you wherever you roam, but something compels my feet to physically travel over landscapes in order to gather information. This restlessness seems to be an as essential part of wrestling with my particularly windy kind of humanness. I have trouble separating myself from the landscapes that shape me—I love change and crave movement. I tried to get as far away from my childhood home in central Florida as possible, and eventually worked in Paris, Ghana, Thailand and India before I landed in Northern California, which is my current home.

The Bay Area hosts a unique intersection of landscapes, cultures and habitats—it's a biological hub that is not dissimilar to the diversity of Grand Central Station ecologically-speaking.

I would call it home except that the weather feels too passive-aggressive in comparison to Florida's regular raging tropical storms. Without a good afternoon tantrum to break the tension, the place just doesn't feel authentic. Day after day is sunny and mild, the seasons come and go, but none of them leave an impression or hint at the passage of time. Like those blond surfers that don't seem to age, I feel that California must be hiding something: no place is this even-tempered all the time. The lack of change makes me restless—my skin is always dry, and my feet are always cold. I miss the diversity of the invisible rainbows of emotions that water infuses in the atmosphere.

If you've ever sat still and watched a flowing river, you'll know that what appears as one congruent mass of water is made up of many smaller streams that all braid together to form an illusion of uniformity. These separate streams weave together just like threads in a tapestry, but instead of colors and patterns, the transparency of flowing water contains only textured reflection. The pattern comes from remembered movement. What compels them to motion is some secret that is felt, rather than something that is seen and described. Some invisible force brings them together, and they collectively decide to move in the same general direction with that one irresistible pull toward the ocean. I have a feeling my gypsy grandmother felt something like this pull that led our family into devastation. I know this pull, and I want to find the freedom to move freely through life so I don't end up creating tragedy as she did.

My friend Rachel recently surprised me when she said I live my life like a river—meandering through majors, master's degrees and cities; gathering and discarding people and ideas at seemingly random times; and generally flowing through life downhill at varying speeds depending on the debris in my path. She's right—if the shortest distance between two points is a straight line, then I've chosen to take the long way around.

In order to live more like a river, I have to learn more about that invisible something that causes me so much trouble in a linear society (not to mention a mountain of student loans). I need to understand the obstacles to the freedom of circuity on levels both personal and collective. As a child, I learned to measure value based on grades, punctuality and my ability to stay inside the lines of the law. This quantifying of value based on objective, external forms of measurement is part of the European axiology, which had its place in history as a necessity.

Europeans may have learned to value efficiency and precision well before the industrial revolution because of the short summers and long winters in the North. There was a brief window in which one could plant food and harvest in order to survive the harsh winters, so the people adapted. The European farmers valued the qualities the earth showed them: stability and predictability. They lived by the fire to stay warm, which taught them to prize quicker, sharper movements with no room for error.

Most of us have inherited, and in some cases had imposed on us, the stress of ancestors and their outdated ways of surviving. This context makes me wonder how modern life, with all of its amenities and engineered sense of time, is shaping us. Are we still being formed by our landscape as it is now? Or have we clung to an expired model for fear of change? Western morals have spread as the gold standard across the world for efficiency and business success. But these ways of judging value can be painful and detrimental when applied to one's personal worth. The need to prove oneself based on societal values causes a dryness of the soul that shrivels a human's will to create and experience beauty.

In areas closer to the Equator, the planting seasons were longer and more forgiving—so people's concept of time was less stringent. The more moderate climates, those further south or closer to the ocean—enjoyed more of the qualities of water and air—a fluid sense of ease that allows for plenty of space for the unknown. Perhaps there is a way to pair these less structured elements with the stability and efficiency of the North that might prove more useful. There has never been more need for cooperation than in these modern times.

For the first time in global history, more than half of the earth's population lives in urban areas. This means billions of people depend on someone else for basic resources—including, or perhaps, especially water. The average consumer has no idea how far the water travels before it comes out of the showerhead or kitchen sink, or what happens to it after it's gone down the drain.

There is plenty of water if we share it, but there will never be enough if the few with power continue to insist on exclusive control and management. Short sighted fixes—such as damming a river that allows a few companies to get rich and leaves entire populations displaced or in water shortage—are leading us toward an inevitable crisis. This axiology of objectifying resources and scrambling for exclusive ownership has also extended its reach to rule over our fellow humans.

I see a connection between the abuse of water as a resource, the diminishment of women, and racism. These are the obstacles to that circuitous freedom: they are all systems based on ignorance, separateness and fear—full of shoulds, cannots and regrets. I wonder where we might find a structure that allows for a paradigm shift toward curiosity, connection, and cooperation—something that helps us move collectively from dominance or *power over* to shared structures of empowerment.

My great-grandmother, a gypsy posing as a housewife, tried to live into a story that was not her own, and when she left it shattered the cultural container for my family. I think of her, and wonder—if the stories that mass culture produces are so powerful, then wouldn't the power still remain if we re-wrote the narrative? If we want to re-write it completely, maybe we need to understand what came before this new story.

I wonder how we can experience the rootedness I longed to find sitting next to those ancient cedars on Mt. Kurama, and also maintain the flow of the rivers that inspire me so much. I know this inquiry has to be driven by body-based awareness; there was a reason I was born female with a fascination for water.

There seems to be an ancient and universal connection between women and water in human psyches. The Cherokee people call the river 'Long Woman' as she curves past their villages. A group of uptown New Yorkers call a woman who is taller than five-foot-five inches 'a tall drink of water', as she sways past their stoop. Myths have portrayed water deities as female since the beginning of time: Oshun from Africa, Aphrodite from Greece, Ganga from India, and the seal-woman of the Irish.

The accepted story of our culture today is one that perpetuates power over one another and scarcity. This is seen in the mistreatment of resources in our dwindling fresh water supply as well as the widespread intensity of dominance against women.

Women's bodies are objectified and used as commodities. Their value is based on their usefulness as a resource. In many parts of the world they are feared and demonized as deceitful and crass. These beliefs reinforce a paradigm that perpetuates acts of violence against women across the globe: female genital mutilation in Africa and the Middle East; bride burnings in India; female infanticide in China; sex trafficking in many developing countries; and soaring rates of rape and domestic violence in the United States. But we as humans have a choice: we don't have to keep falling into the cycle of violence, we can start to fill in the ditch caused by traveling over the same energetic grooves on this collective pathway. We can choose another course.

Myths provide archetypes that guide us through the labyrinth of life. Audre Lorde has written: *Poetry is the way we help give name to the nameless so it can be thought. The farthest external horizons of our hopes and fears are cobbled by our poems, carved from the rock experiences of our daily lives.*

There is an imperative truth relevant to our liberation today tucked into the symbolism of myth, legend and folk tales. The knowledge may have been scattered like the body of Osiris from Egypt, but then my task as a woman, as Isis who wanders along the bank of the Nile, is to reassemble those bits of knowledge. I do this work by weaving stories together.

I've found refuge and inspiration in words since I could hold a pen. My mother came up with a practical solution to my young mind's questions and incessant reflections—one day she handed me a little purple spiral notebook and a pen and suggested I start a journal. I filled that one and countless others since then. She was astute in noticing my need to express my inner world. I've always been quiet—as if the feelings take longer to digest and to rise from my gut and my heart toward my vocal cords. This came from early entrainment of a particular story that was recorded as a need to hold my voice in: *it is unsafe to follow your instincts and speak freely.* I know where that story comes from.

Ocala, Florida. Summer 1988.

It is still dark outside. My mom gathers my sister and me from our room in hushed tones and tells us to get in the car. We sleepily collect pillows and blankets and made a nest in the back seat of the Pontiac. We had left my father before, and we would leave him again. We stay at my mom's friend's house outside of town. Later that day my father is on the phone, and my mother gives us that stern, silent look to keep our mouths shut.

I am three or four and want to say hi to daddy. I do not understand my mom's urgent need for secrecy. My sister gives me a Ricola cough drop and tells me I can speak again once it is entirely gone, and not to crunch it. That is the longest cough drop of my life. I wait until it is almost imperceptible, before I swallow it. I want to cry, but by that time the tears are gone.

This way of being silenced is associated with that caramel-menthol-medicinal taste in my mouth. I want to say something, but it's as if I have to wait for some external factor to give me permission. The vulnerable muscles of my throat hold me back, ask me to reconsider, cause me to question the desire to flow and express. I hold myself in. I find another outlet. The lesson or story was: *it is unsafe to follow your instincts and speak freely.* I built a massive dam at my throat that I am still learning to open.

Today, with this pen in my hand, it is as if the emotions can flow easily downhill from my chest along the veins in my shoulders and past my wrists into my fingertips. The result is visible, the words appear between the lines on a piece of paper I can hold. The ink creates something tangible and lasting out of the ineffable experiences of my body. Those same emotions often refuse to flow upstream into the narrow channel of my throat to become spoken words, and even then sound vibrations dissolve in the air much more quickly than ink on the page.

The lines on this page act as the banks for a river, providing structure so the words can flow.

I peek around the other side of a mass of faceless fear to find curiosity. This is the current of possibility. The intersections of inner and outer landscapes merge. I am the river, I am the sand. Articulating these grooves, these patterns of memory that criss-cross my body and overflow through my fingers is how I learn to move through life with understanding, to leave marks in the sand, to feel my way across a river in the dark.

PART ONE

NEW MOON TRAVELS OVER DARK WATERS

SWEETWATER CREEK

Ripples Scatter Across the Surface

I feel like a river when the tide changes, and for a while the waters flow in crosscurrent, with no direction, only a pulling from all sides.

Christine Downing

Central Florida. Summer 1993.

CLEAR WATER RUSHES over tiny pebbles—gray, brown and tan. Water speaks quietly and rhythmically with taps and hums. A line of cars—red tail lights—stop and go, forming a pulsing river downtown. Blood vessels dance, forward and back, from heart through veins: the gentle whoosh and tsss of the ocean tide flows within my body. These streams bring me home to the Atlantic Ocean, to my low belly, and eventually to a gray house with a metal roof off County Road 475 that I left a long time ago.

No place on earth has clouds like central Florida—they hang lower than any other cloud I've seen, preferring to be fully protruded and pregnant before they release a single drop of rain. When these big, warm, tropical rain drops finally land repeatedly on our metal roof we know they deserve reverence. My mom, sister and I used to sit on the front porch to greet the rain. It was a summer afternoon ritual we cherished.

Rocking chairs creak, steady slow. We breathe in the smell of damp hay and freshly cut grass as an iridescent green hummingbird hovers next to the bright red feeder. We blink heavy lids and look under our lashes where the roof hangs low to cover a modest strip of royal purple sky as she descends to touch outstretched leaves. Waiting leaves turn their lighter green underbellies toward her in shades of shimmering anticipation. Dry with desire, cupped in prayer, begging for her face, her lips, we wait for the kiss of water on trees.

Florida is a state surrounded by saltwater and bobbing right at sea level from the Atlantic Ocean to the Gulf of Mexico. I grew up outside the city limits of Ocala, in central Florida, which was crowded with natural freshwater springs. Natural springs are fascinating in that they are holes in the earth's crust where the freshest water imaginable magically bubbles up from deep in the ground and begins pooling in a basin. Driving down the street in my town you might see any number of mailboxes with the red-and-white dive signs signaling that they have a natural spring in their backyard. That means anyone can visit this house and swim in the spring at any time, because no one owns the springs. Even though the water was a brisk 72 degrees year-round, my dad and I always stopped and swam. We used to take in an extra inhale and fill our lungs to capacity so we could hold our breath long enough to swim down to drink right from the source.

One of my favorite swimming spots was part of the National Forest, surrounded by cedars and pines draped with elegant curling silver Spanish moss at Juniper Springs. We would take wooden canoes out and follow the winding trails through the trees. Turtles lined up to sun on logs, lifting their little green heads towards the sky. Alligators lounged on the banks, and otters would fuss and play in the wake of our paddles. In this tropical climate, water seemed infinite—especially when it came from the sky. The weather was always conspiring: building up as much tension as she could and then pouring herself out fully. There is nothing more comforting than an afternoon storm: wind's fingers trying to pry open windows, thunder shaking your frame, and lightning reaching like a bridge from earth to sky. Later in life, I came to understand why I'm not the only one who enjoys a good storm.

That relaxed feeling you get at the beach, near the water, or after a thunderstorm is a result of the negative ions balancing the positive ones. Research has shown that we are physiologically prone to prefer landscapes with more negative ions. Computers, dry winds and stagnant air in office buildings all create an accumulation of positive ions in the air. This causes our bodies to tense up, which drains our energy. People naturally fill their lungs with fresh air as their bodies receive signals that all is well in the world again. These deeper breaths cause increased circulation and better all-around internal flow. Humans instinctively seek out these negative-ion rich environments because we crave that fluid internal environment.

Our lungs are ninety percent water, our brains are seventy percent water and our blood is more than eighty percent water. Water is defined by science as two particles of hydrogen and one particle of oxygen. It is an amazingly simple structure that sustains all of life. Water regulates our body temperature, moves nutrients through our cells, keeps our mucous membranes moist and flushes waste from our bodies. We need water to live. We need to drink it, swim in it, feel it in the soil and the air, and have it fall onto our heads.

My parents felt that human need to be near the water as a personal calling, like the moon pulling the tides. They were born and raised several hundred miles inland among the endless cornfields of Southern Indiana, but moved to Florida to start a family of their own. I'm sure they weren't the only two Hoosiers who shared a love of the ocean, the need to escape, and the willingness to leave the known boundaries of the small town behind them—but they followed through and actually made the move. Florida was a perpetual day-dream for them, and they imagined that if they lived there they might feel as if they were on a permanent vacation. The future was woven in the lace of a second-hand wedding gown and garnished with a humble bouquet of lavender as they drove an old green Honda Civic due south to the Sunshine State.

When mom got pregnant, my parents settled near the ocean on the Atlantic side. My dad was a lifeguard off Jupiter Beach and my mother was a nanny. Maybe they were happy for a little while, but there was already an ominous cloud of stubborn jealousy building between them. I was two when my dad got a job at a community college and we moved inland to Ocala. Once we left the ocean, the vacation was over. Three kids and a mortgage started to fray the edges of my parent's delicate lace fantasy. Most nights I dreamed of slow flooding, the house sinking, and my family drowning. My whole family swims, but in my childhood dreams, I was the only one who knew how. It was a big responsibility for a small girl.

Despite the apparent abundance of water in central Florida, the land was literally depressed, having had its groundwater supply depleted by years of overpopulation and overuse. Sinkholes could appear almost overnight when we had heavy rains. I was ready to leave Florida for as long as I can remember. I'm fond of telling people that my reason for wanting out was that the culture mirrors the landscape—it's flat. Maybe that's the reason I was restless, but I think it has to do with a deeper wandering that drives me toward the unknown.

My dad always said we were lucky to live in such a water rich area. For my dad, Ocala was a secret paradise. To the rest of the country, Ocala is known for urban sprawl, record-breaking home foreclosures, a few small-time rap stars, and a particularly sweet kind of grass that makes racehorses run faster.

The modern-day Ocala was "discovered" by Hernando de Soto in the fourteenth century, and then officially founded by citrus farmers in 1849. Before that, the Timucua called it Ocali, meaning "big hammock," referring to the large hammock of oak trees that shade the abundant rolling fields. The official report from my school textbooks is that the native Ocale and Timucuan people scattered and disappeared just like the swamp after this site was taken by the Spanish. I know how it feels to be scattered, but I'm not sure how people can disappear into thin air. That seems to depend on who's looking and where.

The style of house we lived in, with the pointed metal roof and the wrap-around porch is known as a Cracker style house. I've heard different explanations for why this style of house is called a Cracker house. My sister said it was because white people lived in those kind of houses and their skin is the color of a cracker. My Uncle Rick said it was because the poorer white people lived there, and they were farmers who raised cattle and cracked whips as they drove the herds from one place to another.

Whatever the reason, our family was excited about the house when we first moved in. It was full of the emptiness of pure potential in the white walls and fresh peach carpet. But over the years my family filled the space up with anger and resentment, and many deaths both literal and metaphorical stagnated the air with sadness more cloying than the muddy waters of a swamp. It is difficult for me to think about the house apart from those lingering, undigested emotions. The walls are punctured, the carpet is stained, and the people are tired.

My family lived on a few acres nestled between the Jacksons on the right: deer hunters and pig farmers who proudly flew a confederate flag on their front porch and whose truck tires were taller than me until I was ten; and the Haitian family on the left: including a great-grandpa and countless cousins, chickens, goats and doves. I never knew their last name; I only knew the name of their little girl, Lauren, who was a friend I only ever talked to from over the fence. I wouldn't understand what invisible force kept us from inviting one another across the barrier until I was much older.

Back then, I had no concept of racism or slavery, and Africa was a place I knew about only through the weather channel. Spiraling red graphics gathered momentum as they traveled over the Atlantic Ocean from Western Africa, which seemed to and predictably hurl hurricanes our way every summer. I was curious about the connection between this foreign land mass and our own, and I was fascinated to watch the satellite images of clouds circle around that still center of the storm before I would go outside and watch the clouds turn purple and the air thicken over our gray metal roof. We would welcome the first big, warm drops of water before the wind started to shake the trees. My Great Aunt Bridgette says that thunder happens because the God is bowling in heaven, and the really loud claps are when he gets a strike. I used to try to imagine that scene, but it always seemed like God would have been sad bowling alone, with no one there to high-five him or bring the nachos.

During the storms, a big, leafy branch or an entire tree would eventually snap and fall, and that first earth-shaking crack of the trunk and the definitive thud shook us out of our reverie. We would head inside like rabbits into their burrows and turn on the radio to wait out the storm from the safety of the house. When the winds shook even the roof, we retreated deeper into the dark belly of the house, to the very back of the closets.

Ocala. Fall 1994.

I'm not supposed to know about it, but my dad keeps a pipe in the barn. Mom says it's okay for him to smoke because it eases his back pain, but if other people do it that would be addiction. He keeps the pipe beneath his tool cabinet. I can imagine his face glowing warmly and then disappearing as he lights the wooden pipe and inhales. He is surrounded by wood, the dusty assortment of nails, screws and utensils neatly stored in their cubby holes.

A young finch mother has chosen one of the empty cubicles as her home, gathered bits of hay and laid three eggs. Dad has four heavy boxes of lottery ticket stubs on the floor; in case he wins, so he can show his investment to the tax office and maybe they won't charge him so much. Sometimes if the door is unlocked, my sister and I carefully slide back the roll-top desk and dust off the watches, hand-written notes, and pictures: my beautiful Grandma Florence when she was young and smooth, Dad's goofy, tall brothers, and a sacred image of our Great-Grandpa Henry with his pipe in his hand as he stands in front of the garage.

Saturday morning. Dad's back is toward me, facing the window. He sits at the table, newspaper unfurled over the edges, and his plate of eggs neatly on the left. My black-and-white cat purrs as he offers an absent caress to her forehead. She closes her eyes and rubs her nose against his fingers. Mom rushes to clear the table and spills the cup of tea across the words. My father explodes, "Goddammit, Anne!" He clenches his jaw and thrusts his chair back as he stands and tightens his fists.

I disappear into my room to avoid the scene. Outside, purple clouds cover the sky and move closer to the ground. Fire, water and wood form a fury, their instincts intersecting and each struggling to stand, to breathe, to live. My parents are louder than thunder, more piercing than lightning. I wait it out in my closet, holding my knees close. I hear a thud against the front door, a loud crack, and my father's expletive. I peek out a slight crack in my door: he's escaped like sunlight in December. I hear my mother crying in the bathroom.

The air in the house is heavy and tense, as if it is about to rain, but it's different from the storms outside in that the release afterwards never comes. The tension builds and spins and builds again. The spiraling red graphics from the weather channel always move, and even hurricanes eventually pass, but the inside of our house seems to be situated under a static system that keeps us in one unending moment before the storm.

My mom cries all the time, but the first time I saw my dad cry was when his Grandpa Henry died. The second time was when his collie, Sandy, died. I was seven. Sandy lived with him when he still had the tipi, before us kids. Dad said it was Mom's fault he got out onto the train tracks that night. He made a wooden cross for the grave. I had never seen such beautiful, curving letters: *RIP Sandy, 1980-1992.*

Dad built the barn too. I imagine he spent so much time out there because he liked to build things, and that's where he kept all his tools. But I think he also wanted to get away from us kids. He likes adventures and loves to share things he finds inspiring. One time we all slept in sleeping bags on the trampoline, and he kept a fire going all night so we could watch a comet pass. Except Mom didn't want to. Samantha fell asleep, and of course Jason was too little, but Dad and I saw the fleeting moments when fire flew across the sky and escaped into the depths again.

Sunday morning. A flock of finches landed in our backyard this morning. They look like a herd of buffalo grazing in the early sunlight, if you squint. Mom is excited because they eat the insects that kill the grass. "Where did they come from . . . ?" I wonder out loud. My older sister Samantha pronounces their small, brown feathers plain. Dad says that they're smart: they can learn songs that are whistled to them precisely, to the note. We watch them while we finish our oatmeal, before the golden retriever goes outside and chases them away. They scatter, we forget.

Mom opens the oven and pulls out the banana bread. She grabs the ringing phone and hands me my backpack. She is telling the caller, "Yes, I'll be there in time to help set up." The phone hits the receiver and makes that lovely tinging metallic sound that feels like ripples over a pond. She exhales sharply, grabs the keys to the Toyota, and ushers my brother and me into the back seat. Samantha takes the front seat because she's oldest. I look out the window and sing to myself. I think my mom is afraid to stop moving sometimes, like a creek hurrying down a mountain—maybe she worries that if she stops she might disappear underground. I don't think my mom would like it underground: she says that's where Satan lives. With my mother's small frame and delicate features, I think she'd rather be a bird than a woman.

I daydream through most of the grocery trip, and snap back to attention when Mom announces, "Home again, home again, jiggity-jig!" My stomach tightens as we pull up next to the porch, and I crack the knuckles on my fingers in order from left to right. My sister makes a twisted face and tells me to stop it. I ignore her. Another grocery whirlwind is over, the sun's going down, and Dad's got the TV on. He's lying face up on the floor because his back hurts again. Everybody grabs a plate of tofu and squash, and Mom shuttles back and forth to the kitchen. Eventually fed and bathed, we nestle together on the couch for a story while Mom massages Dad's shoulders.

Dad's big toe where he kicked the door is cracked at the nail and has turned an angry kind of purple, not unlike the sky before a storm. He falls asleep with the TV remote in his hand. Mom is back at the desk in the kitchen. The gray screen of her computer reflects in her glasses, and her tired blue eyes stare off into space.

I slip quietly out the back door. The sun is almost gone, and I call for my lost cat. She hadn't come for dinner yesterday, and my mom was starting to give me the talk about giving up. But at my age giving up is not an option, it is betrayal. I go to bed with a salty taste in my mouth and hope Mom is wrong.

The next morning, Sheba magically appears on the front porch, but her spine is cracked. She pulls herself along with her front legs, but her back end is limp, and she is leaking all kinds of fluids. My mom gently talks me through it and lets the decision to have her put to sleep rest on my shoulders. As we return from the vet's office, I sit in the back seat with my cat in a box, a tan towel covering her body. I can't cry yet. We bury her under a maple tree in the front yard. Then I retreat into my room, calmly close the door, and fall apart in the back of my closet, safely hidden behind my brightly flowered Sunday school dresses.

My dad said probably an owl had tried to get her, but my mother (a good Catholic) was sure it must have been some "voodoo" from the black neighbors. I had seen the owls; they were big barn owls whose hooting helped me drift into dreamland. I had seen the neighbors too—a big family always speaking a foreign language almost louder than their herd of animals. I didn't know which parent's theory was right, so I just decided I didn't know what happened. (I think it was probably my fault though.) My mother's suspicion about the neighbors made me curious. Something about our dark neighbors scared her. Why was she afraid?

I didn't know the answer, but an overwhelming wave of new understanding was washing over me. Through the death of my cat, I felt the pain of loss and started to question the explanations I had been offered for why things were the way they were. I was becoming a woman, but that was something I never wanted to be. I dug my heels into the ground in rebellion against the way things were. I was so adamant that the heat and friction in my body made my temperature rise and my internal waters dry up. I shut myself in my room with notebooks and pens and wrote and wrote and wrote, but it wasn't enough—the rush of ranting, sad, angry and confused words that wanted to be voiced caught at my throat.

I developed strep throat and came down with scarlet fever every fall for the next three years. Even as my parents tried to pull me back from the edge, I felt a magnetic force in those fever dreams that allowed me to stretch and explore the paradoxical dance of life and death. It was too intriguing to resist. My parents took us on vacation to try to help me get better, and we ended up at Sweetwater Cabin in the National Forest.

Sweetwater Cabin, Central Florida. Fall 1996.

Time and tension turn the roughest rocks to the smoothest stones. Water's constant motion transforms everything she touches. I feel the cool, even texture of a river stone between my thumb and forefinger, and I study the lines and shades of yellows, pinks and grays. I drop the stone at arm's distance and watch. The little stone sinks to the bottom of a shallow spring, I stare into the water at my reflection. I hear sounds coming from the cabin—my mom pulling out pots and pans, and the cicadas start their evening chorus. I smell the grilling fish from the windows, buttery and stark with lemon.

I'm not supposed to be down here by myself on account of the alligators and my small size, but I dangle my eleven-year-old toes into the crisp water and hum a little to myself. I watch the miniscule waves of water wrinkle the surface softly as the circles widen away from the center and disperse. The center dissolves, and I think I might do the same.

I see a hungry log stir out of the corner of my eye, and feel a surge of movement in my gut. Excitement and fear compete in my muscles. I scoot closer to the edge of the deck to tempt the alligator, and in a flash of understanding I feel how easy it would be to disappear, to dissolve and be done with the discomfort. But a fish jumps out of the pond and shatters the moment. I stand up and realize I am taller than I remember. Something in the water's rearrangement after the fish submerges tells me I am no longer the same, and I go into the cabin to face my family.

Between the hard cracking of the trees, my father's toe, and the cat's spine, something in my childhood home was broken and crying out for repair. It is incredibly frustrating to find that none of my square shaped blocks of reasoning fit into the spaces left by circular and winding questions that arose before me. My inner feelings were not mirrored by the outer world. I felt isolated, insignificant and lost as a lone piece of driftwood on the open sea.

The internal tension of trying to make sense of complicated realities is uncomfortable, squeezing too much into a tight space and at the same time being stretched too thin. Ambivalence becomes my mode of operating. It is too easy to blame my dad for everything. At one point, in an attempt to come to terms with my conflicting feelings toward him, I made two lists—one with Dad's positive qualities and the other with his negative qualities, but they came out about equal. I never made a list about my mother.

I can look at my father directly in this way, in the sunlight, but something holds me back from examining my mother face on. The light I use to catch glimpses of my mother is like moonlight: ambient and hazy. She is so close to myself it is difficult to see where she ends and I begin. I once tried to decide which parent I loved more and decided I would always have to love them in different ways, but this was always somehow dissatisfying. Why can't I choose? And which parent am I? The answers are clear as mud.

My internal churning is so constant and chaotic that I develop a mask, a surface that appears extra smooth and subtle like the surface of a stone softened by years of turbulent waters. Underneath I am a swirling mess of stormy emotions and conflicting impulses. There is a split in the psyche that enables one to tolerate violence, but I resist creating that chasm within myself. I do not want to learn to tolerate hate and injustice. I do not want to paint my external features as a flawless mask over my internal feelings of pain and vulnerability. I want to be angry when I see pain and suffering. I want to be whole.

Part of this wholeness requires including unpleasant feelings, places and situations into the reality of experience. I did not know who I was or where I belonged. It is difficult for all young children to find their place in the world, and more difficult without the feeling of being held in a safe, stable structure. I was born without a strong container or definable clan, as are many modern humans. Our psyches continue to search for the support of a village that no longer exists in the way it did for most of our evolution.

This story is offered within Native American communities as a way to help the children who are of mixed blood (and therefore considered clanless) to understand where they belong.

The Story of the White Potato Clan, from the Mvskokee (Creek) Nation

The old ones remember when The Others first invaded the land of The People. There were only a few of them, and they settled into farms with families. The first wave of foreigners came peacefully, and there was plenty of land for all to live side by side, so The People let them come.

For several years, The People and The Others lived in harmony, neighbors became friends, and of course daughters and sons met and, in time, fell in love. The marriages between The People and The Others brought children who did not fully belong in one culture or the other, they were considered without a clan. This is a big problem because the collective rules of marriage and society have always depended on each person belonging to a particular clan.

The mothers of the clanless children were especially saddened by what was happening to their children, and so they went to the elders and asked for advice. The elders told them to go out together and pray to Creator, and if their hearts were pure Creator would hear their prayers and show them how to proceed.

The women departed from the village and went out to a place of prayer in the trees near the mountain. They made offerings of corn and tobacco to Creator. They prayed and fasted for days until Creator saw the sincerity in their hearts and listened to their pleas. Creator told the women to go to the place of soft ground and black waters and to search until they found a plant that would cry out to them from deep under the ground.

If they found this plant and did as the plant instructed them, they would not only find a clan name for their children, but they would also give The People a gift that would feed them forever. The women thanked Creator and left the place of prayer and went back to the village. As soon as they returned, they prepared to depart again. They said goodbye to their husbands and children and went to the place of soft ground and black waters. The place of soft ground and black waters is a place filled with biting insects, snakes, thorns, mud, spiders, hungry logs, and strange spirits. This was a place that would test the hearts of the women.

For many days they searched and listened for the plant that would call out to them from under the ground, but they heard and saw nothing. Just as the women were about to give up all hope of finding the special plant, they prayed again to Creator for guidance. After this prayer, finally, they heard the voice of the plant calling out to them.

It was difficult to find the plant because it was hidden from view, but eventually they dug it up. The plant told the women that even though it was from under the ground, Creator had given it the ability to see in every direction simultaneously. What's more, it felt the connection of all things, even in the darkness.

The women were told to take the plant to the village of The People, and once there, they were to take a knife and cut out the eyes of the plant. The eyes were to be planted in a small mound. If the women followed these instructions the plant promised to grow and it would feed The People forever. The women followed the instructions of the plant. Ever since that time, the potato has faithfully continued to feed The People and the clanless children started a new clan of their own, known as the White Potato Clan.

There is a lot of wisdom in this old story. I see the value placed on the women's compassion for their children in this story, and their need for answers other than what was being offered in the village. The women are willing to leave the comfort of their lives and routine and travel into the unknown for answers. They are hungry, they are tired, but they are also determined. They do not talk, but get very quiet and listen. They are given power because of their silence. This story promised me an answer to the questions I had about violence and paradox if I was willing to wait and listen. It gave meaning to the landscape, and placed value on quiet contemplation and endurance.

The place of the soft ground and black waters is a fertile meeting of two elements: earth and water. The two mix and become a third kind of substance: mud, which is not fully water and also not fully earth. The children of The Others (Europeans) and The People (Native Americans) have also become something other than the two elements that formed them, and so they have to look for answers in a landscape that mirrors their innerscape. I was formed by a landscape rich in water and air—the hurricanes that blew through central Florida made me who I am: a woman who is not afraid of challenge, disagreement and change. I have gifts to offer just as the potato in the story offers medicine. I am also from the swamp and made of two elements, water and earth, sun and moon, mother and father.

It is no mistake that the plant that comes to The People to bring wisdom is the potato, a root vegetable that grows deep underground in the darkness of the earth. It absorbs the earth's nourishment in a way that is fundamentally different from a peach growing on a tree, or a tomato on a vine. Those colorful fruits are full of water and sunlight, but something about the potato requires darkness and moisture to develop. Aren't humans the same? Eating this vegetable connects one deeper into the ground, to a feeling of being rooted perhaps more so than the other sun-fed nourishments.

How do we digest, nourish and root ourselves? The children without clans need a deeper connection to the earth for the lives they would lead outside of the traditional village, in a place and time without stories and elders to guide them. Modern people are mostly born without clan and without village, and we are desperately in need of roots, stories, and wilderness experiences to bring us back to health, to connection and to sustainability.

The soft ground and dark waters are a place less of reflection (as a clear pond or river might be) than of soaking. Experience is not based on sight in the swamp, but on unseen feeling. The marshlands teach us how to feel back into our bodies as something inherently connected to and intermingled with matter, with soil, with the earth. We are literally a part of the earth, and our denial of this fact, our incessant searching for the light and spiritual realms of an afterlife in heaven cause us to neglect the life that is in front of us. Cutting off access to the resource of our bodies is like draining a marsh to put up a bunch of boxy houses.

The elaborate, unnatural family fights that became routine as afternoon thunderstorms in my home may not have happened if humans still lived in community. When we retreated into houses that no longer faced one another in a circle, the actions within the houses became secret. In a circle of village huts, someone would notice domestic violence, and the spouses would be confronted and made to change this behavior. Modern people carry their pain in hidden silence, and in this hidden repression it morphs into something uglier that it would have been in the light.

My parents acted out of denial and projection in their violence toward one another. They were in so much discomfort internally that they in turn blamed their unhappiness on one another. Neither of them had the support of a village growing up, and they both learned to avoid difficult feelings and stuff them further into their unconscious, where those undigested emotions eventually accumulated and overflowed.

The story of the White Potato Clan reminds me to resist the urge to avoid discomfort. I need to take the time to get quiet. I seek out ways that will help me to digest rather than discard the difficulties of my childhood. I go in search of the soft ground where the water is dark internally and find fear in my lower belly, the swamp of my body. This fear is sticky and cloying, dense and immobile. But I have a feeling there is nourishment hidden here in this inhospitable environment. Some glimmer of wisdom, some understanding of life, some growth, maybe even some unexpected gift akin to the un-glamorous potato. I accept the challenge. I step into the waters of my emotions and wait for whatever washing will be offered to me. I feel movement, turmoil, resistance. A push and a pull.

But I stay still as a stone in the rapids. After all, it is through a constant stream of discord that rough rocks are refined into smooth stones. Before I sincerely begin the process of wearing away at the tough outer layers of my psyche, I need to slow down and look more closely at the soft mud of the swamp where I was raised.

EVERGLADES

Binds to the Earth

The unconscious wants truth, as the body does. The complexity and fecundity of dreams comes from the unconscious struggling to fulfil that desire. Truthfulness anywhere means a heightened complexity. But it is a movement into evolution.

Adrienne Rich

RUSHING FLOOD WATERS destroy crops. Crashing waves splinter homes. Water's habit of withholding herself causes drought that leaves skulls in the desert, but she seems not to care how she tortures humanity with her unpredictable whim. She continues over diverse terrain, jumping and laughing on the surface before she sinks into the ground and disappears. She reappears in swamps and surges forward until she meets the sea, gathering minerals, rocks, leaves, fish, birds and garbage indiscriminately.

To humans, nature might seem cruel, but she is only wild— following the laws that keep her alive. Her laws. She gathers what appears to be separate and asks us to reconsider our concept of reality, to look closely at the disparate threads she has brought together, and she asks us to weave her memories into one comprehensive narrative, even if we've discarded large sections of this story fabric years ago. Out of sight may be out of mind, but the mind is only a tiny sliver of all that is. Matter is never created or destroyed, it just keeps morphing into something new.

For thousands of years human survival was based on the whim of nature. Until we learned to adjust our behaviors to her patterns, many civilizations failed. I feel my survival depends on understanding the patterns that shaped me, and so I begin to search my past.

~

Far back in my memory, in those cobwebbed corners where uneventful family vacations are stored, I see my whole family in the old tan Toyota van. "Here we are kids, Alligator Alley." Dad said this every time we drove through the Everglades on our way to visit his parents. I looked out the window, hoping to see a big ol' gator. I never did. But we rarely made it the entire trip without him reminding us to check.

Alligator Alley refers to the section of Interstate 75 that stretches across the swamps of South Florida from the Gulf of Mexico to the Atlantic Ocean. This is a highway speckled with struggling, rusted gas stations, and a long thin stretch of road that is abundant in cheap casinos. The Calusa and Tequesta Native Americans took care of this swampland before the US Army forced them out. Those people who were displaced became their own band of wanderers from varying tribes. They made their way down south and successfully resisted the army in the Sea of Grass, the marshlands of the Everglades.

These exiles are known as the Seminole today—a group made up of those who resisted and escaped the first wave of invaders only to be stuck beneath the framework of a foreign culture as it expanded and eventually claimed the entire peninsula.

Florida has always felt like a land that harbors those without deep-rooted homes; maybe being so close to sea level keeps roots from solidifying as strongly as they might in richer soils. Only those plants and people that can adapt to the constant erosion and salt of the sandy surface stay: the water washes the weaker roots out. The weather along the coast also contributes to a feeling of fluidness from residents and wildlife. It takes a certain hard-spined species to endure the wrath of annual hurricanes.

In fact, land prices in this state have historically been low because of the unpredictable destruction of hurricanes. But a few salty nomads were attracted to Florida because it was a good deal, and so they bet against the weather patterns; they were risk-takers and gamblers with nothing much to lose. The settlers were bent on re-making the landscape to suit their needs. As a result, most of the grasslands have been manicured, the forests fallen, the beaches widened, and the springs sectioned off, so much so that it's difficult to imagine what Florida looked like before pavement, concrete parking structures, pink houses and tall condominiums on the beach. A large portion of the residents in south Florida are elderly—retirees who wanted to get the most out of a modest retirement and preferred to die some place sunny and convenient. The effect modern humans have had on this state's water may be compared to the treatment a corpse undergoes in a morgue. As a result of commercial farming, landscaping and development, the water quality in the aquifer in many places is little better than formaldehyde.

Back up in Central Florida, my mom worried constantly about our water supply. We had an electric well that we had installed ourselves. We spent the better part of a summer digging the ditches to place the pipes. Mom was always getting the water tested, treating it, and fretting over its quality. Eventually she gave up and we were told the water was basically poison because of the years of run-off from agriculture. So we bought drinking water in plastic bottles and used the heavily treated tap water for showers and other nonessentials. We stored tap water in any empty container we could find in the summers, never knowing when a hurricane would knock out the power and leave us without the luxury of flushable toilets.

But the problems of the planet's water supply were far away during childhood. When we weren't working on the farm, summers were spent moving slowly, looking for shade as the reptiles do, avoiding rainstorms and swimming. We used to take tubes down the Rainbow River, jet skis on Lake Violet, and lounge in lawn chairs at backyard pool parties. We would take to canoes on Sweetwater Creek, surf boards on the Atlantic side, and kayaks in the Gulf side.

Anytime I feel lost, I can find myself again at the ocean, any ocean will do just for the smell and sound, but if I can get in the calm, warm water and float I am a new person. I used to imagine I dissolved into the salt and didn't have to worry about the flesh and details of my burdensome body. I was the ocean herself, soaking in the sun. Water reminded me of my essence beneath the layers of cultural programming.

Water offers a mirror for ourselves that is not tainted by the editing of human egos. If we pour oil in the water one day and deny it the next, the evidence will be visible in the stains, sludge and tar on her banks. Our egos manipulate and alter stories about ourselves and do not have the same accountability. Stories from an oral tradition have the potential to act as rivers, but often their meaning is lost as they are passed down and cultural patterns change. As culture dissipates, the integrity of myth and folktales wanes.

Indigenous people know the importance of protecting the stories and truths in ritual context within a village. This way the telephone game effect, the dilution of information and loss of original context and meaning, does not come into play as much. It is a good thing that stories are alive and change with the cultures around them, but it is also difficult when there are no elders to offer wisdom. Without the village container, it is as if we feed the wisdom of stories to the wind, then frantically chase the scattered fragments across the globe. Without the reminders that come from the old stories, we try to make meaning and create morals flawed by our own limited experience. We are a culture of adolescents guiding teenagers, and the results of this lack of tradition cause unnecessary suffering.

Florida. Spring 1997.

I'm about eleven or twelve, and I step into the pool, descend the concrete stairs and touch the soft tiles of blue flowers lining the walls. The water sloshes gently side to side—she is safe, warm, chlorinated. Tame. I enter the water, and she holds me up. I splash, she laughs.

Minutes later my friend Maggie calls attention to the brown stream I'm leaking. I jump out, embarrassed. I lunge for a towel darker than my own. A red towel embraces me. I shiver and hide in the bathroom. Why did I have to be a girl? Based on the information I'd gathered, being a girl was the worst.

The Cherokee celebrate the girl's first menses by covering her in mud, a symbol that she is deeply connected with the earth and part of it, but my skin is white, and I grew up in a conservative Christian household where all I wanted was to be a good little girl. And I was. I was smart and quiet. I was proud of my golden hair, and dressed up as a sparkly angel every year for Halloween, though sometimes I wished my brown eyes were blue.

My mother read Bible stories to us nightly until we were

old enough to read the Good Book for ourselves. And I did. I swallowed it all eagerly—original sin from the lying snake, sneaky Eve, cruel Sarah, dutiful Hannah, deceitful Leah, conceited Jezebel, promiscuous Magdalene—the whole lot. Over and over again the women worshipped idols, seduced and led their men astray.

Jesus' mother Mary was one of the only good women in the Bible, and so I loved and emulated her. But all the men got to have dreams, adventures, connections with God, *and* they were able to write it all down. I wanted to be a writer, and it looked like I was the wrong sex.

I saw these gender roles confirmed in my household too. I adored my father: he was a traveler and a scholar and came and went as he pleased. My mother was trapped—tied to the house by us kids. My father saw her as his cage: he couldn't stand her. She seemed weak to me, and the source of the trouble. I wanted to be strong. I did not want to be a woman. On the morning of my first menstruation, when I saw the reddish-brown flow, I started to cry. *I'm stuck.*

My sister and I were home-schooled for three years, grades second through fifth for me. I loved it. I had my own schedule, enjoyed time with the garden and the animals and was still passing all the standardized tests well in the top national percentage. One benefit of having my mom as teacher was the personalized curriculum. She allowed me to spend more time and even skip ahead in literature and poetry to keep up with my appetite for words and stories. I devoured poems by Emily Dickinson, Louisa May Alcott, Laura Ingalls Wilder, Marjorie Kinnan Rawlings and other conservative female writers. I had role models at last: women who were writers.

That was the up side. The down side of having my mother as a teacher was the one-sided perspective and exclusive control of our educational materials she held. I didn't care for socializing much anyway, but my parents insisted we join a home-school academy called ABCD—the Academy of Biblical Character Development—so that we would not be socially awkward.

Mom decided to give us our health class lesson right before we were dropped back into the world of public school. She pulled out one of the encyclopedias we'd picked up at the thrift store and showed us the internal female anatomy. I don't think there were a lot of details, the main point of her lesson was not to touch ourselves or worry much about what was down there until we got married.

Then my mom got very serious. She asked us if we remember the body armor from the Book of Acts. We'd been memorizing verses weekly in Bible study, and there was even a helpful little jingle about this one. It referred to the body armor of Christ. There's the belt of truth; the breastplate of righteousness; the gospel of peace; the shield of faith; the helmet of salvation; and the sword of the spirit. I had memorized it because of the song, but I didn't know how any of that felt. How do you put on a belt of truth?

The main idea I could grasp was that protection was essential, layers of protection. Mom said it was particularly important for us to remember now that we'd be back in public school. There would be boys around and we have to keep them away from us. If a boy touches us at all, we have to tell the teacher.

I was a little worried. It seemed like she was sending us into a war zone with flesh-crazed baboons. She was almost right though: twelve-year-old boys turned out to be relentlessly obsessed with the female body. I was constantly pointed at and referred to by body parts. In class, boys were always trying to grab or even just touch a girl's skin or flesh like they were starved for it. The school bus on the way home was torture. Two boys sat at the front and grabbed or smacked every girl's chest as she got off the bus for weeks. I walked down the aisle at my stop with my hands in front of my still flat chest, but then they'd smack my butt. I never said anything, but another girl told her parents and filed a lawsuit. I wished I had been braver. And, again, I wished I was not a girl.

God seemed cold and cruel to force me into this shape as a woman, wanting only to punish me and remind me how unworthy I was of divine grace. Freedom was light, spiritual and masculine—not dark, material and feminine. In my understanding, the human 'right' to freedom seemed linked to the ability to control one's surroundings, but natural law often got in the way of that aim. According to the Bible, women were an embodiment of the chaos: to be feared as the power of dark matter. They stood in the way of one's ascension and their wombs opened the gates to hell. This demonization of darkness hurts not only women, but more than half the world's population: those with skin darker than a paper bag. I always wondered why. These days I'm starting to suspect it's because of the link in our modern Western psyches between women and nature, women and matter, and women and water.

Western culture measures water's value based on its usefulness to us as humans—water needs to be transparent, crisp and fluid. Clear, flowing water is what we drink and bathe ourselves in, so it is wise, from an evolutionary standpoint, to make this judgment call. We also measure the value of women based on her usefulness to man—woman needs to be attractive, attentive, and fertile. Most people would say that healthy water is by definition clear, and a healthy woman is thin. But the word 'healthy' here is again a judgment based on the limitation of human perspective and current trends. What happens when we zoom out from the focus of our daily utilitarian goals?

From an ecological standpoint, slower moving water is more beneficial to the overall continuation of the water cycle. Fast moving water, endowed with a fiery quality, rushes away and evaporates, while slower moving water has a chance to sink into the ground and replenish the groundwater that maintains plant roots. The Environmental Protection Agency has determined that the highly organic soils of swamps form a thick, black, nutrient-rich environment for the growth of water-tolerant trees and shrubs that are an essential habitat for diverse and rare creatures. These plants and animals could not live anywhere else: they depend on the dark soil of the marsh. Slow water is such an important part of the water cycle that permaculturists dig little ditches known as swales in their landscaping patterns in order to slow water from rolling downhill and draining the topsoil nutrients.

At the other end of the spectrum, distilled water has too much clarity, and fails to provide nourishment because it has been stripped of life. In fact, it is used to pull toxins out of other cells because it is so vacant as to have a leaching quality to it.

This privileging light and avoiding dark is strongly ingrained in much of the Western human psyche and causes deeply seated problems of inequality, fear and violence. Movies and books take it as a given that that dark forest or the dark prince is going to be evil or scary. This assumption is not part of human nature, but it is part of human culture. It is something we learned based on socialization rather than instinct or biological fact.

The drive of greed and the internal feeling of scarcity led certain nations to create new narratives based on the insatiability of their own needs. Carl Von Linnaeus (1707-1778), founder of modern anthropology, put forward a new classification of humans in his work *Systema Naturae* in which he used color to classify humans, and assigned moral and intellectual capacities to each race based on his limited opinion. James King, author of *The Biology of Race,* points out that race is a concept created by people who stood to benefit from the belief that skin color related to a genetic difference and bestowed inherent superiority to lighter colors.

Race has no scientific merit outside of sociological classification. There are no significant genetic variations within the human species to justify the division of races. European scientists spent centuries trying to prove the superiority of the white 'race' based on anecdotal evidence and culturally biased tests of intelligence. And, in many cases, the 'evidence' was accepted.

The 'evidence' was also accepted when applied to the natural landscape. Humanity basically wrote off the value of the swamps because of their superficial appearance and difficulty meeting our needs. We treat swamps as a disease to be cured. Swamps are held in the human psyche as noxious, unpleasant places to live because the suction of the mud and unpredictable nature of flooding makes it difficult to build a house or plant vegetables.

In countless myths, the hero comes to the swamp just before a big transformation. He enters the forest of no return, or the enchanted marsh and meets with a monstrous creature—think of the swamp creature that rises from the murky depths in *Beowulf,* the haunted house of the old woman in every children's movie or the vast nothing and the swamp of sadness from *The Never Ending Story.* Gunter Grass once said: *We need forests in order to get lost. Without forests, and our fairytales about forests, we can never get lost and never find ourselves.* We need swamps in order to be whole.

Perhaps we should reconsider the importance of swamps. They are the meeting place of earth and water, a liminal space between the surface, the conscious world, and the depths of the unconscious. When we dare to venture into the forbidden forest, the soft ground where the waters are dark, or the house of the witch, we engage with adventures and learn more about ourselves. The challenge smooths out our rough edges, but that smoothing process may be uncomfortable.

The obsession with dominance and the greed for cheaper land has driven developers to dry out almost half of this ecologically rich resource in the swampland of Southern Florida, the Everglades. Selfish policy is causing groundwater reserves to disappear in the state. Almost half of what was once the marshland has been drained and developed into mazes of suburbs and retirement villages. I can only imagine the fears that drive this need to possess and control our environment so drastically. I wonder what we are losing if we lose the wild places where we can truly find ourselves as a part of nature.

Ocala. Fall 1998.

I learned a lot in public school. First I learned that animal T-shirts were not cool. It also wasn't cool to be quiet or smart, but that was harder to change. I was tall and had long shiny hair and good skin, and I was proud of my body once I learned to wear clothes to accentuate my tiny waist and growing hips. My boobs were never big enough, but there were plenty of padded bras and push up wires to help me with that. I wore generous amounts of eyeliner and glossy lipsticks scented like peach and sugar cookie . . . My friends said boys like it when you smell like food. I bought expensive lotions with cinnamon and spice and painted my nails in bright colors. I plucked my thick eyebrows down to tiny lines and rolled up my gym shorts to show off my legs. I was twelve, and spent most of my time worrying over my image.

One of the most popular hangouts in the summer was a water park called Wild Waters. We spent countless afternoons there floating in the wave pool and smoking behind the slides. The turbulent emotions of teenagers took over this place as we rushed around and nearly flooded one another with the intensity of misguided hormones. I still remember the smell of chlorine mingled with Black and Mild mini cigars. It was almost always warm enough to swim, and the girls would obsess year-round about their bikini bodies. The boys got high and bragged about how many blow jobs they'd had or whose boobs they'd grabbed. Most girls spent their time sunning on the lawn chairs, and boys would wander by to scope out their tanned skin.

I was especially proud of my little blue and white bikini that year. It sat low on my hips and had a thick white belt that added to my curves. I walked up to the counter to get another lemon ice, and a group of boys whistled at me from the picnic tables. I ignored them for a moment, but then I realized one of them was kind of cute. So I smiled a little and three of them came and stood with me in line. I put my thumb in my belt loop to seem aloof.

"How old are you?" one of them asked.

"I'm twelve, going into seventh grade." I answered, standing up straight to look even taller than the five-foot five I was.

"Woah, you're really hot for a twelve-year-old," one of the taller guys answered.

"Why, how old are you?" I asked. They were sixteen and seventeen, so they got embarrassed and left. But I was glowing as I walked back to my friends—older guys think I'm hot!

I was so worried about how to act in sixth grade, my first year in public school, that I did whatever everyone else did. During the three-month break from classes that summer, away from the peer pressure, I remembered that I didn't like letting others make decisions for me. I was still awkward in seventh grade, but I realized I wasn't meant for the mainstream. The pain of trying to fit into a shape I was not was too awkward. I found a new group of friends who mirrored my individuality, and we paid less attention to the drama of image and sex appeal.

I went back into the stories that sustained me. I discovered a wider range of literature from my English classes and reminded myself how Jo from *Little Women* was strong minded and counter-cultural in her own way. I also loved Scout from *To Kill a Mockingbird*. It would be years before I found Janie in *Their Eyes Were Watching God* and Joan Didion and Sylvia Plath, but I knew enough to look for stronger female archetypes. This love of learning and hunger for strong female characters eventually led me to study literary journalism in college, where, for a brief moment, I felt at home.

University of Florida. April 2004.

Old growth oak trees line the street on Fletcher Drive, draped dramatically with gray Spanish moss that adds a haunting effect at dusk. The sun is setting to my right, and the magic hour has just begun. Golden light highlights dark silhouettes in all directions. I am right where I belong. I feel refreshed, as if I've just bathed in a crisp spring. College is a long drink of fresh water for a thirsty psyche.

I walk past the Plaza of the Americas where the Hare Krishnas wear bright orange robes, chant to their lord and savior, and offer discounted vegan meals. I've just come from an anthropology class on language and culture, and I'm still mulling over the meaning of the Hopi word for water: transparent life-giving force. I feel nostalgic for a culture I never knew. Indigenous cultures created language based on observation that held meaning, so the earliest languages were often full of lengthy, circuitous dialogues. English is a streamlined language, one that gets to the point like an arrow rather than a moth. In my mind English reflects the way in which modern humans seem to have become obsessed with changing the world that they forget to let it change them.

I'm pulled back from my philosophical musings when I feel my foot sink into the soft ground. I struggle to lift a mud-soaked sandal from the edge of a puddle I nearly missed. I look over to my left side and see two eyes stare up at me as I move back onto the sidewalk. It's a giant, ancient reptile with a head full of teeth, but I am in a hurry and I hardly pay him any attention.

If you've got water, you've got alligators—the campus at the University of Florida is no exception to this law. Floridians know to assume every body of water contains an alligator (or three). My mother even called animal control one summer to have a little five-footer removed from our baby pool when I was young.

Central Florida's water table has been so depleted that sinkholes regularly pop up in people's yards, under houses, and in front of the red brick buildings next to my culture class. A seven-foot gator lives in this filled sinkhole on campus, it's a mini swamp reclaiming a spot where the land used to be all marsh. The water smells like a compost bin, which is the price paid for turning over something rotten into something fertile. No one likes a slimy leaf, and few people care for the slippery frogs that link water and land, but this miniature ecosystem does not worry about glamor or glory. And those dinosaur-brained reptiles seem to thrive here. I start to wonder about the wisdom of the alligator. As an ancient creature whose design has withstood the test of time, I am curious what she remembers.

There is a story they tell in parts of West Africa about Spider who stole all of the knowledge and put it in a pot way up high in a baobab tree. He kept it away from everyone else, but he himself would crawl up the branches to enjoy it.

One time he reached a little further into the pot than he had before, and the ceramic container fell from the high branch of the baobab tree and shattered on the ground. Some of the knowledge and stories were lost, but the rest remained in pieces. All the other animals rushed in and took a little shard with them for their families. Alligator was one of those creatures, as were Elephant, Snake, Vulture and Lion. Since that day, the seekers, the ones who want to know the full story, have to be content to travel from place to place to gather the broken pieces.

The depth of woman, the full story of her strength and unique challenges remains, but it is no longer compiled into a coherent narrative within Western culture. We have to be willing to do the work of gathering the scattered pieces in order to reassemble the wholeness of ourselves. The river meanders slowly at times and at other times she sinks into the ground as a way to digest the nutrients she has gathered over the centuries. The swamplands are a denser store of memories because they constantly hold this rich knowledge in stillness and contemplation. I found this spacious depth that I learned from observing the marshes useful when I listened to stories from around the world.

The Story of Green Tara's Vow, from Tibetan Buddhism

Once there was a great Buddha named Avalokiteshvara, who was kind above all else and whose heart flowed constantly with the waters of compassion. He was the greatest kind of Buddha, because he was actually a bodhisattva—which means he had woken from the illusion of suffering and then volunteered to return to the world of pain, greed and hunger in order to help others find their way.

One day after watching an immense storm, an earthquake and a volcanic eruption, he becomes overwhelmed with sadness. He feels connected to the pain of others as if it were happening to himself. He recognizes an immense suffering coming from humanity—that strong, watery heart filled with unconditional love in his chest overflows—and two beautiful tear drops of pure compassion race down his cheek to be born on earth.

One tear becomes the illustrious white Tara. She is the gentle mother, like the Virgin Mary. The other tear, her twin, becomes the activist green Tara who is known for fierce action, more similar to Mary Magdalene.

Green Tara took on an exceptional birth, incarnating as a princess who was very bright and loved by all. She would wake every morning and make offerings, praying that she would become enlightened in order to alleviate the suffering of all beings.

Her offerings were the sweetest of the village; she would bring jasmine, and oranges, and incense. As she walked from the market one morning with her basket of gifts, a group of monks stopped her. They had taken notice of her devotion.

Being male and fairly advanced in their practice at the monastery, they were eager to show their compassion. They took pity on her—because at that time only males could be admitted into formal devotion as a renunciate—and offered her immediate re-birth as a male, which was a considerable offer at the time.

Tara smiled her enchanting smile and said thank you, but no thank you. *Our outer skins of male and female do not mirror our deepest selves. I can see that any woman can achieve enlightenment as easily as any man.*

And then she vows, right there on the spot: *There are many who desire enlightenment in a man's body, but none who work for the benefit of sentient beings in the body of a woman. Therefore, until samsara is empty, I shall work for the benefit of sentient beings in a woman's body.*

Tara went on to become the mother of all Buddhas, and is known as the embodiment of infinite wisdom and deep compassion. Because she is born from a tear, she is a special kind of water deity. Tara is green like the potent algae of the swamp; the slimy goo that allows digestion of waste into nutrition. She unlocks the power to transmute poison into medicine, and she reminds us that our ideas about our bodies and sex are just that: ideas, and not truth.

⁓

I was born with a heart that craves stories; the stories that saturated my young psyche were of a patriarchal, monotheistic God of revenge and separation. I learned to feel shame and guilt at being a woman and tried to escape my body or use it to gain approval from men.

But at my core, I have always been a seeker of a wider range of stories. It is difficult to leave with the cloying heaviness of the swamp begging me to stay still, but my path as a seeker calls me to wander wider than anyone else in my family before me, to find my own answer to the questions in my soul.

I now know that I am blessed to be a woman. Like Tara, I no longer believe I need to be born male to achieve my full potential. And just like the mothers of the clanless children, I go with a prayer to creation out into the unknown, hoping to find my own understanding from the wisdom of other dark waters. It is my work to learn to listen with the ears of my heart and dance with the rhythms of the moon, and for me that means leaving home and crossing the Atlantic Ocean.

VOLTA RIVER

Melts and Races Downhill

Perhaps if we had found ourselves as we looked at that dark image, and in that recognition, felt part of the whole dark thread of life—the darkness of the womb from which we were born; the darkness of the new moon to which our menstrual cycles entrained; the dark place to which we descended for personal growth, emerging . . . strong and whole and authentic; the darkness of the face of the first African mother; the primordial darkness of matter before the sunburst of creation.

Leslene della Madre

Ghana. May 2005.

I
T'S THE SUMMER before my last semester in college, and I am lost in more ways than one. I sit in the back left corner of a tro-tro (an old van used as a bus in Ghana). It's hot and there are twenty-five men, including my companion, Noah, to my left. The van's tiny ecosystem stinks. Like ripe bananas and weeks of unwashed sweat, oil, petrol and unfulfilled longing. The music is too loud, or maybe it's just loud enough to drown out my thoughts. I have no idea where we are, but the rock paved road keeps unfurling over the dusty landscape.

This is the summer that I take a hard left turn from the paved path that lies straight in front of me. My journalism internship in Accra, Ghana did not go at all as expected, and I've decided to blame the drums.

I had never heard African drums before, at least not in person, and certainly not on a regular basis. The music of West Africa brought me, eventually, to an entirely new way of experiencing the world and opened a path before me that I had never expected to take. Once I heard that deep, pulsing sound, my entire body lifted up and listened. A part of me, I'm guessing the more watery part, recognized the importance of this sound right away. I was taking the first baby steps over a terrifying bridge from being mind-focused toward a body-based awareness.

A steady percussion is the first sound we experience. The watery environment of the mother's womb is acoustically designed to allow the sound of the mother's heart to reassure the fetus. Her heartbeat holds a steady rhythm that helps weave us into form. This time of development (up to about three years of age) is mostly pre-verbal, and so implicit memories are not stored in our minds as stories we can relay in words. Our earliest experiences are stored in our bones, muscles and tissue as patterns of feeling.

Drums remind us of the feelings before language that guided us into life. The instrument itself is surprisingly simple: the skin of an animal, usually a goat or deer, is pulled tight over a wide, open base. It's the empty space of the drum that allows for the magic to happen. Just like in the womb.

There is a stanza in drumming that is known as the "call." For dancers, this is a time to break out from the choreography and improvise. I had taken dance classes before, but I always stuck to the structure of the eight counts. Until I found West African dance and heard the call. This is the moment of bifurcation, like when one cell splits into two and chooses whether to make an exact copy of the DNA or allow space for a mutation, a transformation of potential. My mind is bypassed. Improvisation feels like standing on the edge of an internal cliff, and the next step is walking out into the starry night sky. I have no idea what I am doing or why.

Drums have been used to communicate between communities because of their ability to carry sound over long distances. The drums called me back in time over more than twenty years toward a wider place of knowing in my body that I had forgotten. It is a place where life unfolds from the quiet stillness and uninterrupted darkness of the flesh. In my case, being immersed in the soundscape stimulated frozen memories from a pre-verbal state to re-surface, which was confusing because the memories are inherently evasive for language to capture and comprehend. The feelings rush through my body, and before I know what's happening I find myself somewhere I did not expect to be. I feel the changes inside me affect my entire family constellation even though I am across the Atlantic. It is as if we are a kaleidoscope and I've just turned the handle one degree to the left.

I sit in the back of that crowded tro-tro and let my mind wander over the events of the previous week.

I'd been my mother's most trusted counsellor since I could talk, and as her counsellor I had always advised her to leave my abusive but charismatic father. But now I'm not so sure. It happened weeks ago, her moving out, but I only just made it to an internet café yesterday. My inbox was full of letters from her, but there was also one from my father. He's never emailed me. I didn't even know he had my email address. And he's never hinted that he cares for my mother—he was always picking at her and cutting her down. My whole life he did this. But now, now, he's falling apart. Shattered. Lost. He's never reported being anything other than a happy camper. This is big.

Tears. An avalanche of them before I realize I'm holding my breath. I pull in air, and it's a sobbing gasp that ignites fresh sobs. Hot, burning, sobs. Something about my breath offends my lungs and they sting and grasp. My entire body pulls the emergency alarm. The crying stops and I stare, frozen.

I attract curious eyes from the polite computer users around me in the café. Noah logs off his screen and puts his hands on my shoulders. "Let's go," he says quietly. No need for explanation, he drags the white arrow to the upper left hand corner and pushes the X. My father's words vanish back into the invisible tubes and tunnels they came from. A photo of a nautical spiral appears on the computer screen, and I feel the tightness of twenty years of anger lock in my jaw. I thought I would be happy when they finally split, but somehow I feel rejected and vulnerable.

Outside the rusty dirt makes me gag, and I bury my head in Noah's chest. He happens to be just the right height for this gesture. I let him hold me, sobbing silently, internally, not enough. We decide to take some time off from our volunteer positions and make a plan to visit the Green Turtle Eco Lodge at the other end of the country.

So here we are, six hours into the journey, black fingernails, damp shirts, cracked skin, and an about-to-explode bladder that threatens to burst over every bump—but I feel ok. Except I don't want to be a journalist any more, suddenly the world's pain is too big and that career path is not good enough. The shock of my parents' split has caused a deep chasm to open up in my innerscape, and every decision is up for review.

I've made a list of new possible careers: doctor, teacher, artist, activist, mediator . . . I feel like I'm in ninth grade career class all over again. It's not my favorite situation, but how can I be a journalist when there is so much suffering? My mind had made this safe little equation about how writing helps people. But as I waltzed past the rows of sick and dying people in the crowded hospital waiting room for my appointment with the director just the other week, it felt impossible to convince myself that words on a page—in English—in a country with less than a third literacy rate—was really helping anyone. I wanted to work with people, put actual Band-Aids on the places that hurt. So I decided to do just that.

I switched from the journalism plan to the health care one. I worked with orphans at the Liberian refugee camp outside of Accra. I had always been turned off by the feeling of opposition, struggle and competition within journalism, and the drums were teaching me something else. They were always played together. If you can hear yourself drumming in a drum circle, you're doing it wrong.

The truth is I've been inconclusive as to where I fit my entire life. I just don't seem to fit. Anywhere. I run in a million directions and just skim the surface. I want to do something big. Something that matters. I know almost nothing, and am passionate as a June bug on a mild summer night. I don't seem to have much of a chance in this world of ambitious go-getters and ladder climbers. Tired, I let out a sigh. Noah pats my leg.

"What do you like to do?" asks the man who has always known he wants to be a doctor, since the moment he understood what his father did. *You save people? Cool, that's what I want to do too.* His dad is a surgeon—heart, I think. His parents have a mansion in fancy part of New Jersey and are happily married. His mom doesn't work. She makes necklaces and sells them or gives them away. Easy.

I look at him only thinly veiling my contempt. Then I consider his question. I don't know if it was ever put to me like that. *What do I need to do? What does the world need? How can I use my skills best?*—Yeah, I've been over those. But *what do I like to do?* That is new. I feel the vista opening up before me.

I look out the window at the changing screen of dark greens, tropical tree after tropical tree. A woman with water on her head and a baby on her back urges a goat across the stream, men wait at the crossroads, cutting pineapples and smiling with all their teeth like happy gators. An old man sits on the curb, knees up, hands resting on top, and a little boy splashes in the mud.

The driver is playing highlife music, which is on everywhere we go in this country. Highlife is upbeat but mellow at the same time—with the strength of the ocean waves breaking on the shore and a gentle consistency that's as patient as a mountain. The rhythm is circular and has percussion that keeps a steady groove, like a river rushing down its path—sure of itself. My favorite song, the one that has been following me for weeks, comes on the radio:

do do da do
do do da do
Still I love you . . .

I smile. "I like this," I finally answer.

Noah raises his blond eyebrows and the left corner of his mouth turns down. He's going to tease me about this.

"Riding on tro-tros?" he feigns shock. "I don't think anyone will pay you for that."

"I know, but there is a nugget of wisdom there. I like movement, rhythm. I love to travel, to meet new people, to gather wide and follow my curiosity. I wonder about everything. I ask questions and listen to the answers. I want to know how people and places got to be the way they are. I am interested in the good and bad and the boring mundane, I want to hear both the loud and quiet. I want to see the big picture behind what we do in our routines. I want to zoom out and take in the whole magnificent tapestry of the entire universe. I can't figure it out or really explain it, but this music reminds me who I am and how it feels to be—to just be—without the need to articulate that. Would someone pay me for that?"

"I don't know," he admits.

I move gently to the music and feast on the stories parading past the window. I feel warm in my chest and breathe deep through my torso. Something has woken up, and I am home. The honesty is a relief.

I don't know. *I don't know* turns me into a tiny trickle of freshly melted snow, and the descent down the mountain is tenuous. I pick at one of my gritty fingernails and straighten out a line in my long blue and white printed skirt. I've spent half the ride debating my next move. Should I dive underground, push over rocks, or evaporate into the air? It's a small country, yes, but we are moving slow over rock-laden roads. I just tossed out my boyfriend of two years, along with my dreams of being the next Joan Didion, and my hopes that my parents might step away from the edge of divorce. I am empty as a drum, blank as the sand, and grasping like a monkey to the thinnest branch, way out from the trunk, but I have found at least one moment of peace with all this.

I've spent the summer immersed in moonlight dance parties with drums on the beach. I am pulsing and alive, and I feel sensations much more acutely. I am thawing, and the pool of water I am becoming terrifies me: I no longer fit into the shoebox I had planned to inhabit. This is how snow must feel on the morning of the first sunrise of spring. The water forms and melts, racing in many directions toward lower ground. The pace is fast, and the direction is uncalculated. The warmth, the drums, the crisp moments of a foreign place, and the proximity of nature are working on me, but it is the water that causes the most radical of changes.

My house mother encourages me to go and visit the famous Volta River, the pride of her country. So I take a day trip with my Danish roommate, and that Saturday we stand on the edge of the Volta. I stand by the water and listen. If music is the sound created by the space between the notes, then rivers are the symphony of stillness created by the chatter of constant motion. Who is this river? The Volta is a disappointingly flat river at this bend—quietly slipping away toward the horizon. The water is brown and a small child crouches to relieve himself nearby. I smell must and decay. An old half-sunken yellow rowboat on the shore rests without judgment as witness.

Volta means *many turns*, and she was named by Portuguese invaders in West Africa. No one I talk to seems to remember (or wants to tell me) what she was called before, but the locals say the lake that is at the center of her belly is known as the way home: the moment boats have a chance to turn around and return to where they came from. The Volta travels across parts of Burkina Faso and into Ghana as the White, Red and Black tributaries. White, red, and black: the colors of the goddess—maiden, mother and crone—the cycles of a woman's life. These colors braid together in my mind, and I turn over a new feeling of depth and curiosity that refuses to surface in words.

Tributaries are not actually separate rivers, they only appear to be independent if we zoom in and don't bother locating the source. This is easy to do in the rush of daily life, but slowing down and changing lenses allows for that wider view to return. The steady rhythm of the water rushing past, the circular narrative of the drums, and the reclining nature of storytelling all help us to sink into that spacious perspective that awakens our gut instincts.

Humans often forget they are inherently connected, it is often easier to imagine ourselves as distinct islands rather than a single continent. Drums help us flip this switch physiologically back toward an understanding of ourselves as one organism with separate parts, one river with several tributaries.

Many drumming patterns create tension between the limited notions of self (in the mind) and the vast freedom on the other side of body awareness. Carolyn Brandy, a master drummer and Santeria high priestess, explains that this is precisely the goal of a group of drummers, *they want to throw you off!* The dancer's feet move with the constant beat on the predictable one, two. This is what she calls your main purpose in life. *No matter what, do not lose touch with your main purpose in life.* Then, the hands are clapped in various manners that are meant to test your commitment to that life purpose. This is called the argument. One cannot question her feet once her hands get involved—the body has got to listen and respond without the head. It's a wild ride, just listening to the layers of vibrations that the drums emit. Trying to inhabit the opposition in movement forces my mind to loosen its grip, and my life changes. I pulse between moments of whole body acceptance and conceptual theory.

I return to the river often overflowing with questions. The river touches and then runs from my ten bright pink toenails. One foot reaches the soft sticky sand. The other foot hesitates in the air. *You can never step into the same river twice.* She is already gone. She is alive. And what is alive moves. The home I remember no longer exists. I cannot turn back. I have to look forward, and create a home with what I have here.

Rivers are one of the easiest places to recognize the easily forgotten truth of impermanence and relentless shifting. Flowing water creates an illusion of one steady stream, persistent in motion and constant only in change—a line of traffic, blood in vessels, rain—and even humans, on a microscopic level, move in a similar pattern of fluid motion. Humans may appear solid from the outside, but if we zoom in close enough, the stillness and structure of skin and bones is actually a mass of fluids and space. Our skin is entirely new every thirty days; we re-grow our livers in six weeks; our skeleton regenerates in forty-five days; and our brains renew themselves every two months. We basically have a brand new system, right down to each atom, every five to seven years.

There is a special kind of a vulture associated with the river goddess Oshun who embodies this paradoxical way of moving through space and time. The sacred sankofa bird of West Africa looks back at her history as she flies forward over unknown waters. I feel like a bird flying out over the ocean, unsure of the next time my feet will touch land.

I feel the urgency to put down roots, to belong—but how do I plant myself when the current of thoughts runs so fast? If permanence is an illusion, then what allows for the persistence of self, of home or of culture? It must be the same intangible knowing that allows a river to be what she is. She is a constant rush of new droplets of water called by one name because of the story we tell. Our identity is a story we tell about ourselves. Culture can be simplified to describe a group of people who share similar stories. The water flows in the same places, makes the same decisions, time after time over the landscapes.

Everything follows an order, makes a shape, and then sometimes it deviates. The river has sought the path of least resistance and settled into the grooves of comfort, just like the trails our synapses form from our repeated thought patterns. It's like when the route to the grocery gets into your muscle memory. You've used the same trail for a long time, so you hardly notice when to turn and when to stop. If you take a different route, it will feel longer, because your entire being is paying attention to the details again—making notes to recall this route next time.

In Ghana, I feel the grooves in my brain re-routing, and the possibilities seem endless. Time has expanded. In this tender, open state I take a weekend trip to Elmina Castle, the largest port for human slaves during the Atlantic slave trade. It is a haunted, exhausted place. And the waves are still furious, pounding against the castle walls, eroding the memory of wrongs too heavy to digest with saltwater alone. The sickness of separation and ownership enforced by the white walls rises from my gut and forces its way out. I make it to the shore, but the power of the waves pounding into the sand scares me back inside.

I recognize myself as a part of the problem, the drive to help, fix, or save "others" brought me to Africa. I'm no better than the arrogant missionaries who claimed humanitarian purposes during colonization. Why am I here? The feeling that something is wrong inside me is bigger than I thought. I avoid the ocean because it holds the heaviness of a graveyard, but I return to the Volta River with a new urgency to my questions, and again and again she surrounds my feet with her waters, but I do not submerge myself. There's something safer about the shore.

I am pulled deeper into the scenery of this country against my will one warm, unassuming night in July, just before I fly home. Noah invites me to a movie at the cinema in Accra. I think it is a pirated version of *Pirates of the Caribbean*, ironically. This is our only chance to be alone together, since our house moms are very strict. I take showers out of a bucket, eat frozen rice and vegetables for every meal and sneak to the movies to make out with my new boyfriend.

It's almost midnight when we start to walk home. We hold hands and sigh a little to each other. I point out the delicate crescent moon, just coming into view. An older woman sweeping the sidewalk scolds us, "Go to your room!" We release hands immediately: we'd almost forget how inappropriate public displays of affection are here. I feel a gentle tug under my right shoulder, and then I feel lighter.

I feel my hip—my purse is gone. I turn to Noah: "I think I just got robbed?" I half-ask.

"Uh, should I run after him?" he asks, puzzled.

We see the man on the bicycle turn the corner and decide not to pursue him. The woman with the broom speaks up again, "Did he take your purse?" she yells across the street. I nod, a little confused, and she begins to scold me for being out too late, and then for not shouting out to go after him. "I know his mother!" she says. "She will hear about this!"

I return to my house like a dog with her tail between her legs and knock on the heavy wooden door. My house sister, Noel, scurries across the living room from where she sleeps on the couch and asks, worried. "Who is there?"

"It's me," I manage. I hear her release the lower lock, then the middle wooden frame across the blue door, and finally the metal deadbolt. I notice for the first time the countless woodpecker sized holes along the door's frame. How many times has this door been broken down and reinforced? This is when the fear settles into my stomach. I feel violated and unsafe. My house mother, Miriam, scolds me for being out so late and worries over the lost key more than the cell phone and little bit of cash

I've lost.

I lie in bed awake until I hear the sound of sweeping outside my door. It's just before dawn and I haven't slept, but I'm not tired. I love the sound of a broom across a hard floor. I feel my insides respond, and they are swept clean as well. Each morning I wake to this sound before the roosters, before the sun creeps in through the thin curtains, before the sounds of pots in the kitchen, and before the neighbors turn on Shakira's *Hips Don't Lie*.

Why didn't I yell for help when he took my purse? I felt irritated by the older woman from the street: her loudness and confidence unnerves me. *She's not my mother.* Why do I feel I have no right to take up space, to defend myself, to scream injustice? I just let him take my purse. What is missing then, that the fire in me did not rise to say *No!* I feel damp and weak, but being robbed has brought me out of the fog I've been traveling in. I feel more a part of this place than I had before as a visitor, now, after being robbed, I imagine I've been initiated into the reality of this neighborhood.

I am aware of the spectrum of victim and tyrant spiraling through myself. I am the head of the serpent, devouring her own tail, and I am also the tail being eaten in silent acquiescence. Seeing all the holes where the locks had been broken in the door frame before makes me aware that there is struggle and scarcity in this country to which I had been oblivious. I am ready to crawl home, but first, I need to say goodbye.

I spend the day on my own. I walk more slowly than I have so far, meandering between little shops—open shelters with dogs, kids and music at the front. I hop on a tro-tro to head toward the square. As the driver waits at a stop light, a crowd of merchants rush to the windows. Women have fruits and nuts in baskets on their heads, and men carry large plastic bags full of water. I take a bit of cash from my pouch and motion to the woman with the pine nuts. I buy a bag, then I notice a woman with a whole pineapple and a big knife. My dry mouth releases streams of saliva, and I pay too much for a cup of freshly-sliced pineapple. I haven't had fruit all summer.

I savor the sweet and generous liquid, lick my fingers, and then turn to the pine nuts. The salt tastes good after the sugar. Then I'm thirsty, so I open the small bag of water at the corner and add a few drops of iodine. The clear liquid turns brown, but I know it's safe to drink now. I tilt my head back and manage to spill only a little as the light turns green and the tro-tro leaves the crowd at the intersection behind.

I get out in front of the fabric booth at the market to touch a golden skirt with red roses draped from the overhang. A woman rises from her seat and pulls it down. She hands me a mirror as I hold it up to my hips. "Very beautiful," I say. The lines move like overlapping waves, and the fabric smells like cinnamon incense. The woman has a kind face full of lines and patterns like the landscape in the Western States. She smiles. I nod, fold it up, pay and bring it home.

I was touched by the feeling of community, roots and belonging I felt in Ghana; most people stayed close to their place of birth and knew their entire extended family. The experience inspired me to begin researching my family lineage in greater depth. I had always been curious about my culture, but the longing became more urgent once I moved away from Florida and was on my own.

When I had some genetic testing done and found that one of my grandmothers way back on my dad's side was African, I felt denial and disbelief. How could my family have covered up our own grandmother? A surge of grief follows a slow realization. We must have decided to forget her, to cover her up in our selfishness and guilt—in our belief that survival meant more than memory. We believed we needed to be light to live in the world that rejects darkness. My grief turns to anger, followed by shame. I am frustrated there is no one alive to blame. It was a secret that was passed down and then disappeared. The weight of this understanding pulls something heavy across my low belly, like an anchor dragging skeletons across the ocean floor.

I search for more information, and I find a single shining mirror—a broken shard of glass in my family tree. As I look through the mirrors of myself, I see a forgotten grandmother with darker skin. Finally I find a teacher who remembers the West African river goddess Oshun. The story of Oshun's transformation from Africa to the Americas is part of the human story, it is part of freshwater's story, woman's story, and it is part of my story as well.

The Oshun River flows southwesterly from the mountains in Yorubaland (Nigeria) and spills into numerous tributaries in West Africa. Oshun's name most closely translates as the source or spring. She is the little sister, the one with honey lips, the gentle one, full of grace and ease. She decorates herself in gold and always carries a mirror.

Oshun's healing powers are as renowned as her sexual prowess. Her laughter calls the thunder god home to her bed. Her tears heal the broken hearts of orphaned children. Her sweet water brings life to earth. But long, long ago, at the beginning of time as we know it, Oshun was misunderstood and overlooked, and her neglect nearly ended life on earth.

The Story of Oshun, from the Yoruba People

When the Yoruba creator first brings life to the planet it begins with the rocks and the mountains. The spirits, the *orisha*, of those landforms animate each of their separate patterns to form matter. Then the creator adds the trees and the ocean, and the spirits that inhabit and enliven those parts of nature take up residence.

Oshun is the youngest of the orisha. And because she is young, she is often left out by her older siblings. The bigger, male deities forget to invite Oshun to the celebration of first creation, so for some time the waters of the world are salty, and no life is possible. The male orisha seek counsel with the creator and ask why the world is not yet animated with creatures and plants. The creator says they had better go humbly to their littlest sister Oshun and ask her.

They go apologetically and beg her to come help them create life on earth. She hums and combs her hair, glancing into her hand mirror. She is pregnant, and angry at them for their poor treatment of her. Oshun tells them she will wait until she gives birth, and if her child is a girl she will stay right where she is in the ethereal realms, but if her child is a boy—then she will come down and animate the planet they are begging to save.

Time passes, and she does give birth to a male child, Elegba, lord of the crossroads. Only then does Oshun release her sweet waters onto the earth, and the story of life begins. She brings love and beauty to the earth, and right in the spot where Oshun lands, a beautiful fresh spring appears and flows toward the sea. All the little green things, the ferns and the mosses spring up beside her.

I find it fascinating that the fate of the earth depends on

the whim of one young woman, a maiden on the threshold of motherhood. In Yoruba culture, Oshun is like a spiritual blueprint for the life that will be created or manifested on the earth. This culture emphasizes that there is a special value, and a tendency to overlook, the young women of the village. The importance of taking care of fresh water, of valuing and listening to young girls is essential for human survival. Neglecting the importance of beauty and meaning in our lives is not only harmful to the village, it threatens humanity's existence on this planet. The elders notice how easy it is to write her off, and they place a warning in the form of a story.

The personified Oshun always carries a mirror with her, and this gesture may be misunderstood as a simple act of vanity. But Yoruba priestess Luisah Teish says it is a symbol of her need for self-reflection. The river goddess is naturally fluid and often loses her shape in the containers of others, like a modern day empath. As a result, she constantly needs to check her reflection in order to feel where she begins and others end.

It is also significant that Oshun gives birth to a boy in the story. This is another symbol that articulates the way West Africans view women's power. Because the Yoruba people lived close to the land, they learned from observing nature. Everything in nature reproduces itself. Usually the baobab tree produces another baobab tree, the fish create more fish, and the ferns create additional ferns. It is not so significant, then, when a woman creates a child in her own image—another girl—but there is something especially magical about a woman producing a child of a different biological form than herself—a boy.

This ability had a profound impact on the imagination of our ancestors. In Western Europe a similar story emerged in the Pagan tradition, which also honors the special ability for woman to give birth to a boy during the wheel of the year. (This is partly why Mary and Jesus' relationship was easily picked up when Christianity spread across Europe: it was a symbol that was already familiar.)

Woman's ability to produce her opposite gave her a high rank, and African societies across the continent honored this power as meaningful and worthy of respect. African queens were common across the continent before Christianity and Islam were introduced, and the women often chose the next kings. There are countless ancient depictions in clay and wood carvings of a woman sitting on a throne with a male child in her lap. She is the constant stability of throne, and he is the ever-changing executor of her will.

Oshun is a queen. The little sister, Oshun, is the embodiment of fresh waters. She represents the natural healing salve—the missing ingredient during hard times. She is the diplomat, the sweet water that brings the earth to life and allows us to flourish. When water is present, there is agreement, an understanding and connection. We recognize each other. We are different, but we are not separate.

Oshun, as a perpetual maiden, represents water's ability to flow through difficulty and erase stuck patterns. And as the river, she is not always gentle and happy—her fierceness, rage and strength are just as essential. She forgives both the victims and the tyrants in our blood and invites both to drink from her generous breast. She forgives, but she does not forget the grandmothers my family left behind. She is the honey sweet web of life and love that connects us all, no matter our age or external appearance, and she is also fear and loneliness when we are separating from long held karmic patterns and family dynamics.

I leave Ghana feeling more scattered than ever. I am full of music and stories, but no one has told me what to make of these experiences. I'm swirling in a seemingly infinite eddy, and the spirals seem to lift me from the ground like a whirlwind in a hurricane. It feels imperative that there is a right way, if I could only see further ahead to know which way I'm supposed to flow. I want to read the final page of my story before I decide what's next. I wish some older, wiser person could give me the answers, tell me where I belong and what it means to be a woman.

As the sun warms and thaws more and more of my internal icebergs, the tiny creeks and puddles pool together and begin to create deeper pathways, which join as braids and become their own force of motion. Soon the thaw is a creek, falling and diving toward a common resting place where it has time and space to settle before the next storm comes ashore and scatters my neatly arranged notions of security. My feet continue to carry me away from Florida, but they cannot seem to escape the swamp.

MISSISSIPPI DELTA

Floods into Homes

You know, they straightened out the Mississippi River in places, to make room for houses and livable acreage. Occasionally the river floods these places. "Floods" is the word they use, but in fact it is not flooding; it is remembering. Remembering where it used to be. All water has a perfect memory and is forever trying to get back to where it was. Writers are like that: remembering where we were, that valley we ran through, what the banks were like, the light that was there and the route back to our original place. It is emotional memory—what the nerves and the skin remember as well as how it appeared. And a rush of imagination is our "flooding".

Toni Morrison

New Orleans. March 2006.

WE ARRIVE AT the house in a van full of volunteers. College kids mostly. There is not a single working traffic light in the city yet, and the neighborhoods are eerily quiet on this side of town. We park in front of a modest blue house, and I think to myself that it looks almost normal from the outside. I pull on a white, full-body jumpsuit, put a mask over my nose and mouth, and go inside.

The house is dark as the inside of a cave, with the little bit of cloud-filtered light making its way in through one small window in the front. I can smell the rot and mold through my mask, and there is a distinct stain across the top of the walls. It looks as if a giant child drew a river with blue, green and black crayons held in one hand exactly two feet from the ceiling all the way around.

This is the flood line. This is how high the water flooded into the house and stood for weeks after Hurricane Katrina. As I realize this, I feel as if I am underwater. A fullness in my head, a buzzing in my ears. I close my eyes and almost feel like I am floating. I open my eyes and take a long exhale. This is the wake of the storm, the fury of nature that humans have tried so adamantly to escape with technological advances. We try not to look at the evidence right in front of us, but it doesn't work. I reach into the wall to finish what the storm started.

The drywall crumbles like cheesecake in my bare hands. I put the pieces in a plastic garbage bag and notice the living room that's barely standing. Placed squarely in the center of the fireplace rack, a single Pine Mountain Crackling Firelog waits in its black wrapper to be lit. Vases with roses painted on the sides survived the water, but one brown photo album—full of weddings, birthdays, lazy Sundays—did not. The family's faces are blurred, anonymous. They could be any family, so they are mine. One thousand two hundred bodies have been found, and the deceased are still surfacing in attics and beneath sofas.

I spent my spring break in March 2006 gutting houses in New Orleans after Hurricane Katrina. The city was absolutely devastated and not showing many positive signs of revival, even several months after the storm. This city is one of many affected by the increase in superstorms as a result of global climate change.

New Orleans is a city built on marshland, surrounded by water on all sides, an irresistible port city that gambled big on besting the historic floods of the Mississippi River. New Orleans proudly stands as the last meandering curve, like a sacred pause, for the mighty Mississippi before the river pours herself into the Gulf of Mexico.

The Mississippi is a famously temperamental and muddy river, who grows wide and flaccid at her delta. She seems to carry a heavy secret at the bottom of her river bed, and it keeps her pace gentle and languid. She's so humble one would hardly know she's the largest drainage system in North America. She rises up from a trickle in Minnesota and then slowly meanders southward for 2,340 miles. The Mississippi is the central nervous system of the continent, transporting nutrients and waste across the length of the land.

I stay with a friend from high-school, the red-headed Tim who has just shaved off his mohawk from Mardi Gras. He is a creative type who never fit in in conservative central Florida, but his quirky cooking habits, bizarre photography, and wildly experimental small-scale architectural projects are welcomed with open arms here in New Orleans. He is a passionate host, clearly driven by a love and understanding of this unique place. He says New Orleans is not really part of the United States, she's a little country all to herself.

He's partly right. Because of the city's history as a French and then a Spanish colony, the post-slavery laws were much closer to European values than to the United States. One major difference was the acceptance of a *plaçage*, or a common law marriage between inter-racial partners. It was a half-step; the rest of the country held bi-racial marriages as strictly illegal until 1967. In addition, New Orleans held a more lenient policy on slaves being able to buy or win their freedom. Partly because of the larger number of white men in antebellum New Orleans, coupled with the alarmingly short average age of black males (an outrageous eight years old) and also as a result of a greater number of free black women, plaçages became common practice.

This is a fascinating side note of history to explore, not because the racial relations were ideal, but because as a longer term result New Orleans (at least before Hurricane Katrina) was one of the most authentically culturally diverse cities of the United States. As a visitor, there is a feeling in the city of shared history, of strong roots, of creativity and belonging. Residents take pride in being decidedly from here; many residents of the Ninth Ward in particular had been in the same family home for generations. The city stands on the edge of massive change if the lifeblood of her streets cannot return from the refuge they sought in Texas and the surrounding states during Hurricane Katrina.

As I know from experience, the swamp is a place that is difficult to leave, as the sticky mud literally pulls and slows you down. But having left, it may be even more difficult to return after such a strong show of natural force and engineering failures.

Tim, myself and a few of his friends spend the afternoon barbequing at a riverside park. A little red and brown snake glides right between my feet and I hop to avoid her. I seem to have been more startled than she was; she slithers along on her way toward the cool concrete without speeding up. Her small pointed tongue darts in and out as she sways. A slow-moving cargo train tempts Tim to jump aboard, but the cool iced tea and lemonade in his glass keeps him in his lawn chair. The humidity refuses to be ignored. It's a strong force that slows everything down a bit. In my first few days in the city I had to keep adjusting my walking pace so as to not get too far ahead of my friends, but it didn't take long before my blood thinned out, and I needed to move more slowly as well.

Maybe this slower way of taking in one's surroundings is partially why the city feels so friendly. Even vowels linger, they're drawn out in the mouth before they reach the air and make your acquaintance. I feel at ease with the pace, inspired by the aesthetic of the land, intrigued by the artistic way of life, and detached from my own family's devastation. I pour my unresolved emotions into devotion and concern for the city's future after the storm. I've made my peace that I will continue to pursue journalism after the shake up last summer. I've convinced myself writing is important. I want to do my small part in making this city habitable for its native community, and I want to help avoid the possibility of the entire town being bought up by real estate investors and casinos.

I take my camera and my notepad and go to feel the city's pulse after this debilitating event. I'm not sure where to start, as the entire delta region has been affected. Eighty percent of New Orleans experienced some amount of flooding after Katrina. Water crept in and coated the carpet, ruining stoves and tubs, couches and strollers. The dirty-fish-tank smell replaced the smell of fresh gumbo and Irish coffee.

I decide to visit the epicenter: the Ninth Ward, the lowest ground, right by the levees, and the neighborhood with the smallest rate of evacuation. I wander through the deserted streets before I notice a hand-made sign for an art show. *Maybe I can talk to someone in there.* I walk up the steps of a modest brick home and peek my head in an open door. The exhibit, *After the Storm*, opened at the Waiting Room Gallery in the Ninth Ward several days ago, but there are no names in the guest book. A dark-haired woman, Patti D'Amico, hovers nearby as two tentative visitors view the exhibition of paintings held opposite her fireplace.

Some of the canvases are abstract: yellows that fade into greens, reds and blacks that are heavy and concentrated at the core. Swirling strokes form in just a way to throw one off center. Other paintings are more explicit. A black man floats dead, in the center, a rope is tied from a street sign to his torso in order to save his limp body from being lost in the river of flood waters.

Patti pulls back her long, fuzzy hair into a graceful ponytail and nods at me. She explains each painting was inspired by moments that haunted the artists. She and her husband had both contributed paintings to the exhibition. They had lived in their Chevy Caprice for weeks during the aftermath, after their house flooded past the mantle of the fireplace, but others had it worse. "People either lost their faith or went the other way completely," she says.

The chopping of helicopter wings replaces the sound of neighborhood children passing on their way home from school. I hear at least three helicopters overhead during that afternoon in the Ninth Ward, and each time they startle and unnerve me. I instinctively duck closer to the ground. It feels like a war zone. Patti says the slow recovery makes it extremely difficult to stay in New Orleans, even though she has never called anywhere else home.

I look out the front window and see the dilapidated house across the street; its innards are haphazardly exposed like a zebra being devoured by a lion. There's something incredibly disturbing about finding so much matter out of place, so much of what is inside and private being exposed externally. Patti shares with me that what she misses most is the sound of music made by children playing outside. Few schools have re-opened since the storm, and her corner of the world is quiet now. "This is a musical city," she notes as she crosses her arms and gazes out the window. "Everyone played something." The boy down the street had been learning the trumpet, and he walked home past her house practicing his instrument every day after school. She doesn't know if he was displaced or drowned, but he doesn't walk past her front porch any more.

Seven months after Hurricane Katrina, fewer than a quarter of the population have come home, either because they lack the funds to rebuild their shattered homes or they lack the gumption to risk it all—house and home and life—again. Patti looks at the ground, she shakes her head and says she had a bad feeling before Katrina hit. But she didn't know it would be this bad.

I thank Patti for her story and make my way back to the center of town. I am desperately looking for something, but I cannot articulate what it is. Somehow I need New Orleans to answer questions I am afraid to ask: how does life continue in the face of so much destruction and death? I can't help but follow my curiosity into a hidden Botanica, or magic supply shop, with African music spilling out the front door. Priestess Miriam Chamani, a former nurse who began her spiritual practice thirty years ago, sits cross-legged and casual on a stool behind the register of the gift shop at the Voodoo Spiritual Center. Her voice is barely audible over the African drum music from the boom box.

I notice a tall, elegant statue of what looks like a very tan version of a Barbie next to the register. She wears a golden bikini top and a high-slit long skirt to expose her thigh. Her hair is like Shakira's hair: thick and caramel, as is her skin. I almost don't recognize the Yoruba goddess in this guise. The

West African river goddess Oshun (who was originally black and so wide one cannot fit her arms around her) has been re-born in the West as a light-skinned, blonde, thin woman. She re-surfaced in Brazil as the temptress and the mermaid, and in New Orleans she appears to be a prostitute. I am shocked to feel an angry wave of nostalgia for Africa wash through me.

I recall the spiraling red graphic from the weather channel crossing the Atlantic and can't help but feel the immense distance between Africa and New Orleans. All that water, and all that churning. The warm air comes off the land of the North American continent to meet the cooler air over the water, and the two spin one another around as they create a third micro-climate that blends the two extremes. Either the opposing forces mix, or they continue to hold to their disparate ways, and they clash. This lack of compromise, this struggle to return to balance, causes tension that creates severe weather patterns, a violent churning that solidifies a strong wall, known as the eye of the storm. I feel like I'm waiting in an unnatural calm in my life during college, like the stillness I remember when the eye of the hurricane passes over. It's a moment to catch your breath, but the ferocity is not over.

Hurricane winds can reach up to 200 miles per hour, and they utilize all the elements in their attempt to re-harmonize themselves. Warm water feeds these tumultuous winds and chooses their direction, and the land and trees and homes in their path help to slow them down as obstacles that disorganize the center. The ground ultimately has a calming effect on the rage of wind and water. After coming to shore, the storm eventually loses momentum, the strong wall at the center of the storm dissolves, and normality returns.

All biological systems inherently seek homeostasis, they want to normalize, to balance themselves. The human body regulates temperature this way, and living systems follow the same natural laws. Natural balancing mechanisms work when there are a relatively small amount of changes to correct, but the planet's weather is becoming more erratic and less capable of balancing itself, hence the recent onslaught of wider variations in weather patterns and more drastic forces of opposition. The constant strain of inhabiting an ecosystem out of balance activates our sympathetic nervous systems. They continuously react from a place of stress. The fear that comes from imbalance in turn creates a positive feedback loop that reinforces humanity's desire to control nature's way of balancing herself, thus creating greater imbalance.

Oshun traveled across the turbulence of the Atlantic with the enslaved Africans as a story and a memory from their home. The West African worldview included many spirits in nature, and an inherent valuing of women and working cooperatively. Africans landed on the other side of the ocean in a foreign culture that was patriarchal, monotheistic and driven by capitalism. These opposing cultures and forces resisted one another directly, but over time a creolization occurred. While the orishas' energy remained the same, and some people still held Oshun's original story, her external image was forever altered. She merged into the new landscape.

From a goddess of fertility, she becomes a prostitute; her kindness morphs to gullibility; her great beauty sours to vanity; and her natural wealth turns to all consuming greed. She is a sister to be jealous of, she breeds hatred of the other. She cheats, she deceives. Oshun under the church's gaze is a flirtatious imbecile, a nymphomaniac. Men desire her flesh, but no one respects her. There is still the truth of her story and power underneath the gilding, but she has fallen into the ownership of patriarchy like so many others before her. Oshun, a symbol of women's power, grace and aptitude in Africa, has been reduced to an object of sexual lust in the Americas.

I continue asking my questions in the Voodoo Spiritual Center. I wonder what Priestess Miriam thinks the answer to this mess is? She is surprisingly brazen: she says nobody likes it, but everybody's got to change to adapt to the situation. She sees people who come in asking her to take away their pain, and she cannot help these people. "Religion is not a lullaby," she pauses. "It should be a challenge."

On Halloween in 1999, local radio station WEZB hired the priestess to break the cursed losing-streak of the New Orleans Saints. She brought incense, a pumpkin, and a python, but the Cleveland Browns prevailed 21-16. Priestess Miriam says our pleas to the spirits are not always heard, but all we can do is our best with what we have.

If the biggest troubles in New Orleans before Katrina involved lifting a rumored curse on their football team, then what are the people going to do now? How will an entire city lift itself up and keep on going after so much devastation? It seems like the obstacle barring the way is too vast.

"Obstacles on the road of faith are inevitable," the priestess says.

Obstacles on the road of faith. My mind wanders back toward the spray-painted neon orange X on the houses driving through the Ninth Ward. Red tricycles, Quaker Oatmeal containers, mattresses and clothes are delicately placed in trees and strewn in piles along the narrow streets of the former neighborhood. The priestess is saying that there is something beneficial that comes from this struggle; there is value in being displaced and uncomfortable. I don't feel so sure. I need more answers, and so I continue exploring the post-Katrina landscapes.

We take my friend's Jeep to the Ninth Ward because the mud

and debris are still thick and cumbersome. A perpetual light drizzle cements the melancholy mood required for Ninth Ward visits: the water just won't let up. The numbers of bodies found per building are casually spray-painted on the siding by rescue workers who came too late. These strangers shut the doors to abandoned homes, leaving the orange paint as an awkward sign of despair.

But the colored scars aren't the only indication. We drive up and down the streets at a slow, respectful pace. The neighborhood has become a graveyard. I see a blue Ford turned upside-down and washed under a matching blue home. The roofs of houses look like mushroom tops without stumps, shingles sit on top of bricks and timber on the ground. Crumpled at the middle, other structures have been pushed out into the street like old accordions.

Just past Flood Street, on the stoop of an old white-gray home, stands a headless plastic Jesus, no taller than a toddler. His body is adorned in the familiar robes of peace. His palms are together in majestic prayer, but his decapitated state transforms the message of this messiah into one of menace.

No one feels like talking after our trip, and Tim is almost shaking with rage. We turn back into town for lunch and order coffee and donuts before we retreat back to our shocked silence. I say I need some space, so Tim leaves me to stroll near the Louis Armstrong Park. The sign is crooked and the gate has been swung wide open and bent back by the wind and water's force. I feel I am entering a graveyard as I pass the gate's threshold. I start snapping pictures of the street lamps—three are intact, but the one in the middle looks as if a giant bent it at the neck. I tilt my neck to mirror the lamp post and take another picture. Three out of four of the lamps are cracked, and there's something arresting about the asymmetry.

Absorbed in the landscape, I forget my surroundings until I feel eyes on the back of my neck. I look up and realize I've wandered pretty far into the park and there is a large silhouette of a man coming up behind me. I don't panic, but my stomach drops below my knees. My instinct, a feeling at the base of my neck and in my gut, tells me I am in the presence of a predator.

I hear Tim's voice call me from closer to the gate. I steady my voice and answer him with as much confidence as I can muster, and the man abruptly turns down a different path. I'm glad to see Tim, and my knees are jelly. He apologizes for not warning me. He says he noticed the man follow me into the park so he had to turn around. I'm grateful, and a little shaken. We walk back out onto the street and head for a church to sit awhile.

The inside of the church smells like damp wood, but it is inviting and peaceful nonetheless. There has always been something that feels safe about church. People are on their best behavior, at least while they are inside. I sit in the middle toward the left side and take in the aisles. Three-hundred candles illuminate Jesus' face at Our Lady of Guadalupe Chapel. The colored glass containers shine against the blue and gold mosaic of Jesus and St. Jude as they bless all the children of the world in a space the size of a small shed. St. Jude is the patron saint of the congregation; he specializes in last hopes and lost causes.

Originally built as a funeral church, the tired, heavy building witnessed numerous bouts of fire and disease, including twenty-three yellow fever epidemics from 1817 to 1860 alone. The port-town church was abandoned three times since its founding in 1826. On the second Sunday of advent, a lonely couple here and a hopeful loner there speckle the pews. Father Don stands level to his congregation and preaches about the time God tested Abraham's faith by commanding him to sacrifice his only son, Isaac. Father Don wears a large purple robe with a cross covering his chest. His full head of hair is white, as is his skin. His urgent tone and his excited gestures share the message of God's saving grace. "We are given the joyous opportunity to prove our faith in times of trouble . . . Let go and God will catch you."

The message concludes to applause, but the images of the Ninth Ward surely come to mind as the weary souls mumble, in unison *Thanks be to God.*

I notice some of the congregation cross their arms, most mouth the words to the songs of praise, but even the most fatigued find voice for "Amazing Grace." *Twas grace that taught my heart to fear and grace my fears relieved* hangs in the air and drips down the sides, like gravy on mashed potatoes.

After the service, a man with white shoulder-length hair lingers in the pew. He lowers his head past the required bow of humility and tucks his chin toward his teal Hawaiian-print shirt, clasping his hands as if to squeeze water from a rock. His eyes are deeply wrinkled, closed.

Outside the church, after the last of the stragglers have turned homeward, a middle-aged man of medium height, medium build approaches Father Don.

"I haven't slept for three days, Father, three days," he emphasizes the number of nights with his three middle fingers. "I just need some Nyquil. I haven't been feelin' right."

Father Don asks him to wait and retreats into his cottage-sized office. For a moment the city is dark. Alone on Rampart Street, cars pass and people ramble by, but they make little disruption to the mood of silence that encases me.

In the distance, the Mississippi River reflects fading street lights and the sound of pounding metal on metal. The workers sweat to repair the levee today, and their toil creates a dying musical beat. Hit. Recoil. Hit. Similar in tone to the get-

through-the-day style of "I've Been Working on the Railroad."
June marks the start of a new hurricane season. What does next
year have in store for this unique corner of the world?

Father Don comes back, hurriedly gives the tired man his
pacifier and says goodnight. The two part ways, leaving an
empty bench alone on the sidewalk as the purple evening
clouds slide in. Everyone turns to their own form of comfort
after the storm, but I can't help thinking of the contrast between
Priestess Chimani's advice to seek out the challenges and Father
Don's suggestion to abate suffering. I suppose both are needed
in balance, and that's where discernment comes in. Sometimes
a crying child prefers the mother, and sometimes she may run
to the father. The value seems to me to be in having both—
not exclusively a father or mother figure, but the option to
find oneself in both sides. New Orleans seems to be a city that
embraces this sort of contradiction. The more I try to pin her
down and define her, the more she twists and slips through my
fingers.

Oshun seeks pleasure and enjoyment as a way to heal.
Even a drop of her sweetness is better than none at all, and
this town feels thirsty. Churches and bars checker board New
Orleans. Some locations, such as the cross-filled St. Joe's bar,
even combine the two devotions. The French Quarter offers
an escape into the noise, the lights and the liquor of the city.
Bare-legged girls dance, visible from the street, to a fast beat at
The Cat's Meow. We pass by Bourbon Street without turning
down the famous road. This is the temple of New Orleans'
flashy Oshun. Her natural rights to, and her connection to, her
body are removed. Oshun the perpetual virgin, (from the root
"virago" meaning the one who possesses herself), is no longer

full of herself. She is possessed by man. She lives in a case of fear instead of a temple, any man can take her when he chooses without fear of consequence. She is paid for sexual favors, or to bare her chest and dance on table tops.

And every woman is Oshun. Until Roe v. Wade was passed in 1973, every time a woman became pregnant, she was required to bear the child. Even in the result of a rape, a man was considered to own the child and had paternal rights. She could not control her cycle. She had no access to birth control until the 1950s.

The river is commodified as well. She is a shipping port that has been retrained to the maximum effort of man's powers, and still she rebels. She breaks the levees, floods the French Quarter, and knocks out power lines in her protest. But no one seems to listen. Engineers are hard at work trying to bend her back into a convenient shape at this very moment. Oshun the river goddess has been caged.

It's not that Oshun is no longer herself, but just that the people have decided to limit her to one extreme aspect of herself: a caricature. She is a reflection of those who tell the story about her. There is no great depth and therefore no great mystery, but she is pursued none the less. After passing Bourbon Street, we turn onto a local street, away from the external image and explore the other face of the river goddess.

It's 7pm on Sunday. Music penetrates the city air, and people catch the beat at red lights and on street corners, approving with a snap of the fingers or a tap of the foot. Even the common wail of sirens blends into aching jazz, quick rock 'n' roll, and hearty soul. Jazz spills out into Frenchman Street from The Spotted Cat club in a blue melody that floats both light and heavy, sorrow on the bass and joy from the trumpet. Humidity rules the night, with a thick breeze as sidekick. The melancholy from the Ninth Ward visit has melted away, and our bellies are full of étouffée.

I just miss stepping in a puddle of standing water as we turn into The Spotted Cat—but it hasn't been raining in this part of town. The water table is so high that even if it rains in another neighborhood, the drainage system sometimes floods out of the other vents—so you have got to be on the lookout for puddles no matter where you are.

Waiting for a Pimm's cup from the beret-wearing bartender, a tall man in a suit discusses his idea to offer insurance to the people the government plans to cheat. He came to New Orleans on business from Ohio or Indiana or some other land-locked place and never went back. Something about NOLA seems to inspire this kind of devotion and heroism. He says he feels more alive here. The space is full of women in jewelry and fresh men in wrinkle-free shirts dancing and talking and drinking and sitting and living. Every knee is bent, hips sway, feet tap, arms lift toward the sky.

A grayed man with withering teeth like a jack o' lantern walks in from his address on the street. He straightens his back, gives the crowd an ornery wink, discards his cane and does a jig in the middle of the wooden floor. His face expands as he puts on his best smile and closes his eyes, tilting his head to the ceiling in simple bliss.

This is the face of a city living through the difficulties of severe weather, inhabiting the magical liminal space of the swamp. Some intangible quality settles on the air, and each moment rises and falls with more beauty and grace than the one before. Impermanence has reminded us of our wildness, our frailty, and we dance with gusto in the moment between life and death.

I planned to leave the next day, but Tim convinces me to stay through the St. Patrick's Day Parade. A day when a river-like procession moves slowly down the street on floats like boats on the asphalt. Beer overflows in the streets, and the swamp is leaking out of the drains onto the sidewalk. The city is a saturated sponge, and my bladder concurs. Judging from the smell of urine, locals relieve themselves wherever they need to, but I wait politely in line for a port-a-potty next to a woman in a purple fairy costume who offers me chapstick and toilet paper (*because there won't be any in there, honey*) I decline the molten chapstick but accept the crumpled toilet paper. She's with a man who's wearing a green hard hat that doubles as a beer dispenser. Locals know to wear head protection, because instead of candy or beads, the float riders usually throw material for stew—carrots and cabbage—into the defenseless crowd. I make it through the day without a concussion, and leave with a belly full of stew.

As I drive back over Interstate 10 toward Florida—utterly homesick for a place I'd just met and listening to the New Orleans Jazz Vipers on CD—I regret that I didn't get to see a New Orleans jazz funeral. Death is seen as another reason to celebrate in this city. The coffin is danced all the way to the burying ground along the streets while colorfully dressed friends and musicians escort the grieving family into a new life without their loved one. Just like a snake finds new skin beneath the one she sheds, I am curious about death being part of the cycle of rebirth. A city that lives in such a difficult ecosystem and has seen so much death must find a way to go on in spite of it. If any city understands how to come back to life, it is New Orleans.

I feel a new possibility arising after spending time in a place like this and seeing such a different angle of Oshun. What if I were able to re-write the entire story of myself? Keep all the facts and details, but change their meaning. There is something inside me that knows that the secret to freedom, deep inner freedom, has to come from a revision of my personal narrative. One has to understand the contextual situation of that personal narrative in the context of her culture. I'm tired of writing myself into the role of prey, the helpless victim.

~~

I am the daughter of a survivor.

The daughters and granddaughters of abused women were never meant to survive, so we belong to those grandmothers who, against all odds, chose life—for themselves and for us. We belong to those women who found an internal love so infinite and bright in the eyes of their children that they kept going. We are the daughters of the survivors. Those who died externally and learned the secret of rebirth that the snake taught them. Some of them kept following orders, enduring abuse, shattering themselves with every glance into their child's future. Some of these women dared to hope for the impossible, for change so radical that it would make a life worth living for their daughters. Some of them gave their lives for their daughters' chance at freedom.

My mother did all of this. And she did finally stand up to my father and leave him, calling down all the rage and power of air and water that had stagnated between them during my childhood. They were divorced and lived separately for two years before they started dating each other and returned to couples therapy. They too learned to rebuild an entire foundation after a massive storm. When they moved back in to the house as a new couple, one of the water pipes broke and completely flooded the master bedroom. The water offered an opportunity for deeper renewal, and they physically altered the ground under their feet with more than new carpet and tile.

It takes tenacity to find the uncorrupted stories of strong women and survivors, to place ourselves back into their skin, to understand the suffering and abuse they endured, and the storms they weathered. It is still difficult to see my mother straight on, illuminated by all the abuse she endured. It's almost impossible to hold the pain and misuse her body has held. But without this understanding we cannot begin the process of shedding that old skin we inherited: the skin we have taken up over generations like a thick, dry snakeskin. It served us well, but we don't need it anymore.

The peeling away of the protective layers that keep us bound, the breaking of our hearts, is actually a breaking open, a letting in of light to our bodies which are made of matter. We honor the forgotten ones in our bones, the ones they tried to hide from us in our own blood, and we include them in the tapestry of who we will become.

An infinite line of grandmothers stands over my right shoulder, and I begin the process of re-writing the stories I had accepted as true with the strength of my relationships behind me. The re-writing disorganizes my life as much as any hurricane, but it's this destruction that makes space for a creative rebirth. The snake knows this, my mother learned this, and the people of New Orleans have lived through this. Death is as necessary for life as longing is necessary for love.

PART TWO

WAXING GYPSY MOON
GATHERS LIGHT

COLORADO RIVER

Rages at the Dam

Men may dam it and say that they have made a lake, but it will still be a river. It will keep its nature and bide its time, like a caged animal alert for the slightest opening. In time, it will have its way; the dam, like the ancient cliffs, will be carried away piecemeal in the currents.

Wendell Berry

Colorado. Summer 1992.

Take me home, country roads, to the place I belong . . . West Virginia, Mountain Mama, take me home, country roads . . .

THAT WAS THE SUMMER the radio broke in the old Toyota van and we bought a John Denver cassette. We aren't on our way to West Virginia, but we've somehow made it all the way to the Mississippi *en route* to Colorado. We've already played the entire cassette through half a dozen times, but it keeps playing. I'm not sure anyone is listening any more. Dad's driving, Mom's in the front reading, Samantha and I take the far back and play with our toy horses, and Jason takes a nap in the middle seat.

We can hardly believe there is snow on the peak of one of the Rocky Mountains in the summer. When I stand on the top it feels like standing on the spine of a sleeping dragon. A huge, magical reptile that sleeps in between the two sides of the continent, separating east and west.

Later I thought it was funny that the Eastern hemisphere generally embraced and considered the dragon good luck, while all the knights from Western stories were constantly trying to kill those mythic reptiles as a nasty nuisance. Western morals seemed to need nature to be contained and dominated, and so it is. The soil was colonized, claimed, owned in name and on paper. And the river's water was diverted, polluted and drained.

I peek over the edge of the massive concrete structure at the Hoover Dam—water rages out and falls seventy feet back into a stream like a great serpent reassembling after having been chopped into pieces: re-join or die. I watch the water molecules urgently race back together. I feel the lump in my throat trying to roar against the manipulation of power, but what comes out is a small sound, stifled and broken. Why does the surging dam upset me?

The Celts use the story of the *Cailleach* and her little sister, Nessie, to explain the nature of lakes and rivers. As they tell it, the Cailleach controlled all the water flowing from under the ground. One day she asked her little sister to watch over a well so it didn't overflow while she moved the goats in the pasture.

Of course, the little sister got distracted by a handsome young man and forgot to put the lid back on the well at sunset. So all night the water flooded the fields and created a lake. And when her older sister came back, the girl ran away to escape her anger. The Cailleach cursed her to run forever and to this day Nessie runs as a flowing river.

Even this story seems to feel that constant motion is negative: a curse or burden. I wonder if water was already being re-routed when this story came about.

Back in modern day North America, the Colorado River is one of the most controlled and litigated rivers in the entire world. Re-named by the Spanish invaders for her red color, most of the waters are now green. She was called other names by the many indigenous groups living for centuries along her banks, the Maricopa called her Xakxwet, the Mohave called her Kwhwat, the Havasupai called her Ha Tay, G'am, and Sil Gsvgov, and the Yavapai called her Hakwata. But nowadays most of her waters are re-routed to California to support industrial farms, and the once fertile river valleys are deserted.

Dams create disparity of access and have globally displaced more than 80 million people according to the World Wildlife Fund's study on rivers at risk. Vandana Shiva, a water rights activist and author, calls this need to own and control natural resources *cowboy economics*. This mindset makes a race out of obtaining and hoarding limited resources that by right belong to everyone. It is a little switch in the psyche that disconnects action from consequence, so they experience pure, refreshing denial with no guilty aftertaste. It is easy to see the physical effects. Formerly lush valleys become desertified. The destruction of the massive flood plain around a dam. But it is more complicated to see the effect this worldview has on women when they are turned into commodities.

"We had the river licked. Pinned down, shoulders right on the map." Here, the chief of construction for the Hoover Dam is speaking about a river, but it is easy to consider how he could be talking about a woman. It became popular in the industrialized world to consider it wasteful to allow a river to continue on her natural path, so the leaders wrote policies that protected profit and proudly erected dams to harness her energy. The director of the US Geological Survey from 1881-1899 commented: "It would outrage one's sense of justice if that broad stream were to roll down to the ocean in mere idle majesty and beauty." A few years later, President Theodore Roosevelt noted that we must save the water from wasting into the sea.

Value is measured objectively, which leaves out the importance of health and happiness and includes only a solid concrete bottom line. But beauty is never wasted, and majesty refuses to be tamed. The accepted, popular paradigm causes an immense grief and longing for depth that is often difficult to recognize and even harder to satisfy within a Western framework of patriarchy and capitalism. This obsessive need to control and dominate nature, and by extension women, creates psychological canyons between male and female, mother and son. Leela Fernandes says in her book *Transnational Feminism* that this split and the resulting isolation and pain is the reason that destruction, hate, rape, violence, and inequality exist. We are no longer a part of, or the creators of, beauty. Our only job in the post-industrial age is efficiency and intelligence.

As a result of this utilitarian world view, beauty's connotation begins to merge with excess, and we confuse in our minds the lines between self-respect, pride and arrogance. Maureen Murdock writes that women have internalized the myth of inferiority, and so we look outside for approval. We desperately need to fill the empty space with partner after partner. We are told that the wild, free women are the ones wearing the bikinis and thongs. Not the ones covered from head to toe—they are trapped, man says. *Let the men see your flesh, let them long for a nice, long drink*, he whispers. Yes, this is what they call your liberation.

But I'm not buying it. In my own life, I have turned to the Eastern spiritual traditions for answers based on respect for nature.

Florida. Fall 2004.

I've always been a bit out of place in my body. I'd learned to live more fully in my head, reading books, making up rich fantasy worlds. Western culture encourages us to be dissociated from our bodies, and I am a talented escapist if left to my own devices. But as I mentioned before with the drums in Ghana, there's always been this little, almost imperceptible, invitation into some more expansive way of living. College, my first time out on my own, was a time for thawing some of these icy character traits. My journey into my body began with a yoga class my freshman roommate Corey talked me into.

I am willing to admit I was entirely arrogant at first, judging my ability, flexibility and balance as a means to determine whether I liked it or not. After the first class I thought proudly, *that was easier than people make it sound.* I didn't go back again until a year later, the point at which a new tightly-wound roommate drove me so crazy that I found myself looking for excuses to get out of the house.

My first year or so in yoga classes consisted mainly of stories. I told myself about how good I was at it. I spent the hours telling myself how flexible I was from dancing, how thin I looked in the long black pants, and how clear my mind was during balance poses. I hated when the teacher corrected me—I would get embarrassed—it threw off my internal dialogue of perfection. I think she could feel my resistance and she rarely helped me in a pose as a result. Maybe I simply needed reassurance, as a college girl surrounded by other beautiful and competitive young college girls, but I always felt lighter after class.

Somewhere after the first year or so, though, I started to feel actual changes. I remember being in a triangle pose (a standing pose where one straight extended leg forms an angle with a straight back leg and you reach toward the floor) when my body adjusted itself. I can't remember if there was anything special about that day, but the pose suddenly lined me up internally in an entirely different way than it ever had before. My lower leg pulled itself forward, and I realized I hadn't really been breathing before. My breath deepened on its own, and my body was wider, and somehow cleaner. It's like the feeling you have in your mouth after you brush your teeth, but that freshness spreads over your entire body.

This must have been what they were talking about when they described "listening" to your body. I had had no clue. Once this first little avenue was open in my physiology, I started to notice bigger and bigger changes, and I was hooked on something deeper than endorphins and flimsy self-esteem talks. I took a Buddhism class the next semester, started meditating, and changed my major to anthropology and religion. I traveled to Paris to study art, film, and the Bible as literature.

Next, I took a yoga training program and discovered I was decidedly not a Christian. At twenty, I announced myself to my mother as agnostic or maybe Buddhist. It felt good to finally stand up to her with my words. I had taken care of her emotionally for years and decided she was strong enough that I could separate myself as my own woman. It was excruciating, but in a lot of ways, as we worked through our differences, I felt this was finally the beginning of a real relationship with my mother.

Sivakasi, India. 2007.

From my first rebellion, I followed a winding road further into the Tantric and Shivite lineages of practice and cosmology. This is where I discovered my first image of the personified Dark Feminine: Kali-Durga.

I should mention something about what deities are in the Yogic traditions. They are ways to unlock vibrations within oneself: from the perspective of a non-dual cosmology, there is no such thing as an external savior. There is only one energy that vibrates in many different forms. Chanting a particular sound or name unlocks vibrations within oneself that are considered to have access to the parts of the psyche we shut out. In the case of Durga, she is the courageous feminine warrior in every human who stands in the face of fear and refuses to back down.

I knew she was the one for me: here she was strong and powerful, real and alive, dancing on death and laughing in the face of the feared darkness. This was my ticket out. I took a job as an editor at a small, English-language magazine in Southern India and soaked in a culture foreign from my own. This was a chance to be more myself than the people who knew me allowed me to be.

I learned mostly from the traffic patterns of this small town in Tamil Nadu. There were no signs and rules about where and how to walk, drive, or ride through the streets. There was just an invisible feeling of one's way and a trust that we will look out for one another. I walked, hesitant at first to enter into the hectic currents of auto rickshaws, massive lorries, herds of uniformed schoolchildren, bikers, bone-thin stray dogs, and shirtless, turbaned old men with ox drawn carts. They all co-existed in this little dirt road, with their diverse speeds, agility, and force. Somehow, they were all given space and flowed together to get where they were going.

I recently found an article that reinforces my perception, so I'm not just being a romantic traveler here. Traffic engineer Hans Monderman was also inspired by the no-street-sign, no-crosswalk phenomenon. His theory is that drivers pay more attention when they have to watch out for obstacles.

He's designed roads around the globe, showing up in Austria, Denmark, France, Germany, Spain, Sweden, the UK, and the US, that have lower accident rates than the traditional straight roads with traffic lights. Of course there will be the occasional accident, but the overall movement of this river of pedestrians and traffic works.

The way traffic flowed was mirrored by the pervading worldview in India: everything was included. The older views from Vedanta were built upon by the Tantrics, nothing needed to be denied or pushed down—philosophical and cosmic theories wove together like tapestries and separate streams in the same river. The exploration simply expanded.

Once I built up the courage to ride my own bike into the wild river of the streets, I felt more connected than I ever had. I was part of the one force of movement expressed by a multiplicity of shapes. I knew I was changing when I started reading more than one book at a time and allowed the narratives to overlap and feed one another. Before, I would always start and finish one book at a time before taking on another. This is when the many streams of my ancestral consciousness began to braid together. I felt less blockage, less turmoil; there was a greater space for internal discord.

This is perfect, I thought. If I could just stay here, then I would be happy. I relaxed into that familiar feeling of home and considered staying in Sivakasi indefinitely. But I was ultimately rejected by India. I stayed three months, and then had my visa renewal declined because I was a journalist. I came back to the States deflated, stopped shaving and wearing make-up and became celibate. I had graduated with highest honors, but I waited tables at a fancy restaurant in Florida to gather the funds for my next launch.

Nine months later, I moved to California, enrolled in graduate school, and followed a precarious thread of hope toward who-knows-what: I was racing as fast as possible away from where I had been. As I continued my body practices, I started to feel a pulsing of understanding and confusion happening in my mind that was both foreign and familiar. I realized that I was opening up to a body-based wisdom that had merely been asleep.

One of the benefits of yoga is that it helps smooth out the grooves we create from habitual behaviors, known as *samskaras*. These grooves that our neurons travel along become worn in over time, and cause us to act in a reactionary way rather than a responsive way. The samskaras could be seen as impressions from the decisions we've made before, like footprints in the sand near the ocean. If we continue to step into the same footprints, they deepen. If they are out of the reach of water's tide, they remain.

When we practice yoga, it is like moving ourselves closer to the tide's edge. So the waves routinely come up far enough to wipe the sand clear of these impressions. This allows for a feeling of liberation and possibility, just like I felt in Ghana with the drums at the ocean.

Even with all these new tools and understandings, I was in a place of constant hesitancy and resistance; I had a recurring desire for some external teacher or deity to have all the answers. I was lucky to hear more of the stories that reminded me to look deeper into myself rather than grasping externally. The stories provided a place to land, an image for the body to use as a map. I steeped myself in all the unresolved paradox I had neatly tried to explain away in fear.

Enduring this internal tension creates heat (*tapasia*) that ignites alchemical transformation. When we engage mindfully with the practices of holding the opposites internally we are physically strengthening the container of our body. It is useful to have a strong container for your body because it does more than house your spirit, it is the manifest part of your spirit. It is said that lion's milk was a highly sought after healing substance in ancient times, but there was always a need for an alchemical golden chalice within which to contain the milk because the substance itself was so pure and potent that it would burn through any other material container. In yoga, we strengthen and transform our body in order for it to embody refined spirit. Peak spiritual experiences and other epiphanies often do not last because we have a leaky container. With yoga, we work to change that, becoming a golden chalice that can hold the gift of lion's milk.

During my yogic training, my teacher Sianna Sherman shared the story of the descent of the Ganges River (as told to her by the Sanskrit scholar and Shivite devotee Paul Mueller-Ortega). The way that this story is told, it is important to imagine yourself as every character in the story, as the Shivite yogic perspective is that there is only one psyche with different forms.

The Story of the Descent of Ganga, from India

One of the greatest kings of India was also one of the saddest. Yes he was celebrated far and wide for his balance and fairness, but he was distressed because he had no sons.

He decides to perform a great ritual to ask the spirit world for help in creating an heir. The ritual is a success beyond his wildest imagination, and in fact he ends up with 1,000 sons. The king is so overjoyed that he gives them each a white horse, and on their sixteenth birthday they take these horses out to explore their kingdom.

As the fleet of princes exits the palace, thousands of hooves begin to tear up the soil, and the young men and horses take many of the villages' food and water resources carelessly. They cause imbalance in the kingdom and disrupt the land until a grumpy old sage is finally fed up and turns them all to ash in an instant.

The king is beyond grief when he hears the news. All of his sons have vanished in a moment. He once again turns to the spirit world for help, begging for a favor. He prays sincerely from the depths of his heart, and Shiva, known as the Lord of Yoga, appears and agrees to take on his case.

But Shiva is also at a loss. The young princes had been extremely reckless with the earth, and the nature spirits in turn are reluctant to help bring them back to life. For all of Shiva's entreaties, he is unable to convince the other gods to assist. He finally recalls that the great river goddess Ganga, who lives comfortably in the ethereal realms above Mt. Kailash, owes him a favor, and he decides to ask her for her help.

When he arrives, Shiva finds Ganga seated in the lotus pose, deep in meditation. Her body emits a brilliant blue light, and she appears to be floating. He clears his throat and drops to his knee in her presence, bowing his head. She smiles with her eyes closed and welcomes him to sit at her table and join her for rose water tea. Shiva politely declines and says there is a crisis below, and asks if she would consider descending the mountain and healing the earth for the benefit of all creation. She listens and considers his words, but gently declines his request. She is quite comfortable in her home and sees no reason to interfere in the lives of humans who have abused their resources so blatantly.

Shiva persists and asks her three times, knowing she cannot refuse the third time as she owes him a favor. Ganga agrees to descend the mountain and bring her water to the earth, but she warns Shiva that her power is not used to being contained, and she may cause some destruction on the way down.

Her condensed energy may well destroy everything in her

path, but Shiva offers her a solution. He sits at the base of the mountain and enters into a deep meditation, rooting through the earth and up into the stars. He catches her and serves as a bridge between the spirit and material worlds. He holds her still for a moment at the foot of the mountain until she adjusts to the frequency of the earth, and then watches as she sways peacefully into the villages. She meanders into the valley, gathers up the ashes of the fallen princes and uses the ashes themselves to nourish the land back to health.

Ganga is still present in the Ganges River to this day, bringing nourishment, beauty and magic to people across India.

As in the story of Oshun's descent to earth, the river goddess has to be convinced to come and restore balance. The conditions have to be just right, and her movements come from her own agency.

Ganga is a woman resisting something that she will eventually decide to do, but she needs a balancing or mediating energy in releasing her raw force and power. As yogis, there is a shape we take to get in touch with her energy inside ourselves.

What I love about these stories is the instruction for embodiment that accompanies these archetypes. Each yoga pose comes from a story. When we take warrior pose, it is not just any warrior, but Arjuna from the Bhagavad Gita, and there is a pose for the golden eagle Garuda who flies ahead and sees that everything will turn out fine.

The pose I associate with an embodiment of Ganga is called *Parsvakonasana*, 'bound side-angle' pose. It's a wide stance with one leg facing front and the other leg extended on the ground behind you. Then you wrap your hands under your front thigh and clasp your hands behind your back. This binding of the arms provides a system like a levy, something to press against. The rotation of your spine increases and the space across your collarbone can stretch much deeper than before. Experiencing this shape gives me the felt sense that structure is essential for freedom and this is how I imagine Ganga felt as she came down from the heavens to the earth and Shiva caught her. In contrast, it is when there are a lack of rules and lines I feel trapped.

The structured, stable banks of the river provide a space for water to flow. One area is strong, the other is soft; as in the spine. In the shape of 'downward-facing dog' your arms are the banks of the river and the heart then has space to flow freely.

The balance between opposites comes from this internal spaciousness. Shiva was the contracting element that allowed for the safe expansion of Ganga. This embodied understanding of the masculine and feminine dynamic is always only a breath away. On the exhale, we empty out and contract, and the inhale fills us up and we expand.

Many people in our society believe they are supposed to be living their lives with constant expansion (filling up the house with gadgets, acquiring more and more knowledge, gathering friends) and think there is something wrong when they get sick or are otherwise forced to slow down (contraction). But if the paradigm shifts from linear to circular, then it is easy to see that both expansion and contraction, or inhaling and exhaling, are simply needed to stay alive.

Imbalance is what upset me when I stood on top of the dam and saw the water rushing out. The masculine had harnessed the feminine and stifled her movement in an unnatural way that used excessive force. Nature does not behave that way.

Modern business, cowboy economics, tells us the goddess of the river needs a harness. Ganga chose to descend from the mountain of her own free will and in her own timing. Shiva represents a proper masculine support, a container that helps her to guide her own power. He does not keep her contained forever, and it is her choice when she is ready to continue to flow again. Why can't we emulate this model for sustainability?

Through yoga, I became aware of the power of nature through paradox, dynamic tension, and breath, but I still had a lot of unlearning to do. As Clarissa Pinkola Estes points out, the perspective of the dark goddess is that *both polar perspectives of interior and exterior convene: and right there, at that juncture point, she stands, taking in the two worlds, the mundane world of known facts, and the deeply creative, insightful, emergent world of spirit.*

In the Tantric traditions, this law of pulsation between opposites is known as *spanda*. Every cell in the universe pulses to stay alive, from the tiny cells in your blood all the way out to the rhythm of the stars. The seasons are a way of feeling this energy macrocosmically. The winter solstice is the beginning of an inhale, which rises through the summer solstice, then we ride the exhale back through the fall and the cycle continues.

San Francisco. April 2011.

It's almost 3am, and I'm huddled on my green yoga mat with a candle a few feet in front of my eyes—wide open. I'm seated, rocking back and forth, back and forth. My lips move imperceptibly fast; I'm calling her. *Om Dum Durgaye Namaha, Om Dum Durgaye Namaha, Om Dum Durgaye Namaha. Durga please come*, I plead. I've lit sandalwood incense and have her image in front of the red candle so the light shines through the image of the dark lady wielding weapons and perched on a tiger—jaws wide, tail flicking.

I'm calling Durga for help because I am spiraling down. I have had another dream with the black spider, but this time she was bigger than me and ready to devour me. I woke up shaken and got right to work. I'm leaving for the Mojave Desert in three days to mark my passage into womanhood. The only problem is the spiders—they're everywhere: in dreams, on my altar, my yoga mat, in the pots in the kitchen, on my notebook, webs when I walk out my front door, webs on the bus, webs in my bookcase, my shower and my tea cups.

To say I do not like them is an understatement. I am terrified of them. I avoid them. I always have. I've worked with them, been open to the meaning of this fear, rationalized it, honored them as an ally in the weaving and wordsmithing crafts I choose, but nothing helps. I rationalize that this phobia has something to do with fear of some aspects of myself, but that does not register in the moment they confront me. I see those legs and something visceral lights up my spine. My heart pounds, I squeal and run to find a man to escort her out the door.

Here I was in California, in my early twenties, and I was between the worlds again, a place I felt familiar with as the middle child and family diplomat, but all of my worlds were shattering. I spent all my money on spiritual pursuits, I was broke and digging a hole of debt, plus I was moving a lot.

My roots were frail and damaged—fragile at best. No matter how I tried on the liberation from other cultures, the massive dam in my own psyche showed no signs of breaking. A barrier cut me off from my body, my ability to ground. I couldn't finish anything, even the scarf I was knitting for my brother lay barely started on the couch; the yellow and green cords casually tangled as a reminder of the mess surrounding me. I was like Penelope, constantly weaving all day and unraveling that work in the night. Why did I continue to pace back and forth across this same little bit of my psyche?

Yoga was another commodity, as hard as I tried for a break

through, the answer was disappointing: more time, more reflection, more practice is needed. Spiritual breakthroughs aren't as glamorous and easy to recognize as I had hoped for. And they show up with a bit of a delay. A three-year delay in my case. I had wanted a giant explosion, a crashing mountain, a tidal wave, but instead I got a little knock on the door, an invitation to tea, and a moment of memory in a traffic jam.

Berkeley. February 2014.

I just added additional sessions to my work schedule, which means this morning, Monday morning, I need to be in the city by 8:15am. Ninety minutes earlier than usual. I'm jamming along with my reggae sounds, thinking this new extra early thing is not so bad, but then I stop almost a half a mile back from where the traffic usually gets tangled and hectic. Great. Now I'm stuck and I'll be late.

The shipping port at Oakland to my left is full of the inspiration for the All-Terrain Attack Vehicles from the early Stars Wars movies. George Lucas, or one of his collaborators, must have sat here in traffic and gotten the idea for a skyscraper sized walking tank that demolished anything in its path. The metal structures to my left could have been used on the set. I'm feeling a little more violent than usual myself in this gridlock.

We are too many water molecules waiting to move through a minute opening, and the contraction hurts. My mood turns. Why did I agree to this? My body feels tight and strained. My mind is on the attack. Too many thoughts at once, as if the cars somehow jammed them all through my head at the same moment. I need to change music to match my new pace. I pick a CD given to me by a friend of a friend, it's hang drum (a percussion instrument that is like a bell and a drum), and I ease into the melodic, alien soundscape.

No words, that's good. The percussion is fast, but the tempo is spacious. I take a deeper breath and start to feel a little more fluid in my spine. I open my ears and relax my jaw. The notes seem to bounce off one another, I roll up the windows to slip further in. The raindrops add to the experience of being inside the mystical movements of waves from the speakers. I rub my eyes and stretch my neck. I start to feel connected to the other people in the sea of cars. I can feel past the cars to the warm human bodies enfolded in metal and separated by glass. We are an ocean, riding the waves. Water disperses to settle, learns patience and moves around obstacles. Outside, the bay is glassy this morning, and I'm feeling wider. The space of my womb recognizes the space of the drum.

The musician adds another instrument, some sort of shaker, and I see a band of gypsies—colorful and carrying their homes along a winding path through hills and over fields. I think about my Sicilian great-grandmother, Maria, the one who disappeared onto the road she came from. I feel bells around my ankles. I inch closer toward the toll booth, and daydream of traveling to that little island in the Mediterranean Sea. Something about that shape, the circular island fascinates me. I'm nostalgic for something I can't quite place.

The next track has vocals—a woman singing high and swooping. I am immediately jealous of her talent, but then I rest into the rocking she creates. They are sounds without words, but one is repetitive and feels like she's calling me. I feel connected, invited, included. As I start to head over the bridge, I feel warm. A big truck roars past, and I feel small and cozy in my little bubble of a car. I feel the air under the bridge and the depth of the ocean under that. I am floating and soaring and humming.

Then I am transported back in the mausoleum where I saw

the musician live with my partner on the equinox. She sat on the floor with the blue metal UFO-shaped drum and played for hours. The room was a side room, and the ceilings were high in a new building made to feel old. This place was built for sounds, and there are plenty of them. We had wandered around looking for the drummer around the ashes of the dead, joined a harmonic chant group upstairs and then returned to the garden room for her improvisation.

Her hands move across the drum's belly like rain drops. She has the focus of a small child lying on the floor and coloring. I know her from somewhere. At one point she says a little about her background, from Sicily, a percussionist. My mind wanders back to my lost great-grandmother again, bells around her ankles, my ankles. I feel connected.

My voice is free, and I let myself make sounds that amble along beside her. It feels good to let sound out after holding it in for so long. My hips feel heavier and the back of my throat relaxes. My eyes become catlike. More so than that old John Denver track, this music has brought me home.

I'm almost at the office so I turn off the music and look for empty parking spots. Today I turn twenty-nine. I'm on the cusp of a dozen unfinished ideas and absolutely lost as to the direction for my MFA project. My backyard is flooded and the ants are invading my kitchen.

In three months I will find out I am pregnant. By December, I will complete my degree. I will be a mother by this time next year. I don't know why I am where I am, and I don't know where I am going next, but this morning I feel waves of acceptance for the winding path I am on, and gratitude for the music a friend introduced me to last year. This stillness comes, and then it goes again just like the tide.

The mystical, foggy peninsula of San Francisco proved to be a difficult place to establish roots. I am addicted to change and movement. *Flowing water does not decay.* The ghost of Grandma Maria brings me a feeling of connection and space, but also worries over my settling, becoming stagnant, so I cannot establish roots. For three years I learn all I can about women's spirituality, devour stories and interpretations and chants and go to pujas and get closer to the goddess traditions of India. I had some success, but something always seemed to happen before I took an initiation. Like the old school-yard chant: *I am rubber and you are glue . . .* I seemed to bounce off the communities around the goddess traditions rather than sticking. Something was off, and I still didn't have the tools to really discern or guide myself through the mess of projections and lies. I still wanted a savior, my teacher, my father to have the answers.

I imagine that women look outside for answers because they cannot feel the wisdom of their own bodies anymore. Years of creating an icy barrier to keep out the stares, the calls, the threat of rape and worse. Women take care of their friends and families, but they do not take care of themselves. Women have lost what sustains them, forgotten what brings them to life, pushed down their rage and denied their need for rest. Women have taken to demonizing the feelings, the sensitivity, the ability to mold to the container, the fluid nature of emotions, thoughts, feelings, dammed behind a white porcelain mask. Control and denial are favored. Thin, slight women are prized. Strong curves are out of fashion.

No one admits to being a feminist or womanist these days. I've read that black women are being blamed for the destruction of their family core—they are too strong willed, man says. Women perform for men, like tigresses in cages, and too few of us refuse this option. Durga would never stay caged, neither would Ganga, and my great-grandmother Maria wouldn't stay contained either.

We are the ones who believed, perpetuated and wrote the stories of Western civilization. We've collectively taken to wearing the curse of Penelope, we keep ourselves busy with practice and exercise, but in the end, for fear of being found out to be greater than we appear, we un-do all of our own work. We forget our power and fall into the prevailing currents. *A free river is a waste of potential.*

The urban rivers—the Seine, the Thames, the Arno, the Los Angeles, the Chicago, the Hudson—are contained in cement beds and ailing without grooves that connect them to the land. How can a river feel her way toward the sea when she is cut off from the land?

The laws of nature are changed, molded to fit into fiscal years and annual reports: everything needs to be measured and secured quantifiably. When we believe the false stories we've been told, those stories come to life and live us. We as a culture have written ourselves into the stories as objects, and we see ourselves as cogs in a machine. We, the victims, are too small to make a difference, to matter. We, the debtors, pursue greater pay and higher spiritual realizations, and lose the magic of being human with this perpetual seeking (for things outside and for things in the future). We, the lost, have no feet and float from place to place like parasites, devouring resources and discarding loved ones.

Our feelings are blocked behind the wall of who we think we are. We tell lies and create labyrinths within our psyches. We forget we made this mess, we blame others. Water is meant to move from sky to earth to ground and back again. If the cycle is broken, if the freshwater we have leaves us, we don't have anywhere else to go. Dreams try to wake us. Poets and ecologists try to warn us. The obstacles in our paths are causing us to make compromises we cannot afford.

Isolation is killing us. Denial is causing our souls to wilt. I choose life and freedom and connection, and I know it's time to face the ghost of my great-grandmother, the gypsy Maria.

LAURENTIDE ICE SHEET

Waits as a Crystal

Ice contains no future, just the past, sealed away. As if they're alive, everything in the world is sealed up inside, clear and distinct. Ice can preserve all kinds of things that way—cleanly, clearly. That's the essence of ice, the role it plays.

Haruki Murakami

The British Isles. Prehistoric Time.

AFTERNOON YAWNS AND stretches shadows deeper across a flat canvas of green. A bee rests on a single white daisy, and an oak tree shivers in the wind. The sun slides below the horizon, and a shadowed figure emerges. Silhouetted by the dimming light, a giant woman carries a heavy load of stones in her apron toward the fading orange sun. She pauses and uses the oak tree as if it were a barstool, to rest. Just as she seems to be dozing off, a stray dog barks and startles her. She jumps and accidently places her foot on the white daisy. The bee reacts just in time to sting the sole of her foot before being squished.

The electric shock of the bee's final act zips from the giant's foot through her body. She whimpers and hops on her other foot, thereby dropping her load of stones and thus creating hills in the once flat landscape. This rolling landscape becomes known as Ireland. And the great giant woman is known as Grandmother Cailleach, the powerful crone of winter and water. She is the figure of death, and the queen of ice who has shaped the land and her people since before time began.

She controls the flow of water from wells, decides when and where to form lakes and streams, and welcomes the spirits of the dead to the other side of the river. She is respected and feared, but this face of the mother is seldom loved.

Some of my ancestors settled in Indiana, on Shawnee land, because it reminded them of a home they had left across the Atlantic in Ireland. My Celtic ancestors used to explain the phenomenon of ice carving out the land in the form of the Cailleach, but today science has replaced her.

Southern Indiana. Prehistoric Time.

Water draws in a large inhale, expands her lungs, and holds her breath. She's waited here perfectly preserved as potential energy, as ice, for hundreds of thousands of years. The memories of landscapes and times long before humans are frozen in her crystalline structure, waiting to re-emerge into the collective human psyche.

Temperatures fluctuate on our planet for centuries. The ice feels a pressure to soften, to change, and resists at first, holding tighter to the ways she knows. As parts of her body warm, she realizes the change is inevitable, outside of her control, and she accelerates the melting process with her new certainty. This warming brings a metaphorical sunrise, as a thawing of the slower moving molecules in the ice starts a trickle of streams forming and spreading out across the landscapes.

Humans, too, felt the inner warming and moving of molecules within themselves and spread out across the continents during this time. Possibilities expanded as the earth took a collective inhale and filled herself with life. The earth is so vast that many thousands of years later, the expansion and exploration of wild places continues.

The last of the ice receded from Southern Indiana around 22,000 years ago, and the melting deeply impacted all the land north of the Ohio River. Ice had covered most of Canada, the Upper Midwest, and New England, as well as parts of Montana and Washington for most of the earth's history. As the Laurentide Ice Sheet that covered northern North America slowly receded, the melting patterns formed grooves in the land that in turn created troughs—like giant bath tubs—where water would flow and stand for centuries to come. The carving of the land, these grooves left by the glaciers' retreat can still be seen, like fingerprints from a sculptor, in the islands of the Great Lakes and in Central Park. The Ohio River was also a part of this glaciation, which forms the border between Indiana and Kentucky, where my mother grew up.

Just as the landscape was formed by the water and ice melting over thousands of years, my ancestors also shaped our family-scape over time. The glaciers are long gone, as are my grandmothers, but the imprint they left, the lives they lived, have formed me. Genetic memories, little bits of essential structures of character, physical traits and blood types, are passed through generations in DNA. The frozen memories of my grandmothers on my maternal side are lost to my cognition, but their stories are alive within my bones and my blood. They shape me in ways I do not need to understand with my mind. I feel them in my body.

One fragment of a story from a great-grandmother that my family tried to conceal behind layers of ice re-surfaced recently. My maternal grandmother's line comes from Germany, centuries back, and my inquiry led me to discover the extent to which this town was affected by the witch burnings that took place there in the late sixteenth and early seventeenth century. I learned that only three women were left alive from that town after the burnings. The details are up to my imagination.

⁓

Three women were left alive in the town my great-grandmother claims as her family land back in southern Germany. All the other women were burned, drowned or hung because they were suspected of dealings with spirits as witches. Witchcraft here means talking or otherwise associating with other realms or beings. In those days, gardening, keeping cats (too many), having a fondness for medicinal teas, reading (too much or the wrong kinds of books, i.e. not the Bible), owning coveted land, resisting the pull of inevitable motherhood, or growing contentedly to a ripe old age might land you on the list of suspects.

I imagine, if nothing else, the towns were quieter after the killings. Maybe routine came back naturally. People still woke early, some of them ploughed the fields, others washed shirts, still others ran out for a loaf of bread just in time for supper. The neighbors didn't have to listen to that old mangy, and now abandoned, stray cat howl at all hours of the night—one could simply slip it some poison and be rid of the inconvenience. The rules of consequence were twisted as a wrinkled old tree, bending in favor of those few who held power and the whim of society in their hands.

Perhaps they truly contented themselves with having done the right thing, seeing what a devilish creature the old hag left behind. As they nestled into warm beds they drifted into dreams feeling justified: no God-fearing soul should have to tolerate another's oddities, or live in fear that there may be more than one truth. And so it was rationally decided to end the lives of those who seemed to hint at the possibility that maybe the answers to life's big questions were not all printed so neatly in one book.

And once the passive dissenters were silenced there was no more hatred or jealousy, no more war or confusion in Germany, and the grapes ripened more quickly, the beer turned golden more readily, the hills were an easier shade of green, and the cold stone on the city walls refused to harbor mold. The image of perfection kept a town frozen in silence, and they remained so even when they eventually went looking for another home across the Atlantic.

I think of the time during and after the witch burnings in Europe as a time when once fluid women chose to turn themselves into ice for self-preservation. They decidedly slowed and suppressed their wisdom of ways sensitive to the natural landscape and began to live much further beneath the surface of their skin. They learned to conceal, conserve and control themselves to survive.

Somatic psychologist Peter Levine writes that traumatic symptoms are not caused by the triggering event itself; they are caused by a kind of frozen residue from the event that is recalled in our nervous system which causes an immobility, as is seen in Post-Traumatic Stress Disorder. The event needs to be discharged, or shaken loose, so we can thaw and return to a state of equilibrium. We may not even remember the trauma, but the need to protect, to freeze, that may still be stored as an implicit memory from grandmothers who adapted to survive.

We, as the descendants of the oppressed, live our lives as ghosts floating across an ocean, and we teach our children to do the same. We have created a story that we wear as a mask over our true face, and it becomes our persona. But we have forgotten this mask was meant to be a temporary disguise to get through a particular situation. We start to believe we are meant to be who we have become.

The line from my ancestors in Germany to my Grandma Clara is long but straight. By the time Clara was born, her parents and grandparents had made their way inland to Southern Indiana and settled near the White River. Clara was a learned woman. Always thin, composed, with the lines of discipline and frequent washing in her palms and the lines of piety and fervent prayer next to her eyes. She chose my grandfather, Stephen, for her husband and proposed to him after a basketball game one afternoon. She began work at the supermarket at the age of twenty, and was regional manager by forty. By that time, she had also given birth to one son and five daughters, including one set of twins.

The last time I saw Grandma Clara was at my sister's wedding reception. She seems always to sit at the center of any given room and command power like a spider in her own web.

Grandma Clara has the posture of a deer, alert and ready for action, and her pink shirt is meticulously ironed and pressed. Her legs are neatly crossed at the ankles, right in front of left. Clara's small fingers are wrinkled and soft, resting on her lap. Her fingernails are piously pale and neat as the rain. My always busy mother internalized her phrase, *idle hands are the devil's workshop.*

Clara's daughters, many of them mothers by now, watch nervously out of the corner of their eyes, like anxious fawns, for her approval or disapproval. Their invisible umbilical cords are taut, reeled in close. The threat of a mother revoking her love is a terrifying instinctual reaction.

As an infant your survival depends on her willingness to take care of you. Grown women remember this fear of death in their bodies if their mother often showed disapproval or lack of attention to them when they were young. It is a visceral fear, a tenuous attachment style that takes time to heal. To this day, I never start preparing a meal before the dishes are cleared from the sink, and my mother still insists on washing and ironing the bedsheets on Wednesdays. All of my aunts married Catholic men in the church or had their Protestant fiancés convert before they agreed to be married.

Grandma Clara gave me a crystal clock for high school graduation, and it keeps immaculate time. I still don't think I've ever changed the batteries. I keep it on my altar as a reminder that structure has a place in me alongside all the airy dreams and fluid emotions. I learned to live within this structure before I ultimately rejected it.

When I was six, I grew tired of making my bed so I slept on top of the sheets to avoid the chore. When I was seven, I organized silverware by category in the dishwasher. When I was eight, I set my alarm twenty minutes prior to my mother's wake-up time so I could read my books before it was time for chores. By the time I was ten, I refused to brush or comb my hair and wouldn't let anyone near it with scissors. At eleven, I dressed myself in mismatched socks and clothes and my mother declared me a ragamuffin.

Whatever else one might call her, Clara is a strong, determined woman with the piercing clarity of a river carving out canyons in the land. She lives in perfect alignment with her principles and is clear about her expectations. If Clara is the Cailleach in my family story, then her mother-in-law Maria might be the bee. Maria is a lesser character who nevertheless plays a key role in shaping our lives. Because of the pain Maria causes Clara, there are hills and water in the otherwise flat and dry landscape of our family's story.

Clara's mother-in-law Maria stood for everything she is against. Ice inherently knows if it wants to hold its form it needs to resist the softer, fluid water it could become. The warmth of the movement causes melting—a lack of structure that is disorderly and uncomfortable.

I never met Maria, but I imagine she was a full flowing river, a musician and a traveling woman with brown hands who stopped for what was meant to be a brief time for work as a tenant farmer. But she fell in love with the owner's youngest son, Patrick, and she married him and bore seven children before continuing on her way.

Maria was not usually referred to by name by my aunts, but as "the gypsy" (when she was referred to at all). No one likes to talk about her, so all I know about her is a sketch I created from scraps of story. Maria married my Great-Grandpa Patrick, and they lived in a wooden farm house in Loogootee, Southern Indiana and had seven children: three boys, four girls. One day Maria up and left the entire family. Some of my aunts whisper that she ran off with the gardener. But Clara was the holder of the family story, and she held it tightly in her petite hands, using her entire body as a cork that would plug up the raging emotions implicated behind that thick layer of ice. Clara's official word was that Maria was a sinful woman, not worth our thought or pity.

She was an example of what not to do as a woman in our family. But I was more than a little proud when Grandma Clara accused me of having got "the gypsy blood" because I traveled so much. My mother always tried to stay still, to be a well-behaved girl, but she was something of a rebel herself when she eloped with my father, an agnostic, and moved to Florida. I wonder if she felt more of a push to leave or a pull to arrive when she left that small town in Indiana. And I wonder if she ever misses the structure of her mother's home as I do?

My mother doesn't collect rocks, but she does keep a few special stones around. Of these, she has three unimpressive gray rocks that she keeps in her sock drawer. They are smooth and about the size of a robin's egg. Each one is unique, with long white lines of varying width criss-crossing through the shades of gray with tiny freckles of red. She calls these her glacier stones. Her Grandpa Patrick used to go out in the backyard and help her hunt for them, then he would tell her stories about the ice that carved this land. The lines tell you exactly where the ice used to be, like a marble cake, except that the white swirls contain a memory of former landscapes rather than a flavor of sweetness.

These glacier stones were relics that are sacred to my mother, as authentic artifacts from a time she did not understand. I can imagine Patrick was something of a fascination for her. I always hear a bit of nostalgia and tenderness, a tenuous quake like the sounds of a young girl, in her voice when she mentions him. My great-grandfather Patrick did not live long. The blanket term used to describe him in those days was mentally unstable, though I think it was depression that ailed him. My mom says it was because of his heavy heart. After Maria left him with seven children he seemed to collapse under the weight of his loss. His heart slowed, blood refused to flow, and finally all of his movement stopped.

After their mother left and their father lost his mind, the boys were raised by an uncle, and the girls were sent to an orphanage. I can't believe the girls were discarded so blatantly. I wonder if we can still feel that lack of value in our memory—my aunts, my sister and me. Our family has decided that we are disposable, so we need to earn our keep as *good girls* or better. Grandpa Patrick must have been crushed by the weight of that guilt, of choosing between his children. He fell asleep with a cigarette in his hand and burned down the family home. In some ways it feels like a fire is an appropriate end to their love story, the only spark of heat and drama in a family of conservative Catholics.

Grandpa Patrick was a huge rock, my Grandma Maria a fast moving river. She swirled around him until she felt she lost all momentum and sank. As the momentum of her own grandmothers gathered behind her she found her feet again and continued on her way. I don't know what drives the grandmothers behind my aunts—their course seems to be one that needs to maintain a steady order after an upsetting and outrageous divergence caused by the wake of Grandma Maria's disappearance.

They may be driven, or pushed, by the fear of abandonment more than the pull of freedom that must also be hidden somewhere within them. My mother was one of two braver daughters of Clara who left Indiana and the Catholic Church to carve out her own course. But she is marbled like the glacier stone, with Maria's red yearning for freedom and the white criss-cross of Grandma Clara clinging to truth. The layers my mother chose to reveal and even those she tried to conceal from me have made me who I am.

Once I convinced my mom to show me a picture of Grandma Maria, and in it she looks surprisingly human. I told my mom that Grandma Maria looked kind of like her, and she responded defensively, *what does that mean?* So I dropped it.

I was jealous of the photographer because he got to meet her. Whoever took this photograph was an invisible, now forgotten, witness to her mortality, vulnerability and mutability. This person sliced away a moment from the endless stream of time and froze it, only to have it passed down to cause me to melt. Maria sits at the far left with her husband and father-in-law. Grandpa Patrick has their first little boy, Mike, on his lap. He's wearing glasses and smiling the smile of a proud papa. Grandma Maria has her left hand under her chin, and she leans forward slightly. The picture is old and blurry, and it seems her eyes wander out of the frame. Her attention is elsewhere, somewhere in the periphery. Perhaps a breeze has just lifted the trees and her mind escapes past the edge of the farm into the forest. Maybe she's thinking of her own family she left behind to settle here. She's got the farmhouse now, so there's no more working in the fields. But security wasn't what she had wanted. It must have been hard to live in the ease of the shade when she loved the brilliance of the sun on her skin. Maybe she daydreamed about following the winding path of the White River south where the sun shone brighter.

Joan Didion has written: *A place belongs forever to whoever claims it hardest, remembers it most obsessively, wrenches it from itself, shapes it, renders it, loves it so radically that she remakes it in her own image.* She makes the argument that loving a place makes it yours. I wonder what would happen if we flip the statement around. I might say: *A person belongs forever to the land that claims her most persistently, calls her obsessively, shatters her conceptions of self, shapes her, and loves her so radically that her own heartbeat is felt in the soil.*

I think this flip might have helped Patrick and Maria. I have a feeling he tried to love her enough, to claim her so outrightly, that he crushed the delicate shape of the woman he loved. It's like eating a songbird for the beauty of her voice. Without freedom, Maria collapsed. When a river is dammed or frozen it ceases to be an essential part of itself. Maria knew she belonged to the land, to the road. And she must have needed courage to accept that.

Each child was a joy, but also another link in the chain that kept her bound to her domestic life. I wonder if she went slowly mad with the monotony, the lack of stimulation. Or maybe she always knew she would leave and stayed only as long as it took her to break away and return to herself. I wonder if she ever heard the Irish legend of the selkie, about a man who steals an enchanted sealskin and marries the woman underneath.

The Story of the Selkie, from the Celts of Ireland

Once upon a time in the land of high cliffs, crashing seas and unpredictable storms there lived a very lonely and very clever fisherman. On his way home from another disappointing day, he stumbles upon a group of beautiful women sunning on the rocks by the cove. He watches the women and longs for a wife, and then he gets an idea. He notices that these women are not ordinary women, but are half seal, and they have left their skins to dry on the cliff as they laugh and recline.

He quickly steals one of the pelts. One by one the women return for the pelts and dive back into the sea, except for one woman who looks around distraught and confused. He pretends to be sympathetic, and comforts her. She agrees to stay with him, since a seal without a skin cannot return to the sea, and he promises to return her pelt after seven years as long as she lives with him for this time. The woman agrees and returns to his home.

The seal-woman has a child with the fisherman, and although content enough, she feels increasingly uncomfortable in the outer world. She does not forget the waves, the wind and the sun. Her skin loses its sheen and the spark is drained from her eyes. Her hair starts falling out, her eyelids start peeling and her skin cracks. She begins to demand he give back her pelt. The fisherman becomes paranoid about his hiding place and moves the skin he's hidden.

One night the child wakes up to hear arguing. It has been seven years and the seal-woman is demanding that she have her sealskin back. "I want what I am made of returned to me!" cries the seal-woman. The husband refuses to give his wife back the sealskin for fear that she will leave him. The child goes to sleep, but wakes up in the night to hear the sound of the wind and goes out into the dark.

The next night, the full moon whispers for the seal-woman to wake, and she finds her way to the field. She begins digging in a frenzy and re-discovers her lost sealskin. The seal-woman pulls on her sealskin and heads for the ocean.

She runs to the ocean, but she doesn't see her son sneak out behind her. He chases after her, begging her not to go. She stops at the water, and kisses her son goodbye before she puts on her skin and dives into the waves.

He cannot follow her because of his human blood. But the seal in him turns him into a brilliant musician. He learns to live in between two worlds.

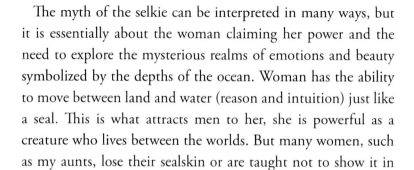

The myth of the selkie can be interpreted in many ways, but it is essentially about the woman claiming her power and the need to explore the mysterious realms of emotions and beauty symbolized by the depths of the ocean. Woman has the ability to move between land and water (reason and intuition) just like a seal. This is what attracts men to her, she is powerful as a creature who lives between the worlds. But many women, such as my aunts, lose their sealskin or are taught not to show it in the outside world because of fear of oppression or punishment. Maria seems to be to have been a woman in touch with her wildness and her need for adventure, a woman who possesses her own skin.

Maybe Maria, who was so easy to demonize, was actually doing something brave, returning to somewhere she felt at home rather than staying trapped in an uncomfortable reality. I came across a poem Sappho wrote about Helen of Troy with a similar theme.

Forgot her kin and forgot her children
to follow however far into whatever luck
the hitherward of her headlong heart.

There has to be some redemption for a woman who has caused so much pain and whose memory has been so beaten down by later generations.

She likely felt regret for most of her days after she left, like a seal missing the ocean and a woman missing the land. She could not be in two places simultaneously, she could not have been both free and connected in the same instance. I choose to honor Maria for her mysterious purpose and bless her for the wildness she brought to our line.

In the end, I am also marbled like the glacier stones my mother keeps in her sock drawer after all these years, with a streak of Grandma Clara's flare for control and precision speckled with Grandma Maria's wild abandon. The lines carved in my psyche remain as the simple pleasure I enjoy after sweeping the floor clean and emptying the dirty laundry bin. And those little red flecks are visible in my refusal to brush my hair or get a job that requires I wear shoes. I am a thoughtful, curious woman who spends her time reading myths about the days when women were giants and glaciers and rivers. I am a woman who values the bee sting, realizes the cost of courageous freedom and remembers the true faces we once wore underneath our masks. I am a woman who wonders when we as women will recall our ability to carve the land mass beneath our feet.

Berkeley. September 2014.

I lost my temper the other day when my partner Sebastian asked me if I would start cooking more. Just because I work from home does not mean I have time to be a housewife. I rebel against the archetype that's coming up behind me like a speeding truck down Smoky Mountain. The weight of the mother, the woman, the housewife terrifies me. I don't want to be trapped in a house without my skin, my ability to dive into the depths of mystery and meaning. I can feel Grandma Maria's hot blood in my veins, pleading with me to avoid the net being thrown over me.

I'm nearly five months pregnant by now, almost half way. The pressure to resist what other people think motherhood means takes more and more energy. I found the best reminder of my freedom is giving myself the gift of choice. I always have a choice on some level, even when my body overrides my mind.

So far the hormones have acted on me like a washing machine. They sweep me away, saturate me, spin me around, and I somehow come out on the other side fresher and clean. I can feel the surges coming, there is a kind of drawing in energetically like the tide before a tsunami. I need to rage against whatever dam is in front of me. Not that the small inconvenience is the problem, but the line at the bank or the internet being down is an obstacle that I can press against to know my strength. My psyche is re-calibrating. My voltage is increasing, my stream of blood widening into a river that supplies two hearts with nourishment. My energy moves like the tide, rushing over me and then withdrawing just as quickly.

I have to organize my day around what my body will allow. She has taken over. At times my reason feels less sharp; I forget words or lose entire trains of thought. My sister calls it *Mommy Brain*, but instead of an insult I can take this as a compliment. I am becoming more instinctive—my senses are becoming more acute—and my awareness has widened like moonlight. No one expects the sun to glow softly and reveal the stars as the moon does. The different qualities of light are valuable because they are complementary. We should not expect the moonlight of a pregnant woman to become sharp like the sun's rays. Perhaps her specialty is not in the piercing light of discernment but in the glow of ambient awareness.

The space of my womb is a tiny ocean, sustaining me as well as my child. I've dropped into my center at my navel and I move through the world from there. It's an intuitive, relaxing place to inhabit, and this new orientation has brought me fresh realizations as well. I can look forward to a fullness during my childbearing years like the full moon phase of the moon's cycle. And when the moon of my inner life begins to wane, my womb will close into itself like a cowry shell. As my hairs turn silver I will be able to harvest the strength and nourishment I used to spend externally on children and lovers, and instead relish the dark moon of the crone.

As a woman connected to this power of my center, my own internal ocean, I realize it's up to me if I resent doing housework. Holding this center is the gift of sovereignty, it is the seal-woman who owns and commands her own sealskin rather than having it taken over by a man. It is my choice if cooking dinner is a chore or a welcome break from the computer, a time to play music, enjoy the smells and colors of ingredients and work with my hands.

The distinction between work and play is that we have the power to define it for ourselves. If work is something we do to achieve a certain outcome, such as changing the color of the wall or getting a paycheck, then play is defined as what we do for the purpose of the action itself. Anything can be play if we enjoy it without worrying about whether or not we will get something from it later. In this play, I re-route my habits and enjoy the journey over new landscapes. It is my choice when and where my waters flow. Having found my own essential movement I explore what it means to move in relationship, to hold my center and shine my light with a partner by my side.

LA SEINE

Reflects the Light

It is as in the inexorable course of lovemaking. When the river rushes toward land's end, it has no recourse. It must re-become, must leave the earth and meet the air. Must hang suspended, fracturing the waning light. And float, rather than fall.

Sandra Jackson-Opoku

Paris. June 2005.

IT's 8:30 ON A SUNDAY EVENING. I climb the double sided cement stairs out of the Cité Universitaire Metro station heading toward my home in the 14th arrondissement. I'm humming Nina Simone's "I Wish I Knew How it Would Feel to be Free" and I'm at the part where she sings *I wish I could say all the things that I should say. Say 'em loud, say 'em clear, for the whole round world to hear.*

Without thinking, I've chosen a coat that acts as armor. It's too big, rectangular and heavy, too warm for this summer day, but it's already dark outside, and my dorm is twenty minutes away. I wear all manner of shields and protection every time I go outside because I cannot assume I will walk down the street without hearing a cat call, without being followed, and without fear of being harassed or touched.

I smell urine and see a man with a big dog walking toward me. I cross to the other side of the street, pretending to be invisible, wishing I were inside already. This is how it feels to be a woman in the city today.

~

Woman has been blamed again and again for sexual assault: society says she was "asking for it." Has a man ever been blamed for feeling handsome in his own skin? One of women's unique powers lies in her capacity for experiencing the world sensually. Women twist and turn in all directions in order to bind and contain these powers in order to fit in in a man's world. The problem is—aside from also wounding men with this limited perspective of their self-restraint—that women of all colors have started to believe this ridiculous lie: *that women's bodies are sinful by nature.*

We, as women, are intact underneath the heavy coat that blocks out inner light, but the wounds are more difficult to mend when we constantly tear at the sutures. Once we realize the layers of guilt and shame that have been placed on us, we can begin to dig ourselves out from underneath the layers of oppression.

No element exists in a vacuum. Especially not water. Water loses herself easily when she comes into contact with other elements, as does the Greek goddess of love, Aphrodite (more on her later). As a transparent liquid, water is highly influenced by the surrounding elements. In the earth, water turns to mud, in the presence of fire, she boils over, in cold air she turns to ice.

If this book were a song, this section would be the bridge. The instrumental breakdown of emotions that connects the beginning of the song, which presents a problem, to the other side of the song that finds resolution. I have to build this bridge from crisis to solution by acknowledging the wound and potential liberation in relationships.

~~~

When my sister and I listened to my mother tell stories, we learned that failure was growing up to be average. We needed to excel not only as women in the home, but also as men in the public sphere. My mother, the perpetual teacher, was truly Clara's daughter in that she set an example as an ambitious worker, never able to settle for just good enough at any task. She was keen on blurring fun and education, and she was an expert at the identification and execution of a teachable moment. Bedtime was her main stage performance. We read straight through the Bible, year-round, and these stories woke up the paradox of morality in me.

Most of the women in the Bible were "good" because of their restraint, suffering and piety, and they were "bad" when they were sensual or powerful. I believed the one-sided opinion that Jezebel must have been a conniving sorceress until an Iron and Wine song revealed the clear misogynist message behind her fate. The "good guys" had set the dogs on her to be brutally torn to shreds—that should have been a clue as to who was menacing and violent. But even amidst the deceitful Rachels, doubting Sarahs, lying Leahs, and that goody-two-shoes Esther, I found a heroine worth emulating.

The story of Eve always fascinated me. I was deeply curious about that snake. And what would it have been like to be the first, and only, woman? I know she was supposed to have turned out "bad," and needed to be punished—but all she wanted to do was share what she learned with her lover Adam. I always felt my mother empathized with her too.

My mother seemed to tell me at once to be a good girl—

so that one day I would find a nice husband—but also that there is much more to the world, and if I am willing to endure scrutiny, I can veer away from the paradise garden into wild and raw self-discovery. Wasn't that what she had set out to do in eloping with my father to Florida? And so the Biblical lesson on original sin backfired, my curiosity was whetted: I felt a yearning to be called away from the blissful garden by a snake whispering something about mystery and knowledge.

The call would come when I was sweeping the front porch, the day after my freshman year of college during my nineteenth summer. There it was, right there beneath the red and pink begonias—a glimmering golden snake. She looked at me, and, this time, I look right back.

I had seen her sisters before, as the black water moccasin next to my canoe at Sweetwater cabin, as the little green garden snake under the orange squash blossoms outside the kitchen door, even my school mascot was the diamondback rattler.

This one is a fast snake who shoots out from under the bushes and over to a clearing, where she begins to grow. Her golden scales pulse in expansion until she is just about my height, and then she begins to spin, creating a little whirlwind about her. The heathers that line our front walkway scatter little purple flowers all about, and I step near her. Dazed by her force and power, eyes wide and mouth dry, I want to say something, but I don't—I can't. She catches me up in a whirlwind, and I am lost in enormous sensation along my spine—currents running up and down like lightning across a wire.

The next thing I know, Jewel is singing something about how she cracks the yolks to make a smiley face, and I am in my bed. *You were meant for me, and I was meant for you.* I hit the snooze button, blink once or twice, and realize what happened. I was dreaming. But why am I up so early? And why did I set my alarm during the summer? Right—I've got a plane to catch! And I am off to Paris.

I sold my car in order to afford that trip. It was the summer of my sophomore year in college, and I needed to be further away. So I sold the white Toyota Celica I had saved for years to buy, and enrolled in summer study abroad in Paris. The dream of the snake on the morning of my departure felt like an omen for transformation. Something had started to move in my psyche before I ever landed and before I took my poetry book and notepad to the banks of La Seine. I had followed in the footsteps of Eve, allured by the whispers of mystery and knowledge I was certain to discover in France.

〜

Thirty-two bridges cross the Seine, an urban river that is almost entirely contained between concrete walls. Many people cross over her, but no one enters her. She is known and yet remains unknown. The last time she raged into a flood was 1910; she's been well-behaved since then. In the summer, locals set up sprinklers and add sand to the sidewalks down by her banks and call it the beach. But still, no one swims in La Seine. She is worn out as a cheap hooker, brown like the cat-sized rats that troll her banks, and still irresistibly beautiful by the dim light of candles.

Somehow a river whose banks are made of concrete is still able to reflect and remember how to inspire feeling. La Seine taught me the importance of including poetry in my life. Audre Lorde has written in her essay, "Poetry is not a Luxury": *Poetry is a vital necessity of our existence. It forms the quality of the light within which we predicate our hopes and dreams toward survival and change, first made into language, then into idea, then into more tangible action. Poetry is the way we help give name to the nameless so it can be thought. The farthest external horizons of our hopes and fears are cobbled by our poems, carved from the rock experiences of our daily lives.*

Poetry allows one to set down her rational mind and enter into a feeling, a dream or an experience. Poetry helped me to reclaim eros in my life. Erotic energy is the energy which brings passion for living, the feeling that a person is happy to be alive. Eros is not necessarily about sex, though sexuality is included in a holistic framework of the body. It is something that can be felt while dancing, singing, performing, making love, or even while drinking tea, washing the dishes or sweeping the kitchen.

It helps to distinguish between pornography and eroticism here, which are often confused. Western society has tangled the experience of the body with something inherently sinful or wrong, rather than allowing it be to a full expression of the human spirit as matter. Audre Lorde defines pornography *as sensation without feeling.* She defines the erotic as *an assertion of the feminine life force, of creative energy empowered* in speaking, walking, and other daily tasks.

Being objectified or used as another person's means to an end reduces our capacity to feel the fullness of ourselves. When we as women allow this objectification, we have sold a part of our soul: we have effectively traded in the juiciness and sweetness that keeps life worth living. If we give ourselves away as objects often enough, we become dry and bitter.

I had spent much of my first twenty years trying to be good, living for approval and thriving on praise. But poetry and the snake invited me to experience my own power at my belly and in my hips, which brings me to the goddess of love, Aphrodite.

Paris is known as the city of lovers, and La Seine, is the Aphrodite of rivers, the Marilyn Monroe of waterways. Most people who meet her are instantly charmed and, if not, often feel the disappointment of not having been enchanted as expected. Whether or not visitors connect with her, there is an implication based on her mythology. I was magically receptive in the summer of 2005 and relaxed into a willingness to be vulnerable, to be touched by a moment. I read Victor Hugo, Pablo Neruda, JD Salinger, and Audre Lorde by her banks and watched countless amber sunsets late in the evening.

I picked up my purple journal and began, with a virgin hand, to write verse rather than prose. My mind constantly interfered and tried to block the awkward flow of sensual words from forming such odd patterns on the page, not even filling the sheet. *You're wasting paper,* I reprimanded myself. But my heart overflowed down my arms and through my fingers with the scent of roses and crêpes, the jazz cello in the air, and the romantic glow of the street lights on the bridge, and poetry persisted.

La Seine was originally named by the Celts, who eventually were pushed north out of Europe and isolated onto the island that would become Ireland. Her name meant *sacred* to them. Today, her name connotes romance, art and love. People come from all over the world to gather inspiration from her, to place themselves within the lineages of poets and painters who fell head over heels and lost themselves in her reflection. The Seine has become the goddess of love embodied in a river, she is Oshun, who has been transformed in Europe into Aphrodite.

Aphrodite is a water goddess, born from the discarded genitals of Uranus that are thrown into the sea. As a goddess of fertility, she bestows humans with grace and desirability. She is the force of creation, the charge between positive and negative ions that cannot resist one another. In the psyches of both men and women, she is the will to live, she is what animates us and brings us into the world of beauty and passion. Aphrodite is so closely entangled with our life force that she is difficult to see as something separate. If she leaves us, our breath gives out, our hearts stop, and we die.

Christine Downing calls her *Aphrodite Automata*: one who is spontaneously giving, but also never possessed. She lives in humans as their quality of personal charisma: bestowing warmth, availability and a golden hue to all interactions. She is an enchantress and a storyteller.

Aphrodite lives entirely in the realm of feeling. She moves through the world with a finely tuned discernment about her senses. Aphrodite stands for the qualities in humans, and especially in women, that need to see themselves through the eyes of others. Like Oshun, she needs constant reflection to feel who she is. When out of balance, she is dependent on being liked and admired. When balanced, she trusts what arises from her body, and she knows sensations will not steer her wrong. She is the ground of the river, the lower organs that touch the earth and use tactile muscles to make their way from one place to another.

Unlike the humble, modestly robed Virgin Mary, Aphrodite (also known as Venus) is almost always depicted naked (*à la* "Birth of Venus".) She is unashamed of her body, and willing to be fully seen. I can hardly imagine the immense shift in the collective human psyche when the pantheon of gods was replaced with monotheism. By the time of Constantine in the fourth century, the image of a goddess of fertility is effectively usurped by a virgin who gives birth *without sin*. But Aphrodite's innocence and vulnerability is unstained by lovers; she is a virgin in the pagan sense of the word: *a woman who always belongs to herself.*

Aphrodite, as the River Seine, inspires those who seek her to let down their body armor and wake up to sensuality in their skin. She is loved because she inspires us to reclaim the eros in erotic. She lessens the toll that constant interactions with machines take on our human softness, our fluidity, and our aliveness. Our bodies are our homes, so she teaches us to inhabit them. Often that means being willing to look back at the places we've left: the dusty corners of our psyche we avoid; the painful, stuck spots we've repressed because we have been told at some point *shame on you.*

Shame is placed on us by others like a backpack full of rocks, and we continue to bear it until we realize it is our choice to set it down. Much of our life force or energy is diverted and unavailable to us because we unconsciously spend great portions of energy holding on to pain.

We live into only a fraction of our wholeness because we don't take the time to reflect and release what we hold. Our bodies remember these early patterns of holding and hiding, but unconditional acceptance causes an internal flow to return to break apart the heavy, frozen areas that have been traumatized by intrusion, guilt, or fear.

We, as women, live layers beneath our surface, cut off from our internal flow, because we were taught to fear our own bodies. When we begin to remove the heavy cloak of shame that has been placed over our elegant and regal shoulders, we have a chance to reclaim the intact fullness underneath.

~

This is not the story of one summer romance in particular.

This is the story of all the summer loves I've ever had, because up to a point they all could have been the same single man. Until I found a way to remain in my own skin while falling in love, every person I dated was a projection of myself.

My first romantic relationship was with Simon. He was

smart, and I wanted to be valued for my intelligence. I was competitive with him, and loved to imagine I outwitted him. In those days, I lived for his praise of my reason and our long philosophical debates. We spent most of our time together in our minds, in the element of air, and our brief interludes into matter and earth in our bodies were awkward and foreign.

Florida. May 2001.

I reach up under the mini blinds, open the window and release smoke and a little breath. You're pale in the dim gray room. I wear white lace panties and you cover your crotch. Cheeks pink.

"Like a jar, I'll get to keep you forever," you said. *Who offers themselves as a keepsake?* I cannot hold you. I will not store you—an object on a shelf. No, I decide you cannot have me, but I give something to you anyway.

I am ready, or I think I am. And, anyway, everyone else already has.

But it didn't feel all that different. Or I don't. I am still somehow only sixteen. And tomorrow I paint my lips red, yawn in early morning fog and wait for the yellow bus.

Florida. Fall 2005.

The relationship I would call my first love was with Anthony. I had just gotten back from Paris and wore a bright yellow skirt with a red top to a friend's house party. I had grown my hair long and wore dangling earrings with crystals that came down from a wide top to a sharp point and reflected light like a prism. We stayed up all night talking, and when he left in the morning we knew we were embarking on a tragic long-distance relationship, but it was perfect.

He wanted to be an actor, and I was an aspiring poet. We

were both in need of deep heartache to influence our crafts. We wrote elaborate letters to one another, and were always on vacation when we visited. We cooked decadent meals with red wine and listened to Etta James on a second-hand record player.

He was Paris personified, a hangover from the romance of the Seine that waited to manifest until I got home. We were romantics and dreamers who shared a common tendency for erratic behavior and eventually took flight separately as a pair of cowardly narcissists. We were broken tea cups made all the more lovable by the tiny crack of impermanence we knew would eventually end us. Seeing our end the entire time made our love all the more freeing.

I was ready for longing
like a stone in the Desert,
cold tea on Wednesdays
and autumn in Oregon.

You smiled like a Cheshire cat
and all I could think of was a
sandalwood flame.

So we laughed at the Lightning
and stole nectar from Midnight:
four sticky pomegranate
thumbs prying open
into starry bloom.

We set out on Canoe
and made altars to Krishna
on the arrow-head prow
but the Sea was Poseidon
and his arms were antlers
and Wind took the pink shells

from our dirt-stained fingernails.
We washed up at sunset
outside the city
of Night Blooming Sand Dunes.

We were foggy yet open
two ghosts on the ocean.
But you tilted my chin up
and said I was Home
so we married our eyes wide
as we glided through red lights.

And we first met as rivers
before we were Sand Dunes
and it was raining that Wednesday
in a tea room in Salem.

And I knew when I left you
that courage took breaking.
So one day I'll thank you
you gave meaning to memory.

But what will I do now with this empty longing
and when will I again be alive like the dying?

California. July 2011.

And then there was the one who broke me open—Joshua—but I am not really going to tell you about him. I am not going to tell you about the day he left me. The dream I had of the deflated dark balloon I rode until I jumped from it before it flew into the sun, and I landed in the sand.

I won't tell you about the way I woke the next morning wishing I hadn't woken up at all. I pulled my red knitted blanket over my head and cried until the sun was strong enough to shine through the velvet-red threads, and I had to admit the deep red hue reflected on my skin was lovely despite my pain.

I am not going to tell you how my insides were ripped out when I heard he was with her. The one with the curly hair, and long, pink painted fingernails. I am not going to tell you that for the first time I understood what it is to be spitting mad, so angry my saliva was hot and metallic, and the venom inside me wanted to be released through my mouth—like a snake in mortal danger.

I am not going to tell you how I broke and shattered like fine china, forever into a million pieces on the tile floor.

I will not allow myself to tell you that I still love him. That even when I wake up next to Charlie's warm face and curly hair I miss Joshua's wide, pooling eyes and dark skin.

Joshua and I were a pot of simmering rice whose water never boiled. No matter how much I wanted it to, the fire was lacking; the rice remained bloated and would not cook. After my shattering experience with Joshua, I was determined to put myself back together differently.

I had outgrown my old skin, the model of beauty I had been sold. I believed I was beautiful because I was tall enough, curved in the right places and slender in others. I believed I was desirable because I was smart enough, sharp in the right places and softer in others. I believed I was good because I was kind enough, strong in the right places and gentle in others.

I'm sorry, but none of this is true. I read somewhere that women defer their power with too many apologies. But rather than an admission of wrong, I look back to the original meaning of the word. Apology is a defense. This is my last apology.

To all the men I've loved, an apology from Aphrodite: I want to control the way you see me. I demand you know my flying. Watch me soar, hear me sing, shower me with praise. Kiss me, love me.

I demand you know my worth, my weight, my sparkling talents and dazzling secrets. I want you to be intrigued, but never to know me. I demand you witness my kindness, my depth, my heart. Look away from my falling, cover your eyes when I cry.

I want to say I am sorry for all the times I hid. The times I forgot that I was big enough, smart enough, strong enough to let you see me, to make a difference, to defend, to honor, to love.

And with that said, I feel impatient. Critical. Tired of talking about feelings. Annoyed with people's need to be seen. Irritated with mediocrity. I'm a monkey among apes; a pear on a grapefruit tree. The river's demand for arbitrary juxtaposition is too much to hold at times.

If only the goddesses and female archetypes could be in dialogue with one another, and recognize they are many aspects of one divine feminine. Certainly Tara and Oshun would remind Aphrodite of the beauty in imperfection.

Buddhist teacher Thich Nhat Hạnh has written that he cherishes one tea cup that is cracked much more than the others; the crack serves as a reminder that the cup will not last forever. It is this frailty, this blatant vulnerability and the reminder of impermanence that brings meaning to life. Maybe that depth and beauty, not perfection, was what I wanted in a relationship all along. I may have loved Paris partially for her brevity—I knew she would be one summer of my youth. Paris herself was not always pleasant.

On a cold summer day, one of my last days in Paris, I went to the little island the river creates that houses the grand gothic cathedral, the Notre Dame. I was quietly happy, but the wear of travel and lack of vegetables had weakened my immune system. I had stayed inside for three rainy days with a fever, and just ventured out to the church to get some fresh air. I sat in one of the last pews and took in the giant structure of the building. The building-sized stained glass reflected a bit of light onto the floor, and abstract shapes and shadows formed on the hard stone. I walked slowly, taking in the excess of it all and still feeling deeply connected to the intention of beauty behind the massive structure.

A nun politely walked past me, and something about her small, slight frame made me miss my mother. I realized with a rush of tears that my mother and I would never be as close as we once were. I didn't need her the way she needed me, to define her. We were learning different languages, and there were fewer and fewer ways to translate between her reality and mine. This church didn't move me the way it would move her. I felt her absence and the grief of growing into a woman for myself. The space she had occupied in my heart would need to be filled with my own internal parent now—I stepped into mothering myself and speaking my mind. That's when I noticed how far I had come from home.

I realized I had bought what was sold to me—the image of a perfect woman—and I sold myself short in order to be accepted by the keepers of culture. I love to be in the fresh currents of air that swirl quickly from the Pacific across the Bay Area. Back in the swamplands of Florida thoughts are thicker than mud, and it may be more difficult to question what has become accepted than it is in San Francisco.

Florida. Fall 2013.

I was a bridesmaid at the wedding of my dear friend Amber a few years back. She is a brilliant, passionate woman who allows herself a lot of space for neurotic ticks and minor compulsions. She keeps two of almost everything—vacuum cleaners, toothbrushes, and favorite pajama pants—just in case something happens to one. She exercises religiously, diets consistently, and has a breezy way of agreeing with all spiritual pursuits.

Amber's wedding was at an old plantation house outside of the Ocala city limits. The land was complete with a colonial-style house: towering white columns and a long front porch accentuating the authority of the master's quarters. I could almost feel the ghosts of slavery on the land. The older woman who owned the land wore short shorts and high heels. I think she said her name was Cindy. Her hair was dyed blonde. She smoked, she flirted with the groomsmen. She employed African Americans to move the tables and set up the tent. The workers were quiet and stayed out of her way as best they could. She barked orders to them, and snapped her fingers and pointed to direct them.

I felt the layers under which they protected themselves and lived far from the surface. They seemed to want to be invisible; I knew that feeling. I got the chills when Cindy had one black man climb up into a towering oak tree and hang a rope for the chandelier that would light the dance floor. *That tree has seen other hangings*, I heard the wind whisper. But we were here to celebrate love, so I tried not to pay too much attention.

The bridesmaids got into their bright purple gowns in a tiny cottage filled with baby dolls—frozen images of girls with long lashes and tight corsets. We drank mimosas and chatted about new and old loves. A cousin came to do our hair, and a friend of a friend came to paint our faces. It was surreal for me—like peeking back through a looking glass onto a parallel universe of another potential self—*what if I had stayed in Florida?*

But it was fun to play dress up, and all was well, at least until Amber got dressed. She put on a modern day corset: Spanx, which is a kind of spandex suction suit that is designed to firm and tighten the appearance of a woman's body. Amber is in good shape—she is healthy—but she has always had trouble with her body image.

We help her into the dress, a fashionable mermaid style with a fitted center that flares wide around the knee, and she does look beautiful, but she is holding her breath and sticking out her bottom lip. *If Grandma Clara were here, she would threaten to sit on that lip.* It is a tight dress that hugs her hips and lifts her breasts like an offering of two fleshy jello mounds just beneath her throat. Amber looks in the mirror and cries: "This isn't me!" as she shakes her head. "I can't go out there like this. I don't dress like this. I feel naked. I can't breathe."

The bridesmaids, one by one, come to her aid: they gently talk her into wearing the dress, reassuring her that she looks stunning. The dress was expensive, and she does look like a princess. I state the obvious and tell her she doesn't have to wear it if she is uncomfortable. The other women shoot me a look— *don't tempt her!* She considers my proposal for a moment, as if it hadn't been an option before.

I imagine she has a moment where she realizes she is in a cage, but the door is wide open. She pauses there on that threshold, wavering, and then decides to slam the door shut for herself. "My parents paid so much for this dress, they would kill me if I didn't wear it." And that's it. She stuffs her feelings into her gut and the wedding goes on. She looks like one of the dolls from the cottage the rest of the night—smiling stiffly and refusing to dance. I wanted so badly for her to choose freedom this time, and it hurt me so much to watch her go through the motions all evening.

I refuse to stuff my feelings down. I want out of that cage. I will not be a slave to the favor of others. Once I realized the key was in always reminding myself the truth about my power of choice, I solidified that commitment to re-make myself through body practices and poetry. The poetry I found in Paris helped me feel my way into a new understanding of how I might inhabit myself. Audre Lorde has written: *It is through poetry that we give name to those ideas which are, until the poem, nameless and formless—about to be birthed, but already felt. That distillation of experience from which true poetry springs births thought as dream births concept, as feeling births idea, as knowledge births (precedes) understanding.*

I found, among other poets, a Native American and European woman named Joy Harjo who helped me give birth to these intangible ideas. Her use of symbols provided me with a sense of safe exploration, like a rope to use as I descended into a cave. In *Book of Myths* she points to the discrepancy between how American and Native cultures see their women. She places her people in the foreground and calls them beautiful even though they do not have the kind of mainstream beauty of Marilyn Monroe. Harjo contrasts Western ideals of beauty with those of cultures closer to nature.

There is Helen in every language;
in American her name is Marilyn
but in my subversive country,
she is dark earth and round and full of names
dressed in bodies of women
who enter and leave the knife wounds of this terrifyingly

beautiful land;
we call ourselves ripe and pine tree woman.

The images of earth and nature and roundness provide visuals that empower women away from the objectifying and limited symbolism of one-size-fits all patriarchal systems. Harjo also points out the limiting and terribly painful view that one particular woman has it right, implying that all others are wrong, broken, or fall short. If a woman is held up next to a model she is sure to fail in likeness, but if she is held up against the earth and seen as beautiful in her unique qualities, this is liberation.

Marilyn Monroe is an example of a woman who was destroyed because she poured herself into too narrow a model of beauty and her true self, her wholeness, was cut off at the cost of living as a single archetype. She appeared to have everything that society told her she needed externally, but there seems to have been a deep interior sadness and emptiness that ultimately led to her suicide at a young age. She lived herself into the story of Aphrodite so fully that she was consumed by her, and Marilyn, Norma Jean, disappeared.

<hr />

Armed with a body-based system of discovering truth and a new found self-respect, I returned to one of my favorite stories from childhood, The Little Mermaid. This story is a perfect example of the way changes in culture affect the stories we tell to the next generations, and at the same time we can see that the depth of meaning may still be uncovered.

Like most of my generation of young girls growing up in the mid-1980s, I was mesmerized by the story of Disney's *The Little Mermaid*. It hit a deep vein in my soul that inspired longing for adventure, and a thirst for some other, magical world as well as some deeply satisfying love. I let the story into my psyche, and it became a blueprint for living. I wanted to be different, to be special. I grew out my bangs and pinned them to the side so my hair would sweep wildly over my eyebrows—just like Ariel's hair. I imagined meeting Prince Eric and literally expected to be lifted from my feet into a new life, leaving the chaos of the ground and deep waters behind once and for all. I felt entitled to this escapist's version of a happy ending, and disappointed again and again when life and love refused to sweep me off my feet.

I discovered the Danish author Hans Christian Andersen's original version of The Little Mermaid while studying Depth Psychology decades later. Unlike Disney's version, that is considered to be more suitable for children, the original fairy tale ends in death rather than marriage. We as a culture re-wrote the story to have what in modern times is considered a "happy" ending—a beautiful young woman is rescued from her current situation by a dashing prince. It is worth noting that in the modern, Western version, the prince causes the transformation. The heroine must wait for his intervention, but this is not the case in the original story. There are complex symbols of wholeness and wisdom in the original story that had been discarded with this re-invention. Luckily, what is discarded in the river of memory has a way of re-surfacing as it is needed.

The Story of The Little Mermaid, by Hans Christian Andersen

Far out in the ocean, where the water is as blue as the prettiest cornflower, and as clear as crystal, it is very, very deep; so deep, indeed, that no cable could fathom it: many church steeples, piled one upon another, would not reach from the ground beneath to the surface of the water above. There dwell the Sea King and his subjects.

The great Sea King is a widower who lives with his six daughters, each more beautiful than the last, and his aging mother. Each of the sea-princesses has a garden she keeps on the ocean floor, and each princess is allowed one glimpse of the surface world on her fifteenth birthday. The youngest daughter, Ariel, is most fascinated with the dream of the other world—the surface above her world of blue. Her grandmother had told her about the evil world of the humans, but she had also mentioned their souls were immortal. Mermaids, unlike humans, live only once. The only way for a mermaid to have an eternal soul is if she falls in love with a human and he, in turn, falls in love with her.

Ariel was considered to be a strange child; she was quieter and more thoughtful than her sisters. She did not care for the treasures found in wrecked vessels as they did. She cared more for the flowers in her garden, especially the red ones. Her garden was not in a square like the plots of her sisters—it was in a circle. Her only man-made possession in the garden was a peculiar statue that was a representation of a human male.

She planted by the statue a rose-colored weeping willow. It grew splendidly, and very soon hung its fresh branches over the statue, almost down to the blue sands. The shadow had a violet tint, and waved to and fro like the branches; it seemed as if the crown of the tree and the root were at play, and trying to kiss each other.

The youngest sister waits impatiently for her fifteenth birthday so she may explore the surface world, and eventually the time comes. She peeks her head above the water and is immediately enchanted by the flying fish and great floating serpent of a ship. She watches in fascination as the people dance on two legs and listen to music which sounds entirely different from that in the world of water she has known. Her eyes are drawn to one handsome young man who bears striking resemblance to the marble statue in her garden. She leaves as she is supposed to, and eventually returns to the depths and the palace of her father.

Unable to forget the man from the surface, Ariel travels to a sorceress and trades her voice for two legs so she may walk on land. She has got to get the prince to fall in love with her in three days or else she will die. Every step on the earth is painful as glass pricking into her tender new feet, but she learns to dance and charms her way into the human world. She cannot speak, but shares a deep, silent connection with the man on whom her affections have fallen.

But Ariel ultimately fails in winning his love. The man marries another, and on the night of their wedding Ariel is presented with one final chance to save her own life. Her sisters make a deal with the sorceress that will return their sister to the sea if she is willing to take the life of the prince's new bride. Ariel accepts the dagger from her sisters, but uses it instead to end her own life rather than to harm the woman who has married her love.

Because she has learned true love in this moment, she falls back into the ocean not as a mermaid but as a sea fairy. The spray that lifts from the foam of the waves. The mermaid is dead, but in this way, she is given another chance to gain her soul over time.

On the power of another hangs a mermaid's eternal destiny. But the daughters of the air, although they do not possess an immortal soul, can, by their good deeds, procure one for themselves. We fly to warm countries, and cool the sultry air that destroys mankind with the pestilence. We carry the perfume of the flowers to spread health and restoration. After we have striven for three hundred years to all the good in our power, we receive an immortal soul and take part in the happiness of mankind. You, poor little mermaid, have tried with your whole heart to do as we are doing; you have suffered and endured and raised yourself to the spirit-world by your good deeds; and now, by striving for three hundred years in the same way, you may obtain an immortal soul.

The little mermaid lifted her glorified eyes towards the sun, and felt them, for the first time, filling with tears. On the ship, in which she had left the prince, there were life and noise; she saw him and his beautiful bride searching for her; sorrowfully they gazed at the pearly foam, as if they knew she had thrown herself into the waves. Unseen she kissed the forehead of the bride, and fanned the prince, and then mounted with the other children of the air to a rosy cloud that floated through the aether.

Recalling this story in Paris synthesized something within my psyche. I realized I was a co-creator, authoring my own experience in life. I was posing as a lake, waiting for a man to rescue me by taking me away to an exotic land. As Sandra Burke writes in her Jungian analysis of The Little Mermaid, the character Ariel lives out the feminine search for the missing aspects of her soul. The void that is created from suppression of the anima, or female part of the psyche, causes women to project the divine savior role onto the masculine.

In both versions, Ariel is searching for something she desperately needs: love, and a part of her soul that is missing. In Disney's version, Ariel continues to find satisfaction in the external world. But the projection inevitably fails in the original version, and Ariel is forced to transform through her death and return back to the depths of the water to find her fullness as something internal.

Ariel's quest, this search for an invaluable part of the soul, deeply affects Western women. We recognize ourselves in her search; we identify with this need, even as very young girls. Burke argues that: *Acquiring a soul for both the Little Mermaid and Western women becomes possible when they are able to take up their own life and voice in the world and not look to the masculine for salvation.*

I had been looking for a savior in my previous relationships too, so I knew I needed to find my own shape and give myself a structure. When I started to feel my way outside of the oppressive model I was told I needed to fit into, I looked to the moon and the water's relationship as my teacher.

The pull the moon has over the ocean tides and a woman's menses solidifies a close connection between woman, moon and water. The moon has been a symbol for watery emotions since symbols existed. Water became associated with feelings and emotions partially because of its natural ability as a conductor. Electric currents move easily through water, and emotions are transmitted in a similar way.

The Seine has absorbed and transmitted countless invisible ideas and dangling emotions from one artist to another. She is a wellspring of inspiration that is fed by the pilgrims who continue to write her story and reinforce her lure. We feed her with our own unknown potential, and in so doing, we lend her our magic, our power to enchant, and she merely reflects that back to us.

Aphrodite is born from the ocean; she is a feeling goddess. At her best, she is an energetic signature within each of us that invites us toward the freedom of actualizing our own internal sense of authority. She shows us that we do not need a lover to show us who we are, instead we learn to steep ourselves in self-love. We become full of ourselves so no one other is needed to patch the holes. We are willing to be naked in front of the world and make no apologies.

Paris. June 2005.

It's 8:30 on a Sunday evening and I climb the stairs out of the Cité Universitaire Metro stop heading toward my dorm. I smell the roses that twine over the fence by the stairs. I've just come from a walk along the left bank of La Seine, where I watched the city lights dance in her reflection. The roads are lined with artists and eateries, and I take a moment to sit and sketch out a few ideas for a novel I'll write one day. I want to capture this feeling on the page; I want to share how it feels to take the time to enjoy life. Samba music is playing from one of the booths, a couple stops to check a dinner menu, and a black cat is lazing in an open window.

As I turn down the street with the red flowers vining their way up to the top of the building, I start to hum Nina Simone's "I Wish I Knew How it Would Feel to be Free" and I'm at the part where she becomes a bird *I'd soar to the sun and look down at the sea. Then I'd sing 'cause I know . . . I know how it feels to be free.* I chose my Aphrodite coat this morning—the one with the lacing at my back and the high collar that makes my neck feel regal, queenly. The coat is a warm yellow, almost golden, that emits a gentle glow in the slightly foggy street lights.

It's cool outside, but the fresh air is invigorating. I am so bright nothing can intrude into my space: I am full of myself. I smell fresh bread and see a man with a big dog walking toward me. I look at him and nod, walking straight toward the intersection. He nods back. This is how it feels to be a woman in the city today.

RIO GRANDE

Divides in Silence

Living on borders and in margins, keeping intact one's shifting and multiple identity and integrity, is like trying to swim in a new element, an "alien" element. There is an exhilaration in being a participant in the further evolution of humankind, in being "worked" on.

Gloria Anzaldúa

New Mexico. February 2012.

I T'S WINTER, and I'm on the move again. I feel the tension between my outer stillness and my inner turbulence grow, and I know I've got to get out of California. My nerves are tight and my skin is dry. I tap my fingers on the tray table on a Virgin American flight heading east. A storm is coming in my life: I can feel it.

The internal clouds of self-loathing, emptiness, and dissatisfaction have blocked out the light of my heart, and the waters of my creativity have been diverted into meaningless jobs. I've left the earth and evaporated into the sky. It's uncomfortable and disorienting. My mind is full of psychological theories, subject-object relations, and all the things my parents did wrong during the first three years of my life. I cannot hold any more, and so I bolt.

I look out the window as we fly over the Western States, watching the patterns in the land wrinkle, rise and soften. A half moon is visible as the sun sets into an array of reds, oranges and blues. One river sways across the earth's surface in a pattern that exactly mimics a snapshot of a snake—her floodplains are wide and sprawling like branches and dendrites, but the current rises in the center and forms what looks like a giant serpent slithering across the desert. I hope to rest and recharge here.

Still longing for a place to belong, I go in search of the soft ground where the waters are dark, just as the women of the Creek Nation did. There aren't any swamps that I know of in the Western States, but every river has an edge. I end up on the shores of the Rio Grande in New Mexico for my twenty-seventh birthday. I'm feeling lost, and I'm not sure why, but I need to be alone with the rocks.

I soak under the stars at the hot springs in Ojo Caliente and saturate myself in the wide open sky. I walk through the canyons and hum to remind myself of my internal sounds; my organs wake up and brighten. My vibrations prove my existence in this dusty, ancient landscape. The nomadic tribes used the stars to navigate: for them the sky was more stable and reliable than the drastic seasons of the ever-changing earth. I trust the stars like a nomad tonight.

My ears are full of silence, and the stars pulse back and forth with my heartbeat in a private symphony. It's quiet enough to hear them shine across all those light years, and time slows down long enough for me to appreciate their tune. I am poured out into the landscape.

When the sun erases the other stars, I walk the trails over the hill, following old cracks where water would have or could have flowed. I sift through the sand and find tiny pieces of pottery.

This is the land of the Tewa people, who built large pueblos on this site and held as sacred the warm waters bubbling up from the earth's center. The shards of memory that remain on the solemn, basket-shaped hills are not buried so deep as in other places on this continent. I lift a handful of sand and watch it sift gently through my fingers, letting the wind take it at a slight angle.

I feel the mourning of words that have not been said scatter over hundreds of years. Apologies are withheld and poems remain unwritten. My sleep is full of dreams. I feel the sun rising before I have time to shake off the night, and the dreams continue trying to pull me further into a web built by the spider at my throat. My lips are sticky, like honey, and I cannot find the words. The sparkle in the red stones shimmers and reflects like sunlight on the ocean, a mirror for the sun that separates one light into thousands.

I can't quite remember something, and I am sure it is important. I dream of a canoe and a leopard in the sky, refusing to come down to the earth. The spots of the leopard create new constellations, and I promise to remember this time, but I wake up and forget again.

~

Both sides of my family have been here on this continent for hundreds, and in some cases thousands, of years. How does it still not feel like home to me? I know myself to be a complicated mixture of tyrants and victims: my ancestors were Irish Catholic and Sicilian Gypsy; French and Shawnee; German and Jewish; English and African. Before I started to dig into the stories that were offered to me—and sent in a saliva swab for testing—I hadn't known anything other than being white and European. All the other stories, all the colors, all the textures were discarded like broken shards of clay.

I started putting together the odd shaped puzzle pieces of stories when I heard my grandparents calling me from the other side of the river during the fever years. Once I started listening, they had a lot to say.

One grandma comes and braids my hair in my sleep. The structure of the braid teaches how separate strands come together to form a strong and beautiful shape. They make one whole, and at the same time they maintain their own identity as three unique groups. Each is enriched by the relationship to the others. But dream fragments are not enough, and so I return to the land.

I descend down the canyon walls at a slow, steady pace. The Rio Grande is low this February, and I feel the strain of stooping down to meet her. I follow a deer trail to the water and part the curtain of tall reeds. No one else is awake this early, so it's just me and the ducks. I cup my hands into the cold, gently flowing water and wash my face. The blood in my cheeks circulates and brings me the pink color of youth. I watch the currents move; the edges catch and spiral and smooth, but the stream's center rushes decidedly in one direction.

I feel this center flow as my inspiration for yoga practice this morning. I begin with a few sun salutations, welcoming the internal sunrise as well as the external one. This movement and warming of my lungs brings air wider into my chest, and the blood from the faucet at my heart turns on full force. Fullness returns to my fingers, my low belly, and my toes; it's like an internal bath—warm and liquid like the Gulf of Mexico. I make low, gentle sounds—*aum, hum, laa*—to help the blocked places loosen.

My body holds a landscape of memory; I always carry all my relations with me. I protect my right side (the moon) and show my left (the sun.) I habitually turn away from the vulnerability of my feminine self, I value reason over feeling—but yoga teaches balance. The frustration I carry for my father melts into understanding, but the dam holding up the anger at my mother is more stubborn. It sticks in my low belly as an oiled rock, and around my throat as if I'm being choked by a spider—each of her eight legs strong and scratching as she narrows my voice. I try to bring sounds up again, but they are indignant.

I habitually avoid the intense emotions only a mother could spark. Of course she failed when society's expectations are so high. We set our mothers up to standards of impossible perfection with collective stories of super moms that "do it all." This keeps them scattered and worn out, always not good enough. Never mind that mothers channel starlight through their wombs, weave spirit into matter, offer their body as home and then food for their littles ones. That is not enough.

Mother was always meant to fall, like Eve, it is a comfortable destiny. My mother is a happy martyr, a character in the story she offers herself to. No matter how much gratitude I give her or love I share, she denies it and continues to reinforce her beliefs. She works harder and longer hours until she passes out or needs surgery. Nothing she does is ever good enough for the tormenting voices she has internalized. At this point she has had her gall bladder, uterus and thyroid removed. She is feeding herself to a hungry ghost of a dream that will never be satiated. If I am not careful, I easily fall prey to the same trap—a feeling of being lost even within my own body that continues to chant *not good enough*. The burden society places on mothers is crushing, but yoga helps me to find where I am within the massive messiness of family karma and convoluted collective consciousness.

Hatha yoga is the practice of unifying opposites within

ourselves and in effect within the world around us. We, as humans, occupy the space between heaven and earth, constantly rooting into matter and rising from it into formlessness. Hatha yoga is a form of bringing the invisible internal world to life in a material way. *Ha* means sun and *tha* means moon, and the word yoga can be translated as union.

In *tadasana*, or mountain pose (a basic anatomical way to stand that doesn't look like much is happening externally), I stand still and take in the medicine of balance—symbolically uniting heaven and earth, the inner divine masculine and feminine. Even if our spirits are born of the stars, our bodies come from the earth, and I need to learn to be rooted in this material form.

I place my hands on the warm ground and feel the firm earth. I arch and lengthen my spine in rhythm with my breath. If the exhale is set up properly, the inhale comes naturally. The exhale is the active part of the breathing cycle; I round my spine and draw my belly button in to press out all the stale air. It's like emptying a cup of mud before you fill it with clear drinking water. You've got to pour it out and clean it before you try to fill it up again.

I inhale and lengthen like an accordion; the air floods in. After a few rounds of the rhythmic movement I become still and feel the pulsing continue internally even as my outer body has stopped. This is a sweet reminder of how fluid my body is. I am like a bucket of water being carried from one place to the next. When you set the bucket down, the water remembers the movement and continues to slosh gently side to side until it comes back to rest at the center. My waters follow the same natural laws.

A green mallard duck keeps an eye on me as he flaps his wings and shakes his tail. I finish my movement practice and sit still on the ground. As I slow into my center, I feel like a clear, shallow pond. I can see straight to the bottom, and the pebbles resting there are smooth and soft from the currents of water that have passed. My fingers make their way back to my long hair and begin to braid the loose strands as I remember my grandmother and hum to myself. As my fingers teach me the lessons of the braid, I watch the water of the Rio Grande with a cat-like gaze as she slips steadily away from me without words.

Further down the course of this river is the border between Texas and Mexico. The Rio Grande is used to divide one land into two countries: North and South. The geographic North and South are like the head and body of the world. The mind imposes rules on the body, and the body suffers under the control of the mind. The resources, the waters of this river, are mostly diverted to the people with money and power in the North, and the scarcity and poverty created to the South cause desperate situations that lead to chronic violence. It is an unnatural separation that this water was not meant to create.

Gloria Anzaldúa writes that this convergence has created a shock culture, a border culture, like a silent third country closed into itself. This separate space, this third country of the borderlands, has preserved the tension between the opposing forces so we can clearly see the struggle between traditional ways and the foreign invaders. It is a snapshot of the moment a cold air front merges with a warmer one, there is disorder and struggle as one tries to preserve itself over the other.

When the struggle begins, women are the first to be subdued, often through systematic violence and rape. Conservative Christians see woman as an animal, undivine, and in need of protection, protection from herself. Woman, in this narrative, is the other. She has to be controlled and contained. Over time, the stories are twisted to show the victim as the perpetrator.

Perhaps the most difficult of betrayals lies in making us believe that the native woman in us is the betrayer, the one who is to blame for the way things are. *La Chingada*—"the fucked one"—is the word used by Chicano women to describe other women as the betrayer, the one who sold out her people by sleeping with the European men and creating a mixed race. This is a tactic used by those who want to eliminate a culture: they create internal division and supply feelings of guilt and shame that become internalized and enforced by their own people. The silence of shame is a heavy boulder that anchors spirit to the ground so it will never soar.

However, in the midst of all this pain, somehow the image of the Virgin of Guadalupe survived in the borderlands along the Rio Grande, protected by the fluid waters of the river. The Virgin stretches her arms wide in a gesture of true grace, like cool water on a hot day. Her arms are open to those who have been abused and turned against themselves and their own people. She is a synthesis of the old ways and the new ones. She is the mediator within women's psyches who helps to mend the wounds between the internal conquerors and conquered that wrestle in mixed blood. She is a symbol that tolerates and embraces paradox and complication. She inspires women to treat each other with respect, as sisters.

In other places, further north, the image of the goddesses who preceded the Christian Mary had long been erased by Protestant invaders whose male god saved even less space for the feminine. These places in North America were not conquered by the Catholic Spaniards, and their female deities found no safe shelter in the masculine trinity—Father, Son and Holy Ghost—of the Protestant church. Without this kind of warm embrace offered by a loving divine feminine, families are divided by canyons as deep as the ones out West.

⁓

I visit my older sister in San Diego about once a year. I know I should make more of an effort, but sometimes it is easier to stay apart. Samantha and I have an unmistakable bond that is seldom acknowledged, like the reflection of the sun's light in the moon. We affect one another, but we hardly know one another—we are light years apart.

Samantha has always been more physically embodied than I am. She is athletic and coordinated, she danced on the varsity dance team in school and picked up most physical activities quickly. She is shorter than me, closer to the ground. Her body seems much more certain it wants to be a part of the earth, whereas mine still considers floating away on the breeze.

She knows what she wants and how to get it. Samantha makes definitive pronouncements whether she knows the answer or not, and she sticks to her convictions. She is a forceful river, pushing past obstacles and bounding over stones while I, the little sister, apologetically meander behind her rages. Once we were approached by a canvasser for gay rights outside of a museum, and she told him off with a righteous spew of Bible verses. I stood still with my mouth open, hardly believing what I was hearing. I had no idea she had become so angry. I disagreed strongly with her and my insides were boiling, but I said nothing.

My sister had her first baby last year, a daughter, and I attended as her informal, untrained doula. I wanted to feel close and celebrate this new little girl in our family, but I felt surprisingly overwhelmed by all the little differences between us. I wanted to feel more generous, kind, or warm, but I mostly felt glad my childbearing years (I thought) were far away. It felt as if I needed to put up a wall between us; *now she is a mother, and I am decidedly not a mother.* I chose to write our parts as sisters who live on separate sides of an impenetrable border.

She inhabits one side of the river, and I take the territory on the other. I don't really know the details that bring her pain or joy. And she does not know what makes me happy or contorted. We avoid the discomfort of deep communication, and we imagine ourselves as separate countries. It is as if we are on a see-saw and need to balance one another out by occupying opposite ends on the board. But it wasn't always like this.

Adrienne Rich says it so well, *how we dwelt in two worlds, the daughters and the mothers in the kingdom of the sons.* When we were young, my father and younger brother were in even more distant worlds than we were, and that greater distance from them created a relative closeness between Samantha and me. This closeness faded as we got older and felt the need to define ourselves. We chose to determine ourselves in opposition to one another. If she was the outgoing one, I became shyer. When she danced, I studied harder. If her hair was short, I kept mine long. If she stays put, I travel. This energetic agreement is binding as a contract. We can feel the invisible force between us even over great distances, across continents and oceans—wherever we are in the world we automatically go to the opposite ends to balance the other.

At a fairly young age, I discovered a tactic to assert power over my sister: I could control my emotions when she could not. I used to make her turn red with anger by staying calm when she tried to fight with me. I would simply back into myself and widen out as she came further and further out of her skin and began to spill out in all directions. I create a space, and she rushes out of her center to fill it. When I look back now, it seems like a cruel way of feeling my way into my power, but it is a useful tool I understand better later in life.

Samantha and I are two divergent tributaries of our mother. We share a common source, but branched off long ago. She flowed south to the conservative lands of San Diego, married a military man and settled in as a home maker and Sunday school teacher. I flowed more slowly, wound around curves and explored a variety of landscapes and have come to rest in Northern California, at the other end of the state and the political spectrum. I've stayed in school and teach yoga and offer massage to pay my way through my studies.

Samantha embodies the side of our mother which needs structure and security, and I am willing to compromise stability for pursuit. Our mother wrestles with these two sides of herself internally, and she ended up showing us neither fully. So we set out to find our own ways.

~

My mom, sister and I used to watch *Gone with the Wind* after Thanksgiving dinner as we put up the Christmas tree. It is my mom's favorite movie. She likes the dysfunctional romance between Scarlett O'Hara and Rhett Butler: the traces of Irish cultural identity, and the feeling that some romantic era from our past has been swept away. My sister identifies with the feisty Scarlett, flirtatious and manipulative. I prefer the more submissive Melanie, the martyr. If nothing is my sister's fault, somehow everything is my fault. I am *La Chingada*. I feel a constant mountain of shame and guilt for actions I cannot recall. I often woke in the morning and scanned over the previous day to see if there was some wrong I had committed for which I needed to amend. I know my mother carries the weight of this guilt as well. She told me once that she stayed with my father even through the worst of the abuses because she believed she deserved to be punished. She believed her flesh made her sinful, *La Chingada,* but she worked hard to be pure like the Virgin.

In the world of my younger self, the women I see in life and in stories are the only options to emulate. Dualism tells us it is one or the other, and once we've chosen our archetype, our definable personality, we are not supposed to change course. This neat little box of shoulds seems innocent enough, but it causes problems on a collective level.

Gone with the Wind is one example of many stories that reinforces feelings of internalized misogyny and repressed racism. At the time, I didn't stop to consider the even less appealing options represented in the movie by black women. There is Mammy or the annoying, idiotic little girl Percy. The entire movie glorifies a time in the pre-Civil War South, longing for an era when the accepted order openly embraced systematic violence based on the color of people's skin. It is the essence of divisive, competitive polarity: Mary or Magdalene, Virgin or *Chingada,* Scarlett or Melanie. There is no space for complex, paradoxical truth in this film. But in real life, we are all a continuum of opposing forces. I think the world would be a less violent place if they taught a version of understanding of this spectrum between opposites in church.

San Diego. May 2013.

Samantha prepares an elaborate feast. Steak, lobster and scallops from Costco. Samantha insists I join them tomorrow morning for the church service. I delicately say I prefer not to go, but she says it will mean so much to her if I come along, so I decide I will sit through it with an open mind.

The sermon that Sunday was the worst possible choice for

a visitor like me to witness. It was a painful interpretation of the later books in the New Testament, including some of the Armageddon imagery from Revelations. Pastor Todd, a young James Van Der Beek look-alike with gelled hair, was excited to share with us about the final judgment, and the wrath of God that would inevitably fall on non-believers. He used evocative music and newsreel images of catastrophes on a projector to support his message. Revelation 20:15: *And whosoever was not found written in the Book of Life was cast into the lake of fire.* It was just that simple: if you disagree with this one way, you will suffer a terrible, eternal death. I cried steadily from anger through most of it.

I was shocked. I don't understand the need to condemn and convert. I had left the church for lack of resonance, but still made apologies for Jesus and tried to point out positive aspects of the message before I heard this sermon. It was more divisive, arrogant, and violent than I remember any of the sermons from childhood being. The central theme strongly perpetuated both the cycle of violence and the cycle of self-loathing that is so hard to uproot in a soul. There is a clear way to fail in this world view, and the motivation is avoidance of punishment. John 3:36: *He that believeth on the Son hath everlasting life: and he that believeth not the Son shall not see life; but the wrath of God abideth on him.*

I kept thinking about the way these beliefs were employed to kill indigenous people and poison their living systems of relationships and spirituality. The creator role was taken from women and handed to men, the redeemer also turned to be exclusively male. It was duality at its worst. Conformity, violence and entitlement were established as the accepted means for survival.

As a result, indigenous traditions are fragmented or lost in the time when we need them most. They've been smashed and scattered, fed to the wind, by a paradigm that insists on power and control. A wellspring of hurt rose as my life's aim became clear, and I desperately wanted to fight. The blood of my own, our own, ancestors raged in my veins. *How could my own sister not feel this is wrong?* I cried and breathed and tried to make myself as invisible as possible so that the words would simply pass through me. The entire wave of injustice and misuse of power surged through me until it felt like too much, and then I found a surprisingly calm spaciousness. What if I were curious instead of angry?

I looked at the young, tan Pastor Todd. How is this man feeling as he stands and preaches at the front of the room? He looks concerned with his appearance: he is physically stiff and tight. I am not sure he is breathing into his low belly, in fact he's barely breathing into his lungs. How were the men writing, so many years ago, feeling when they secretly, in fear of persecution, put down these books? Hurt, afraid, powerless. They felt the world was out of balance, and they were crying for justice and fairness. They had lost traditions and stories just like so many others, and they had nowhere to turn for guidance.

They want the same things I want, we've come to different conclusions, but they are looking for peace and connection. My sister too. This is what her culture offers her, and it fits for her. The fires inside me soften. I hold my tongue about the details of my rage after the service, but I told her I will never go back.

I prefer our dad's ideal of attending church in nature. He had been influenced by the Navajo's spiritual system of earth-based spirituality and always reminded us to consider the Native people of the lands we were on. He often went back to New Mexico to visit our friends on the Navajo Reservation, and we were always invited. My sister declined every time, but I always went eagerly.

The last time we visited was just before I moved to California. My dad and I flew out to Albuquerque and rented a truck to pass Tohatchi and enter into the forgotten lands of the Native Americans. Most of the inhabitants live in trailers or mobile homes without heat and running water, but everyone I met called me sister or daughter. The roofs are covered with old tires to keep the heat in, but there's always enough food for guests.

The temperature was hovering below zero degrees when we visited. My dad and I slept in the living room and took turns tending the fish-tank sized wood-burning stove every hour or two all night to keep the trailer warm. We slept in sleeping bags on the floor and shared our boiled eggs with the stray dogs in the morning. We chopped firewood from up on the mountain for most of the afternoon. At night we enjoyed filling dinners: deliciously greasy fry bread and fresh lamb and corn stew, while our host Tommy told stories about the turkey who saved all the animals from the flood or the coyote who got stuck in the stars. I decided to share a story of my own that had touched me deeply and cooked internally long enough for it to change me. And in turn I changed the story.

The Birth of Reina is inspired in part by my reading of Martín Prechtel's *The Disobedience of the Daughter of the Sun*. I imagine a wide re-interpretation that shifts the main female character from a passive to active agent in her destiny, liberates the mother from her role as captor, and encourages death to be seen as part of an endless cycle of rebirth.

The Story of the Birth of Reina

This story takes place a long, long time ago, when the Sun and the Moon first met. Theirs was a love unlike any other, it lit up the sky and brought songs to the birds, and it inspired love on the entire planet. The daughter of the Mountain and the Ocean was born as this divine love began to blossom. She was a being unique in the universe. The daughter of the Mountain and Ocean was the most beautiful girl who ever existed, having come from the strong, rich Mountain and deep, shining Ocean themselves. Her fresh waters bubbled up gently from a place high in the mountain, and she animated the face of the earth with green and gold. Her name was Reina and she was divine royalty, and as her parents were quick to tell her, no common man would ever be worthy of her. Any suitor would need to match her divine heritage, elegance, beauty and talent, but where on earth was such a man to be found? And so Reina was lonely, but she was happy.

Reina grew up in the land of her father and felt connected to her mother but had never seen her. She wondered what her mother was like and sometimes felt a sudden urge to seek her out. But the forest was her home for now, and she trusted she would find her mother when the time came. As she wondered, she often wandered through the forest on the mountainside and talked with animals and trees. On her daily meandering, she made friends with every living thing, and they each in turn adored her for the ease and peace she brought their spirits. As she walked, violets blossomed under her feet and peach trees released juicy, ripe fruit into her palms. She took care of creation, and creation took care of her.

One day, as she wanders through the forest she happens to meet a tiny man who lives in a mushroom. They recognize one another as two threads of one fabric and begin to meet regularly on her walks. The two create a world unto themselves, but Reina's heart is sad because she knows her parents would never allow her to marry this tiny, common little man.

As she falls more and more in love with her mushroom boy,

she feels a tension between keeping the will of her parents and following the dream in her heart. Holding this internal conflict and keeping her love hidden makes her ill. Her father, already suspicious, insists she stay at home through the season. Reina misses her love with all her heart, and she puts the fullness of her emotions into her weaving. She leaves nothing out, bringing together wild oranges and dark greens, lonesome blues and luscious purples in her great story tapestry. She recalls the animals and the forest where she used to walk, and she puts all of this joy and beauty into her work. After some time alone with her weaving, she hears the unmistakable voice of her love. Her heart jumps with delight, and she sees her mushroom love peeking in through a crack in the window.

The lovers continue to meet in secret until Reina's heart is ready to burst open. She can hold the secret no longer. And so the two finally decide to run away to the great unknown land of her mother Ocean where she hopes her mother will be empathetic. Reina uses the tapestry she had been weaving as protection over the two of them. She wove beauty, innocence and love into the threads of her work, and because of this had created an entire universe with her weaving. The result was a magnificent coat of fullness that blended into the very fabric of the world. In effect, it was a coat of invisibility, and so that night the two lovers covered themselves in this magical coat and ran away toward the Ocean.

During their flight, they are hidden from the Mountain by the cloak, but Reina's father is furious and his emotions cause a storm of relatives to rise from all directions. The two continue their flight to the sea as the wind howls, rain falls, trees crash and thunder booms nearby. The two lovers, against all odds make it to the beach, and their feet step into the Ocean on the sandy shore, but suddenly Reina is gone. Reina the river has been scattered in all directions and no longer exists. The mushroom love is confused and lost, unsure of what happened or who betrayed them. He mourns her in every cell of his being.

The forest withers, the flowers fade, and the animals turn to skin and bone. The little mushroom is immobilized with grief and almost dies. All of creation cries over her death, the world dries up, and life refuses to go on for hundreds of years in this unimaginable drought. But time is their only friend, and finally, after lifetimes of grieving, her sweet mushroom love finds a brief moment of shining hope that is born from a drop of water at the bottom of his heart and begins to sing Reina back to her home inside the mountain with the help of the rest of the wild creatures.

His heart is so sincere, he eventually wins even the assistance of her parents, the Mountain and the Ocean. The drops of water come from tears, clouds, dew, stardust and every memory of love and beauty from every corner of the universe to gather inside the mountain and become Reina. It takes cooperation, patience, devotion and time, but she is brought to life. Reina eventually re-emerges in a burst of fresh life from her source in the mountain, and the world is able to continue on with beauty, magic, joy and love once again.

On one level, this story is the story of a family that gets caught up in shoulds and restrictions and forgets the power of beauty and love. It is a story about losing what is most precious when we hold it too tightly—flowing water cannot be contained or ruled by the laws that govern the sun or the moon in the sky, and she is not a mountain; she is not meant to stay still. She follows her own laws. Families—whether the core family or our larger human family—often forget to celebrate the differences that make life possible, and in this way we scatter ourselves and doom ourselves to feeling perpetually lost.

Reina—like Oshun, Ariel, Tara, and Aphrodite—is a maiden and a goddess of love and beauty. This is profound in that it shows the importance and value of the young feminine energy. She is often overlooked, but her innocence and sensitivity are needed to bring the world back into balance. Finding the maiden in our psyche brings us optimism and reconnects us with play, wonder and joy. Her weaving is the magic of life itself, the reminder that we are not separate but deeply connected as the very fabric of what makes life continue.

Back in Tohatchi, I watch the sun rise over a long horizon and inhale fully: *I once was lost, but now I am found.* There is a different promise that comes from a sun that rises slowly over the mountains. It seems to promise enough of everything in that day: enough time, space, food—all is taken care of. The mountain trusts the sun's warmth, and so do I. The clouds stretch wide like pulled-out cotton balls, and the water tastes crisp with the piñon nuts we gather.

My dad and I drive down to the market for groceries, and on the way we see a herd of buffalo fenced into an otherwise wide open prairie. We pull over to take in the animals and see if they will come closer. I snap a picture of my dad walking along the road, his hands in his pockets, his head down. *Where is he going?*

He was told he could be invited into the tribe if he completed initiation rites, and his first task was to bring the tail feathers of a water bird. He used to joke about trying to catch one, but I don't think he ever really tried.

I used to think maybe I would complete this task for him, I would cross over the line and immerse myself fully into the culture and stories that he loved, for him. I think that drive, that longing for a way of living that was lost brought me toward this path of searching, but in the end it couldn't be for him. He has to walk on his own road. And my path is a watery one with many eddies and tributaries I'm meant to weave together in a way I don't yet understand. Maybe I'm not meant to ever understand, but I keep drawing the bits of yarn together because I must. My fingers know the pattern: red over white and black underneath—maiden, mother and crone do not move as a linear pattern but as spirals where time has less influence. Two far away points on a line might end up next to one another if that same line is coiled. My DNA is coiled, and the grandparents in my body do not all get along.

I see that my blood contains pattern after pattern of oppressors and victims, and so I know these two fated enemies dance within me. It is an ancient, torturous dance that has drawn on for far too long. And I am tired of those warring memories, frozen imprints in my bloodstream. Their restrictions and pride make it impossible for me to connect: I am a spiral being told to move straight, a river told to move as the sun, a young girl in love told to stand still and wise up. I feel isolated as Reina before she decided to go to the sea: I am immobilized by my own indecision. I've trapped myself in a labyrinth of memories from lived and unlived pasts. How can I ever find the root of such a large tangled mess?

The most intense personal trauma I've endured was watching my parents fight. It started a cycle of internalized violence against myself. Subconsciously, I identified with my father: I wanted to be the one who got to come and go as he pleased. I did not want to be the trapped one, the martyr like Melanie, the Virgin or *La Chingada*. My inner masculine abuses my inner feminine, demeans her, and stifles her. It seems at first I wanted to be him, and then I wanted to fix him, until finally I just learned to accept him and do my own work.

But the body has a long memory when it comes to family patterns, and even today I am incredibly hard on myself—I tear myself up over small mistakes, I call myself the worst kinds of names, and sometimes I even wish one side of myself would finally end the other. As I became more self-aware, I identified more strongly with the victim I had internalized. It felt safer to reject the piles of guilt associated with the oppressors.

Today I know I have to live with both the privilege my skin affords me as well as the deep feelings of loss and powerlessness that come from being on the receiving end of violence. The inner turmoil is what I imagine a small plant must feel like when it is being choked by weeds. The sun is blocked, and the roots are dry, and death comes slowly. The only thing I can do is keep looking for the root of this wound to remove it completely from my family's garden.

I feel the original wound, the deep, powerfully strong root of the lie, that starts this traumatic cycle of violence spinning, is the feeling of intense isolation that comes from not recognizing oneself in others. A ripping away from the connectedness of the cosmos is required to live as an incarnated being, and this separation, though necessary, is incredibly painful. As pure light, we feel constant connection, but when we mask ourselves into flesh we have to forget some of that oneness. We forget and remember our inherent connection again and again. Like a cosmic game of peek-a-boo, we are fooled by the dualistic appearance of a veiled reality. We are lost and then found, over and over, except that when we are lost it seems like we will be lost forever.

My understanding of hope, my way of practicing being found, is a return to empathy in action. My dad and I took turns maintaining the fire in the minus zero weather because each of us valued the life of the others in the house. Too often in modern culture we are removed from the effects of our actions. The priest ranting about original sin in San Diego may not realize how his narrow, judgmental dogma shrinks the psyche of our planet. He does not see how missionaries in New Mexico robbed the Navajo of their language and their way of life and brought them to a poverty that forces them into mobile homes without heat.

My sister and I are little better, we pretend we are separate when really we are two streams of the same river. We see ourselves as individual agents in the world, selfishly thinking of our own gain all the time, refusing to kindle the inner fires of the hearth to connect in compassion. We as a culture of relatives suffer because we isolate ourselves. We do this in our families first and then in the world, and we may be killing our chances for survival on this planet because of this profound disconnect between ourselves. We need to braid ourselves back together, a new weaving that invites our differences to remain distinct even while we enter into relationship with one another. Reina, the sweet water, is a master weaver because she uses all the threads of life and creation. Her cloak is magical because it contains every color and brings them together in a constructive relationship. The maiden rejects nothing in her artwork. Braids, tapestries, and currents in the river show us the way again and again—it cannot be one clear way or another, it has got to be both ways and together.

PART THREE

FULL MOON GIVES BIRTH

MISSION CREEK

Disappears Deep Underground

There is no shortage of water in the desert but exactly the right amount, a perfect ratio of water to rock. Of water to sand, ensuring that wide, free, open, generous spacing among plants and animals, homes and towns and cities, which makes the arid West so different from any other part of the nation. There is no lack of water here, unless you try to establish a city where no city should be.

Edward Abbey

Berkeley. October 2014.

I T'S TOO HOT, my throat is parched. I kick the covers away and reach for the cup of water on my nightstand. Empty. I pull myself up and drag my feet across the floor to the kitchen. I press a mug to the water filter's lever on the counter and glance at the clock on the stove. It's 3am. Why am I awake again? I drink the full cup, and head to the bathroom to empty my bladder.

I've got a water balloon in my low belly, and it requires a lot of extra fluid to maintain. I'm supporting two circulatory systems and two heartbeats, so I am almost always hot—which dries out my internal ecosystem like the sun on sand. The drought isn't helping. Every morning I see the fog and clouds, and I wish it would rain. Every night it still refuses.

Sometimes it is easier to understand an element with a little distance from it. I never realized how much I took water for granted until I moved to California. Most people think of sunny California as a paradise of land and sea, but we've experienced record droughts the last few years: 2013 was the worst in fifteen years and 2014 was the worst in more than a hundred. It's so bad this year I stopped watering the plants outside. I felt selfish as I turned on the hose and water obediently leaped from the nozzle, wetting my garden shoes. I hurried to get the water onto the sandy soil, but later noticed the slightly darker concrete and thought better of splurging on the decorative plants in front of a rented yard.

I spent the spring watching the yellow wildflowers bloom, the lavender blossom, and the rosemary sprout. Then I spent the summer watching the flowers shrivel and crack, the herbs dry out, and the lavender turn to twigs. It was especially depressing to watch the purple Japanese maple I'd carried from three prior apartments start to shrivel. I had just decided to plant the tree I had kept potted until we had the space, and despite numerous attempts from the puppy to dig her back up, she had sprouted the most delicate green and purple leaves. Now half of those leaves are curling in toward themselves, and they are a thin kind of brown, lighter than a paper bag. John Steinbeck writes that people from the East Coast are deeply distressed by the months of brown (sometimes referred to romantically as golden) hills in California. It's true, I still haven't gotten over it.

Joan Didion writes about the unnatural eerie-ness in the California summer air in her essay "Some Dreamers of the Golden Dream": *This is not the coastal California of subtropical twilights and the soft westerlies off the Pacific but a harsher California, haunted by the Mojave just beyond the mountains, devastated by the hot dry Santa Ana wind that comes down through the passes at 100 miles an hour and whines through the eucalyptus windbreaks and works on the nerves. October is a bad month for the wind, the month when breathing is difficult and the hills blaze up spontaneously. There has been no rain since April. Every voice seems a scream. It is the season of suicide and divorce and prickly dread, wherever the wind blows.*

Even though the Bay Area is surrounded by water, most of its inhabitants' drinking water comes from the Tuolumne River, which was dammed in 1923, 167 miles northeast. The dam flooded what is now known as the Hetch Hetchy Reservoir, a delicate ecosystem that was once home to the Miwok, Ohlone, Tamyen, and Chochenyo people of Northern California before the gold rush, before California was a dream land to which East Coasters hoped to escape and reinvent themselves.

Natural California appears to be scrub land and desert that has been turned to farmland by expensive irrigation projects that re-route rivers from as far as the Rocky Mountain range. The Sierra Nevada mountain range supplies a large portion of water to Northern California after it melts, but at the start of 2014, the snowpack was thirty percent lower than average. The major water reserve sites at Folsom Lake, Shasta Lake, Lake Oroville and the San Luis Reservoir are all at no more than thirty percent of capacity. All this dryness makes way for fires. In 2013 Yosemite National Park experienced the largest wildfire on record. The rim fire burned from August to October and destroyed more than 400 square miles of land. Brown, cracked and charred earth replaces green, golden and blue in our modern surroundings. And that's when we can see the ground at all. More than likely the horizon is a metallic skyline and the dirt is covered in gray concrete.

The gold rush of 1849 was followed by the rush to Silicon Valley just before the turn of the twenty-first century. The prospectors of the gold rush crossed their fingers as they sifted sand and rock in the hopes of spotting a golden nugget. Later, they got greedier and decided to blow up mountains to look for that priceless gold-colored rock. The prospectors today chase fame and fortune in a different way. They place bets on the power of their intellects, hoping to make a more elaborate technological invention than their competitors. They flood the peninsula of San Francisco with ideas, fast cash, and large commuter buses.

Though the gold mining frenzy has passed, the overuse and pollution of water resources is not a thing of the past. A recent study by the Campaign for Responsible Technology found that processing a single 6-inch silicon chip—which is commonly used to power computers, cellphones, and many other devices—uses 2,275 gallons of deionized water. This translates to an average of about 236,600,000 gallons annually from one production plant. That's enough water to fill 360 Olympic-sized swimming pools. This is the cost for the convenience that our modern gadgets charge.

One of my high school friends was present in the first wave of young engineers who flocked to Silicon Valley, and he was lucky enough to win big by building Facebook from the start. It seemed like a wisp of an idea, to move out to California to start a social website. What did that even mean in 2004? But he dropped out of college after freshman year and followed the call of California's golden dream to the Pacific Ocean.

I benefit from technology's excessive valuation as well: I am part of a tech company's wellness program. The company where I offer stress-relief yoga and massage has a full kitchen and a staff of chefs in addition to the health and wellness program myself and three other instructors offer. The suave building is located in the heart of The Mission, which used to be the home of immigrants, artists, and dreamers. *The New Yorker* reports that between the years 1990 to 2011 1,400 Latino families were displaced, and the black community of the Mission District was cut in half. The winds of change are scattering dust in all directions.

It is worth considering the structure and personality of silicon and other metalloids because modern city dwellers may have more silicon per square mile than greenery. Silicon, which is used to make electronic circuits, itself is a chemical element, a non-metal that is semi-conductive. It is found naturally as an amorphous powder and in a dark gray crystalline form.

Electronics work best in a cool, dry environment and they require precision and control to function. Creatures adapt to fit their environments. Lizards are dry and scaly like the ground where they live. Mushrooms are soft and moist because they are part of a damp environment. Butterflies are light and spend their time in the air. Humans who live in a wild jungle are lush and alive internally. Humans in cities often complain of being wired, anxious and "always on". The water within us works over time to conduct the electricity, Wi-Fi and excess sound waves all around us.

As my mother would say, *you are the company you keep.* When we work in front of computers all day, we become more like the machines. And we are not meant to be machines. We are part of nature. We need nature, and water in particular. But, as anyone who has ever seen the warning label on a hair dryer knows, electronics and water do not mix.

The elements in water are highly conductive, which means they facilitate fluidity: energy moves easily across water. When drops of water come in contact with the intricate wires and circuits of most electronics, the energy suddenly has a greater number of options for where to move. If the power supply remains constant, the device will have a greater capacity to use energy and will become so full of energy, so charged, that it may overload the small circuit's capacity and cause heat, fire, or even an explosion. The more fluid we are, the more water we take in and surround ourselves with, the greater number of options we make available for ourselves. We too have a higher potential to channel energy when we are well hydrated. And the reverse is true. Physiologically speaking, we have fewer options and less energy when we are dehydrated.

I wonder if there is some lesson here, some hidden medicine in the dry soil and parched psyches of modern California. I am inspired by the Jericho rose, which has adapted to extreme desert environments like the Sahara in Africa. It appears dead and travels with the wind for decades. It may remain dormant for up to a century, but as soon as the water returns it finds its way into the smallest puddles and sprouts to reproduce. The resurrection plant blooms when the conditions are right. I wonder what kind of seeds of hope, what stores of internal water we hold in the vases of our internal structures. How do we need to adapt to create a greater potential for miracles? And what elements cause us to blossom, to wake up?

As babies, our needs are met by caretakers. As we drink from our mother's breast, or a bottle, we have no thought for where it comes from or if it will ever run out. It won't. We learn to take without needing to replenish the source from which we drink, which is fine when we are babies.

But it seems the majority of Westerners do not progress past what child development scientists call "the egocentric stage" onto the stage of understanding causality. We have a limited amount of fresh water on this planet, and it was meant to be reused for all generations of humans, plants and animals to come for eras. The land is literally burning up, like a child with a fever that doesn't break, and there appears to be no way to escape the sun's glare.

Dagara elder Malidoma Somé writes that the modern world is out of alignment with the elements: there is too much uncontrolled fire and not enough free flowing water. Civilization seems to encourage a disease where the mind constantly needs to move faster and pollute more. The germ is driven by the internal emptiness caused by a feeling of profound isolation. We are prone to rampant consumerism, trying to fill the emptiness with material goods. Reconnection with the wisdom of the past helps bring the energy of the fire into balance, like a campfire that soothes, warms and nourishes us. Fire in balance has the potential to bring back a feeling of the internal hearth, a place of inherent connection.

The dry, fiery air of California makes me tense and restless. I look for challenging experiences, hoping to find some peace, and one of those experiences led me to the desert. I felt the presence of my internal connection to water stronger than ever when I spent time fasting in Southern California, in the Mojave Desert in 2011. This land was named by its native inhabitants of the same name, Mojave. Its name means "beside the water," but that water is only a memory. This is when I begin to write my own myth as the woman who cries for water in the desert.

Mojave. May 2011.

On the third morning of my fast, the sun rises and struggles to melt the desert ice. I swallow my lace dreams with a spoonful of honey and pack up my camp.

Water is my saving grace. I could say she is a woman, thin bow slung over her shoulder, or a buffalo prayer mumbled by an overflowing heart struck by the light of a rising moon so bright she tears a hole in the sky. But on the hard, dusty earth that morning Grace simply promised balance. I once again understand the delightful paradox of birth.

On the fifth night it rains. It sounds at first like Wind, until it curves and hits the sand, drumming with tiny hands. Water's weight compresses my tarp to an inch above my body.

I am glad my little triangle burrito structure has some sense, but part of me wants to be rained on. Disappointment wakes me, sunny and dry, I peek around the edge of the plastic green onto the blanket of the monochromatic dead tan palette of the Mojave. Here I am, a softly shaded mushroom surrounded by armored creatures: Lizard, Snake, Turtle.

I use my scarce bit of drinking water for a bath. I sit on the sunny rocks, naked and quaking in the persistent Wind and pour handfuls of water from carefully cupped palms over my scaly skin, rubbing at the dryness to help it peel off. Like a snake, I think to myself. And then She is here.

Snake. Right here, sunning like Egyptian royalty on the big stone above me. Red and tan and somehow golden, sticking Her forked tongue in and out to taste my thoughts. I feel the mass of Her kin gathering beneath me, writhing like the rainbow roots of a psychedelic tree.

This is it. I prostrate myself on the earth. I lie prone on the ground for lifetimes. Quiet. I don't get up until I can listen with the stomach ears of Snake. Then I listen to the future.

The year ahead of me shares the black of fertile soil and the inside of a cave, two dark eyes peering back into mine. She's been corralled in the dusty states for hundreds of years, kept as a prize like a stag on the wall, drowned by the twins, Arrogance and Ignorance. And this occupation is not over.

I hear Grandmothers' skulls beneath church pews next door,

and her bones under Emery malls, and Geary lots. She ticks, rolls and tolerates under layers, layers, layers of cement and asphalt and tar and brick and stone and rot. We live on her bones, dance on her bones, die, are born and die again on the necklace of her spine.

I look through the mirror of myself: alternating patches of sun and shade light the winding forest path. A waking huntress stretches before me. Glittering sidewalk specks argue over my direction, but these feet hear only Her straight arrow voice beneath.

Fierce Wolf, Dark Eyed Deer, Brave Poet, Playful Nymph, Wise Witch, Elusive Huntress—a maiden steady as the crone. I speak from the ground, voice moves through me as water through thirsty roots—shoots from me, branches reach and bloom.

Gaze steady, our eyes adjust to the dark.

⁓

What do I do with all this? After I've recounted the experience of the desert, I feel emptied out and tired. I enter into a new kind of trance that is foggy and sad. What have I lost? I've left some essential part of myself in the desert, but the sands cover it before I can take a real look. The small troughs of hills and the repetition of two kinds of shrubs and low bushes create a surreal effect that is disorienting. Wherever I am is simply here. I can walk west to the mountains or south to the road. Water is east, and our camp was north. I watched the sun and the moon for clues to my whereabouts, and these celestial bodies in turn gave me a new internal compass, a wider perspective. I felt profound sadness at leaving these anchors behind, like a tree must feel after being torn from the roots. I've lost my place, my people—I could blow away anywhere, like a tumbleweed.

I get into the gray Volkswagen to drive back to the city. I take a seat behind the front passenger. The moment I slam the door shut I am contained. Tears waited in the ducts for this instant, and now that the door is shut, my fate is sealed. They flow steadily and I don't try to stop them: they've waited too long. I cry most of the way back, and the rest of the car is quiet. It's not supposed to feel like this, something is wrong, broken, lost.

Years later I found Martín Prechtel and made a connection with his words on the watery soul. *To the Tzutujil there is only one water which rushes, puddles or is captured in a multitude of diverse forms like plant leaves, hot springs, rivers, lakes, ponds, ice, tears and streams, and like the amniotic flood at our births, all this water is trying to get back home to the original mother of life, the Great-Grandmother Ocean, the great dream pool . . .*

Our inner landscapes mirror the outer landscapes in which we live. Our bodies are the same as plants. We are like the trees, grounded in the earth and extending toward the sky. Water moves through us. Water is willing to remain trapped within us and wait in the dryness of the wood to bring us back to animation. The devotion, the urgency of stories helps us to feel our original place between sky and land. The stories supply a wellspring, a source of spiritual richness that awakens the memory of cultures from the past in our blood. This memory infuses us with connection and reaches out to the branches of diverse peoples across the world. But what if the water dries up? And what if the stories of where we came from are lost?

The tears that came after I got into the car to leave the desert were because I was mourning the loss of a village. A container for the stories. Embedded in the old stories is not just the memory of what was, but the patterns of what will be. Just like the grooves in our brains, the pathways of the river bed, and the vibrations in the air. I knew this time was past ripe. Our tribe in the Mojave was impermanent, full of rootless trees who returned to their far-reaching corners. The vase broke when I closed that car door, and the water it was holding spilled and scattered without a container. It hurts to be discarded.

I looked at the moon differently after that time in the desert. Now she has become an oasis in the sky. A refuge for the watery parts of my soul to be quenched when the thin dryness of San Francisco's concrete and metal threatens to shrivel me like a California raisin. My eyes widened and softened, and though they still forget how today, I can always remind them with a poem, a story, or a walk with the trees.

When the last of my temporary tribe leaves me at my door in The Mission, I notice the newly-empty rooms at the base of my apartment. The Million Fishes Art Collective sign still hangs above the door, but it's easy to see the evidence of construction through the wrap-around windows. Ladders over the sink, half torn-off wallpaper. My landlord has just evicted this artist collective in favor of higher bidders. Scenes like this are common all over the city since the tech boom, but especially in The Mission.

My neighborhood sits in a valley between Twin Peaks and Potrero Hill, so even when the rest of the city is cold and damp, the sun shines on Dolores Park. The Mission has historically been a Hispanic spot, but over the last fifteen to twenty years the original residents have been pushed further and further toward the fringes as a new wave of hipsters and engineers take over. The little river that once ran through The Mission was the first eviction. Mission Creek was once centered around what is now the Mission Dolores, but it was drained and filled in as early as 1874.

The morning after my return, I convince myself to get out of bed with the thought of breakfast. I make oatmeal and smile as the opera singer across the way practices her songs. She makes my morning routine epic: oatmeal feels like a special event with her in the background. As I stir the pot, I notice the lines in my hands like the desert ground: deep, cracked and strained. I add more coconut oil to the pot and rub the remainder over my hands. I take a quick shower with the hourglass timer: five minutes flat, and drop off a load of laundry at *La Lavanderia* on the corner. The older man who attends the space nods at me, as always. He speaks no English, and I speak no Spanish so that's about the extent of our relationship: nodding approval and gesturing thanks. I hear the Spanish language soap opera on the TV. *Estoy embarazada!* yells a big-haired woman at a frightened man. He nervously drinks a glass of water, eyes shifting side to side. For a moment, I almost feel like I'm in a different country.

Then I'm out the door, and a smiling white girl hands me a menu for the new restaurant opening on the corner. It's called The Local, and it has a rustic chic decor with refurbished barn doors and a brunch menu of oysters and farm fresh eggs with mimosa on Sundays. Too pricey for me—$12 for cold melon soup and $8 for seasonal pickles—but I never liked oysters or cheese plates anyway.

I'm following the migration of many former Mission residents to the East Bay. This time next month I'll be an Oakland resident. The city is too expensive, and too crowded. I start to treasure my daily walks as only a visitor, or someone who knows she's leaving, might.

One of my favorite murals is in danger of being painted over. It's just past Florida Street, painted on the side of yet another laundromat, where I've just noticed the red letters on the "for lease" sign in the window. Coin-operated laundromats can't make the rent these days, so their lease expires and the buildings are converted to apartments. It's a huge mural—covering the entire side of the building facing west. The water caught my eye first, then the line of dark-haired women washing clothes in the river. Their backs are turned away from the viewer on the street. I always loved that about the painting—the subjects are seemingly unaware they are being observed. Their long, straight, shining hair offers no clue as to their expression. The women could be anyone, and so they are everyone. I imagine they sing together as they wash the clothes, and for a moment I feel the lineage of washing as something sacred, rather than a chore. It was an act that women performed together, where they shared stories and traded gossip. The ritual of carrying clothes to the river with sisters was a time for internal cleansing as well, rather than the burden that now isolates us from one another.

I snicker to myself, wondering if the new store front will paint a fiery mural with abstract, sharp geometric designs to replace the image of the women in the river. A sketch by my brother Jason comes to mind. He always works in black and white with sharp, abstract shapes. The lines are thick and heavy, and the overall feeling I get from contemplating them is one of discomfort and disorder searching for depth. There are descending stairways that float into nothing and foreign creatures that overlap the view of the center; like a marsh that desperately wants to climb out of itself and move as a stream, if only he could find the will and the guiding banks. But it seems he has invested his future in the world of cold metal, distinct edges and intellect rather than warm soil, curves and instinct. These lines do not contain and support like the banks of a river, but separate and isolate like spears and armor. How does the young masculine fit into this unnatural culture?

Humidity is a natural force that brings rain and moisture and moves through leaves and the ground in cycles. Except when the soil is covered with concrete and the trees are cut down, then humidity stagnates and stews because it cannot move. My younger brother is surrounded by concrete, walls and machines. My father was not a strong role model for him. Even though dad was no longer physically abusive to my mother by the time Jason was born, he was emotionally abusive well into our teenage years. Jason has no outlet. When he looks out into the world, he sees disconnection, when he turns on the TV he is bombarded by consumerism, and when he asks for guidance he is handed a cure-all pill of patriarchy and capitalism. He is a unique shape that does not fit into the grid, and so he rejects this paradigm entirely. Because of that rejection, he inhabits a liminal space, living constantly in-between as one who has the instinct to say "No, not this" and still has not found the courage to say "Yes, this".

I interact with him behind layers of mental fog that we cannot penetrate. He has taken on the role of the family compost: he absorbs and digests full time. And we allow this. We use his sensitivity to our benefit. We as a family and as a culture don't want to look at all we've enabled or the places we've failed him. The rest of the world overwhelms him, floods him with emotions and confuses his senses with *should, supposed to* and *must*. He replies *Okay, no*, or *I don't know* to just about every question I ask. Jason is at a loss for words to express his inner landscape. He refuses his options in silence and lives within four walls.

Society does not care about these young men, but chews them up and discards them, labeling them misfits, deadbeats or in some cases locking them up and medicating them. Jason spends his nights (he sleeps during the day) playing Japanese video-games on the Internet and lives in a virtual reality with a community of other lost boys across the ocean. My brother is not an isolated case, he is at the crest of a fast-forming wave of change. There is an entire generation of young males living as shut-ins in Japan, known as *hikikomori*.

The term *hikikomori* refers to a person sequestered in his room for six months or longer (some have been documented for as long as fifteen years) with no social life beyond their home. It is estimated that about eighty percent of the *hikikomori* are male, some as young as thirteen or fourteen years of age. Somewhere between one hundred thousand and one million Japanese live as shut-ins. This is momentous, and it may also be prescriptive. An entire generation of an entire country has decided not to engage in society. We have no idea of the ramifications that this massive movement into stillness and sequestration will have on the world in the years to come.

There are several theories in place that try to explain this modern phenomenon that range from sociological: blame the parents; to economical: blame the country; to psychological: blame the individual boys themselves. According to *The New York Times*, the Japanese themselves blame ". . . everything from smothering mothers, to absent, overworked fathers, from school bullying, to the lack-luster economy, from academic pressure, to video games."

I don't know what causes healthy young men to refuse to take a place in society at large, but I see something meaningful in their refusal. Joseph Campbell has said that if we as a culture do not find a way to add the fiery passion of the youths to the hearth of the community fire, the youth will burn our culture to the ground. I think his statement was true a few decades ago, and in the time since he noticed this urge toward violence, we as a modern, global society have continued to fail to bring the passion of youths to valuable use. Some, in turn, do burn down the cities in rage, riots, and violence. Others hold the other end of the spectrum and lose the fires within themselves. These boys are collapsed in futility, a kind of impotence and hopelessness that surrounds them just as clearly as if they were lab rats in a maze.

A single chip of silicon is a square structure that looks like a sharp maze. It cannot operate if even a tiny drop of liquid touches it. It follows rules that do not belong to water. Separation, control and manufacturing. My brother daydreams about transferring to the literal fog of the Bay Area. I've told him there was a time when he could have made it out here without a Bachelor's degree, just living on a prayer, but definitely not now. I can't even make it out here, and I'm more or less established with three advanced degrees, but I still need to move across the bridge to make rent. Silicon Valley is unforgiving, a harsh master that demands his devotees fit into an extremely precise mold.

California has chosen to create a segmented wasteland disguised as ingenuity that is entirely driven by the mind. Value is defined by reason and profits control the course of growth. The rest is rejected or objectified. Buildings grow taller, bridges grow wider, and rent soars past the clouds. Water is rejected or commodified and needs to be contained. Intuition is scorned. Women and minorities struggle at the edges. Evictions displace more and more homeless men into the parks and under overpasses. Even the sandy soil is thirsty for diversity, roots dry up and plants collapse. The Bay Area proudly advertises this mind trap as a spiritual paradise, on the cutting edge of cultural advancement. Some days the *smug* is so thick I can barely breathe.

Analysis—literally, "to separate into parts"—is rampant, and the cells and minutiae of trees are obsessed over while the forest is cut down and sold. The extreme state of disharmony that modern culture has created is like chopping up a snake into little pieces and selling off each broken fragment as an entire snake. No one seems to care that the snake is dead, but they are happy to have and hold their very own portion of it.

Too many young boys have been brought up in a desertified culture that rejects the fluid. The concrete of our culture in urban settings drinks the watery parts of their souls, refuses to let them sink into the ground, evaporate into the air, or run off down a hill, and so these boys have only a slight chance that they may discover a path that will lead them back to the forest, the ocean, the feminine, the wild possibility of standing confidently in the sunlight and drinking inspiration from the moon. The journey to inner freedom comes from a connection between their intellect and their instinct; their head and their guts. They are desperately in need of an image, a friend, a teacher or a book that shows them what a society that values the masculine and feminine alongside one another might look like. Some miraculous drops of raining grace must soften and disarm the tangled sparks and wires around their hearts and liberate their warmth, their beauty and natural penetrating fiery passion for life so that they can love again.

The only antidote for the isolated *hikikomori* and cultural desert of California is connection. Real life, flesh and blood, earth and heart connection.

Isis is the goddess who specializes in reconnecting what has been cut apart. Her story comes from ancient Egypt, another once lush land turned to near desert by overuse and loss of culture. The painful wound inflicted on the masculine, as well as the way to heal the damage, is articulated in her story.

The Story of Isis of the Nile, from Egypt

There once lived an exceptionally greedy prince named Set who desired to dethrone King Osiris. He devised a plan in secret, and presented himself as a friend to the court. Set had a beautiful chest brought forth to the palace and declared that it would belong to the person who fitted himself into it perfectly. Who could resist such a playful offer? Once King Osiris was inside, the rival prince immediately sealed the chest and had it dropped into the Nile. Set then promptly assumed the throne.

When Queen Isis hears this news, she sets to walking along the Nile, mourning and searching for the chest which contains her husband. She finds friends along the way whom she is able to bestow her wisdom on, and she is often at the edge of discouragement. Isis meets a magical old woman in the forest and is initiated by the crone into the mysteries of the goddess.

Eventually, after years of searching without reward, she hears news that chest has surfaced along the river's edge and had been held within the root systems of a tamarisk tree.

By the time Isis makes it there, she realizes the queen of that land, Ishtar, holds the trunk in store with her jewelry, and so Isis puts on a silk veil as a disguise and pretends to be a servant to gain the confidence of the court ladies. She teaches the ladies about perfumes and finery, and eventually acts as a nurse to Ishtar's infant son.

One night Isis attempts to perform a magic ritual to make the baby boy immortal by burning away his mortal parts, but Ishtar interrupts the ceremony and the spell is not completed. Angry at being rebuked by a mortal queen, Isis reveals herself as a goddess in all her glory and asks to have the chest brought to her immediately. Awed and apologetic, Ishtar grants her request, and Isis returns to Egypt to bring her husband back to the palace. Isis is considerably skilled in the magical arts, and she uses charms and potions to conceive a son, Horus, by her dead husband Osiris.

When the rival prince Set learns of Isis' doings, he is furious. He searches for the hiding place of the chest and cuts the body of the king into fourteen pieces to prevent Isis' spells bringing him fully back to life. Set throws the pieces of Osiris' body into the Nile to be lost and scattered. Isis is appalled and nearly gives up her husband for lost this time, but after passing through her own dark night she pulls herself back together for the sake of their son and returns to work. She again walks patiently along the banks of the Nile and collects the pieces of her beloved Osiris' body in order to reassemble them and bring the king back to life.

The story of Isis is a story of feminine devotion and strength. She, as a latent river goddess, has the power to reassemble what is broken and lost in the masculine of the world today. The rival prince can be seen as the modern world that cuts up and scatters the indigenous knowledge that gives us the right as humans to enjoy our lives with sovereignty (a metaphor for royalty). The repeated violence committed by the jealous, greedy aspect of the masculine against the divine masculine, the King, is repeatedly met with the patient healing of the feminine, Isis. In this way, she provides a model for behavior in healing the split between modern and ancient technologies. Isis spends time alone in the wild places, and brings the wisdom of the crone, the old woman witch, back to the court and society. She brings intuition back in the age of analysis. And intuition reconnects what logic has severed.

This story also reminds us that the feminine is strong enough to protect and conceal information when needed. Isis has learned magical arts from the old woman of the forest, but she conceals her identity to get closer to her goal. She only reveals herself when she is ready. Isis teaches the women self-care and beauty rituals: it is the work of the feminine in each of us, and women in particular, to re-enchant ourselves, and in this way we reconnect what has been so brutally fragmented in our culture.

There seems to be a subliminal celebration of paradox with sacred and profane in this story in particular between the connection of life and death, masculine and feminine. Isis, like Oshun, is traditionally associated with the vulture. Both are fertility goddesses with a shadow side of promiscuous death, which points to the nature of polarity and balance. I never quite understood why the most beautiful healing goddesses were associated with the vulture, but now I see that Her great beauty and fertile power comes from her ability to digest the grotesque shadow aspects of her nature. Like the vulture, Oshun and Isis are transformers. The river goddess is often dismissed or overlooked as frivolous, the little sister, but in her myths, time and again, she brings balance and peace.

As we saw in New Orleans, death and life dance as two sides of the same serpent. Structure provides freedom, as Grandma Clara and Grandma Maria struggled to learn and as Ganga and Shiva have shown. We must first be lost in order to be found, scattered to be reassembled, and live through drought to appreciate floods. The destruction of storms allows for creation, love is the other side of fear, and the feminine contains the masculine just as dryness must be related to moisture.

Back in San Francisco, I walk east on Mission Street from the BART station toward my school. I move quickly so the smell of urine and the sound of cat-calls from men who smell like booze fade behind me. I pass a giant red brick building to my left, the Armory—an old defense that stands like tight shoulders and a collapsed chest at the corner. It was once the fort of military men and now it is a production studio for porn. One form of violence gives way to another.

Two teenage boys skateboard on the generous concrete stairs leading to the entrance of the red brick building. I think about the CEOs of the myriad tech companies who are not much older or wiser than these boys, but society values their untested intelligence and daring, and rewards them with wealth. What happens when we build our foundation on air, ideas and start-ups? Where are the elders of the village who have seen a full cycle from start to completion?

A man on the other side of the street hoses down the sidewalk. *Hosing off cement? No wonder Californians lead the world in water consumption.* As I look up, I barely miss a pile of shit—*human or dog?*—in my path.

The Armory casts a shadow in this late afternoon light, but I can see a three-quarter moon above me in the sky. The moon reminds me of the water beneath the concrete. I can feel the meek flow of the river that disappeared beneath my feet. The leaseholders offer historic tours of this landmark building, and it's one of the only places you can go to view what remains of Mission Creek. The river still gathers the stories of the native bones buried under the historic mission churches. She's keeping them secret, like the tumbleweed in the Sahara, hidden under the veil of Isis, until the village container returns.

BATH SPRINGS

Returns to the Source

The White Fathers told us: I think therefore I am. The Black Mother within each of us—the poet—whispers in our dreams: I feel, therefore I can be free.

Audre Lorde

London. August 2007.

I ARRIVE AT THE TRAIN STATION with long, dark hair and forearms covered in red-brown henna. I have cellulite on my stomach and acne on my face for the first time in my life, as a result of a full summer spent eating heavy creams and curries. I do not feel like myself at all.

I see my curly-haired friend Anthony on the quaint, open-air platform and head toward him. He waves and then steps back a moment when I try to hug him, "Uh, what happened to your skin?" he asks with a nervous laugh. I roll my eyes and explain to my less-cultured contemporary the ancient practice of temporary tattoos. He rolls his eyes back at me and then offers a brief hug before he picks up my large red suitcase in a grand show of chivalry. He looks thinner than I remember, and I already wish I was back in India.

I've been re-routed to London on my way home from India.

After my visa got canceled, I had planned to renew it in Sri Lanka, but was advised against the trip because of the civil war. The magazine I was writing for was based in the UK, so they offered to put me up in Brighton in the meantime. I, however, thought it would be fun to visit my friend in London while he worked on a Master's degree in Shakespeare.

I wake up the next morning feeling bruised and tired—like a ripe pear in a bag of pineapples. My neck aches, my back is stiff, and I wish I hadn't woken up at all. I push myself away from the floor and assess the situation. I am in Anthony's tiny living room, the vertical mini-blinds are pulled shut over the small window—but it doesn't matter—very little light makes it inside even when they are open. I bend my knee and knock it against the glass coffee table. I hug it in close and cringe, *oww*. This morning couldn't get much worse, but then I smell the cigarettes in the ashtray.

I do not like London.

Outside I can hear the traffic humming and honking, and next door I hear the neighbor's cat begging for breakfast. I am claustrophobic, surrounded by people and thin walls. My head is buzzing, my throat is dry. I put on some hot water for tea and step into the shower. My recently dyed hair bleeds into the water and circles the drain as a brown stream. Just as I'm easing into the lukewarm waterfall, the shower turns off. I soap quickly, shivering, and press the faucet again. The water stays on just long enough for me to rinse my hair, and then goes off again. I repeat this process several times until I am just warm enough and just rinsed enough to call myself clean.

Water usage is controlled in this urban apartment complex— the faucet stays on for less than a minute at a time—which is meant to save water and teaches people to wet, wash, and rinse succinctly. It seems like a well-intentioned notion, but it does ruin the relaxation a steady stream of water wasting brings.

I know better than to hope I'd be back in India soon, but I make a silent prayer under my breath nonetheless. I had unfortunately argued with the customs agent about my status as a journalist, and she had accused me of lying to conceal information. Who knows what notes she had made on my application and how long I might have to wait here in limbo. But I decide I might as well make the best of it.

After nine days of seeing all the current shows, visiting every museum, catching up on countless movies, and binging on stand-up comedy routines, I am getting restless. The damp sinks in. The water here has no boundaries like the storms of Florida that announce their arrival and then leave—London is constantly wet and pervasively foggy. The rain is sticky and cold. There is no friendly heat or humidity, just a kind of invasive moisture that makes one's skin slither. I want to escape underground.

I don't like the water here, and nature is a hassle. Weather is an inconvenience that ruins my shoes. This experience is destroying the beautiful, spacious effect India had on my inner landscape—I am still trying to hold on to that hot, red earth. I use both hands to reject my current situation and grasp desperately for one directly behind me, which is draining my soul's fresh water reserves. I am almost out of money, but I decide to take a train to the south-western spa town of Bath. I thought all I needed was to get out of the city and soak in the springs.

Bath, like so many other sacred springs, was re-named by its Roman conquerors. Before the invaders came, the spring was dedicated to the Celtic goddess Sulis, who the Romans interpreted as Minerva (the Greek Athena). She is a powerful mother goddess who has the ability to place intense, irreversible curses on her enemies. I wonder if she's blessed or cursed this island nation.

I had rarely considered the land of England as having been itself invaded—it seemed the British were the ones colonizing other countries most of the time. British historian Stuart Laycock recently published a book, flippantly titled, *All the Countries We've Ever Invaded: and the Few We Never Got Around To*, that claims the British have invaded all but 22 of 200 countries worldwide. When I stopped to think, it made sense that a small, crowded nation that had endured numerous wars and oppressions would in turn travel the world spreading that same violence. That's the way our world has worked so far. *An eye for an eye*, and the cycle continues.

I make myself invisible in the train station and try to sleep sitting up. The oil from unwashed bodies has stained the commercial blue fabric of the chair next to me, and the smell of greasy chips lingers from the passenger in front of me. I arrive in Bath and sigh in disappointment—the town is much plainer than I had imagined, and the food more blandly boiled than in London. I eat my daily fish and chips on the go and then check into the spa.

My feet cringe as they feel mold in the changing room and cold rejection from the hard floor. As I slip into the concrete, contained, square-shaped springs I find myself increasingly irritated rather than relaxed. I am cold, my bones are thin, and I feel enraged at my situation.

I am stuck in limbo in a country I can't stand. I am a river forced to act as landlocked as a lake. The water I steep myself in is full of ghosts and greasy guilt. Even my skin is uncomfortable and erupting in rage. I wish I were anywhere but here and anyone but me. I pinch the little pouch of my flabby stomach and actually hurt myself a little before I stop and zoom out.

I've uncovered a deep sense of self-loathing that had been hidden beneath my cheerful surface due to the momentum and freshness of travel.

I consider the original goddess of these springs, a mother goddess, and my mind connects her to one of the most famous Celtic goddesses, Danu. She is a figure cloaked in mystery, as none of her official myths seem to have remained intact. Nevertheless she has a devout following and is known as the mother of the *Tuatha de Dannan*, a race of Irish gods who perfected the use of magic. Danu lent her name to the longest river in Europe, the Danube that flows through the central and eastern parts of the continent. Her name has several interpretations that almost make an entire poem of themselves: flow; swift; rapid; violent; undisciplined; wisdom; teacher; wealth and abundance. As the mother goddess of rivers, Danu wields the magic of divine flow. She clears stagnant energy and removes blockages so that our dreams may become manifest. Effort moves with ease to fruition. The river is destined for the sea, and Danu reminds us that we are destined to move in the direction of our dreams.

I got side-tracked when I tried to learn more about her: it seems she is also a Vedic Goddess, or maybe that's an earlier incarnation? Either way, she is ancient and wields considerable power as a triple goddess, embodying aspects of maiden, mother and crone all at once. She is also associated with the element of air, and maybe this is why she is so difficult to describe. I begin to postulate that her vastness may be part of why she is invisible today: she expanded and encompassed so many aspects of woman, life and nature that she blends in, like a river turning into the ocean. I feel connected to this widening feeling that eventually dissolves as I watch ripples scatter across the water's surface in the spring water.

Being surrounded by white people makes it difficult to ignore my own color—I blend in here. I look at my wet arm in the tub and notice the henna is almost gone. It makes me want to cry—the pressure builds up at my throat, but I refuse to release it. I see a middle-aged white woman with brown hair enter the room, and her suburban plainness repulses me. At the base of it, I realize I am frustrated at being white, at having English as my native tongue. I reject being identified as the privileged, the oppressor. I have been in deep denial and was clawing desperately at any evidence of otherness I could find. I didn't want the guilt of generations of ancestors who had raped and pillaged. And I hate being plain, boring or dull. I want to be heroic, generous, exotic and sensual.

My realization might be likened to finding one was related to Hitler. How does the sun rise the next morning after such an insight? After the first dawning of understandings about the enormity of that realization—once I got past the denial—I knew this new perspective would profoundly shape my life. I feel a huge amount of responsibility to learn as much as I can about what actually happened during colonialism and in particular slavery in the southern United States. I have also felt the need to understand how social norms around race drive me to perpetuate white supremacy. Just assuming that because I have never personally harmed or said something cruel to a black person, does not mean my work is done.

As a white woman, I have often felt a fear of being considered racist that—in my own experiences—has seemed to hold white women back from getting too far into discussions about race and inequality. It's strange how the fear of "other" transformed over the decades now to be a fear of self—we are afraid of being outed as someone who is so ignorant of ourselves as to be secretly hateful. In my observations, it is as if white people can't trust themselves enough to know whether or not they are harboring sympathetic views that support white supremacy. I think this is in part due to the historical lack of dialogue regarding race, and the feeling of displaced guilt within somewhat self-aware white people who now recognize themselves as the ultimate "bad guys" throughout history.

And this is where the goddess Danu comes back in. She approves of all feeling. She is the first river goddess in my searching who is a mother. She teaches us to flow through the toughest places with compassion and grace. She is invisible because she has been covered up, like Isis disguised in her veil and like my African grandmother. They are hidden because they will choose another time to be revealed. And while they are concealed their stories are changed, the words are erased and only a feeling, an intuition about her remains. Danu greets me, and encourages me to let my heart break. She removes my fear of death, and I trust her entirely. I finally let the centuries of tears come.

It breaks my heart over and over again to learn the depth of the trauma that separation, ignorance and abuse of power has caused more than seventy percent of the world's people. My heart has been broken steadily over a lifetime of witnessing injustices to many indigenous people, and my first genuine response is usually to freeze. I hold my breath until the tears come—which may be days or years later—and then they seem like they will never stop.

I leave Bath early, feeling disappointed by the waters. Nothing magical had happened; I am still frustrated with my situation. I walk through the city back to the train station as the sun is setting in a cloudy pink and gray sky, but I hardly notice. Night is perpetually falling here—few colors announce the transition from gray to black.

I wear mental blinders, staring down at the gray cobblestones as I walk. I can hardly recall any image of this city—it is surrounded by my mental fog even now. I feel damp and chilled, as if some final ember in my heart has been snuffed out. I hear the clock tower chime seven times and realize I am ridiculously early for the train, so I duck into a used bookstore to kill some time.

Used bookstores have a unique character all their own. I love the musty smell multiple oily fingers leave on countless browning pages. I take off my black coat and begin to browse. And there it is, tucked back in the myth section near Arthurian legends, *Ladies of the Lake* by John and Caitlin Matthews. The cover is a well-worn image of a moon-colored woman standing at the prow of a boat on turbulent waters. Someone loved this book, and that love turned over the fading embers in my soul. I re-ignited in a flame of curiosity again. Who is the mysterious woman on the front? I dive into the text on the train ride home.

When images of the divine feminine were cast out by Christianity, the goddess fragmented and became subsumed in multiple stories. One of the preserved archetypes of the Western goddess tradition has been passed down through the legend of King Arthur. In older versions of Celtic lore, there are nine ladies of the lake, rather than the one who is often referred to in modern tellings. These nine women represent distinct patterns and offer specific guidance for how to move through womanhood because of their close relationship with water and other realms.

Caitlin Matthews writes: *The element of water has feminine symbolism attached to it: it is a flowing, weaving, uncontainable force which invades and moistens. In the Celto-Arthurian myths, water is seen as emotive, dangerous and overwhelming.*

I wonder how I hadn't read about this women's traditional lineage before. The legend of Arthur largely diminishes and demonizes women. But then I recalled the legend takes place as Christianity is popularized. The bards who repeated the stories over these years were men who lived separate from women and may have been intimidated by their complexity, so they repeated the parts of the stories they resonated with and left out the details about women that puzzled them. The stories were passed down with emphasis on the masculine players because they are less threatening and less occult.

Caitlin Matthews explains that women's natures are latent in the everyday and potent in the inner realms. Men's natures are potent in the everyday and latent in the inner realms. It seems obvious then that they are complementary aspects of one sacred whole. She was outlining a lost mystical tradition of Western Tantra; I was fascinated. I had spent years thinking there was something wrong, broken or missing with my Western background. I had built up the Eastern philosophies as being the only true keepers of deep wisdom and body practices, but now to discover that of course my European ancestors had one too. That changed something in me. Many Westerners look to Eastern traditions to find mystical branches of spiritual practices, but if we circle wide enough, and deep enough, with persistence, we find the lost tantric practices of the Western world as well. I felt an opening in my solar plexus, quickly followed by anger. Again, why, and how, was this tradition lost?

Fragments of the Western stories themselves offer partial answers to this question. One reflection of this feeling of having lost something of value in Western tradition is found in the story of the Holy Grail. The grail itself is a round, womb-like or breast-like symbol that is considered to be an image of the divine feminine. It promised redemption and renewed life to the wasteland of the Dark Ages, if only one could find and capture her. Of course, this is impossible, since it is a metaphor for reinstating the value of the feminine in culture and spirituality.

Another commonly told story in Western Europe, that again points toward the answer for why the divine feminine withdrew from religion and society, is the story of the rape of the well maiden. There are numerous holy wells along the British Isles, and the story goes that the wells used to be kept by maidens who acted as priestesses. They were sacred to travelers because they offered passersby a drink from the water, which made long voyages possible. There is a commonly held belief that the evil King Amangons raped one of the maidens and stole the cup with which she drew water.

Any violence committed against the divine feminine ripples out across all of humanity. After this travesty, the water in the sacred springs dried up, the temples to the goddess were abandoned, and the land itself experienced severe drought. The masculine principles of the world have not taken care of the feminine, the resources of the earth herself, and so she decided to withdraw her magic and ability to animate the world. This is exactly what happened before Oshun and Ganga descended, and what happened after Reina merged with the ocean. When the river maiden leaves, the world cries out in pain. As Mara Freeman writes: *Disconnected from our spiritual source, we thirst for life-giving waters in the desert of modern life.*

While it is easier to blame this loss of a strong female lineage on the jealousy of men, the truth in part may be that women played role in covering up their own powerful mysteries as well. Women often fear the depths of themselves, and as a result leave parts of themselves unclaimed. Women who become fixated with superficial daily routines live in fear of the power of their dreaming, their ability to weave formlessness into form. The struggle of balancing an internal and external reality is the work of weaving masculine and feminine aspects together as a cooperative whole. As I've learned, it is supposed to be a struggle—we need this tension as humans to grow—and this weaving of stress and relaxation forms a web of experience that shapes who we are. This web, this weaving action can be called a *tantra*.

I want to explain a little more about what I mean about Tantric practices here, as it's a commonly misunderstood term. *Tantra* most literally can be translated to mean 'loom' or 'weft.' It refers to the structure of reality itself, how formlessness is woven into form—like breath (formlessness) moving through the body (form) or wind (formlessness) moving through trees (form).

Traditionally, Tantra refers to a wide collection of practices detailed in the Indian texts called tantras (like sutras). Some of the most common features of these practices are secrecy and worship of the divine feminine. The aspect that has most intrigued and shocked observers—both Indian and Western—is the sex. Tantra employs sexual visualization and some branches practice ritual intercourse. The purpose of this conjugation, often depicted as the union of Shiva (formlessness) and Shakti (form), is to reach *samadhi*, a blissful state of consciousness devoid of any sense of personal identity.

One could say that Western yogis are all Tantrics now since the most popular form of yoga today, Hatha yoga, has been a central feature of Tantric practice, and its creators were affiliated with Tantric sects. But as with most cultural imports, Western assimilation of Tantra has involved a lot of interpretation and invention. Tantric practice is no quick route to sexual gratification. It's traditionally demanding, complicated, highly formalized, and at times, tedious. And only some types of Tantrics (known as "left-handed" Tantrics) engage in ritual sex at all.

Tantra presents a paradox: it can involve sex and yet its prerequisites mitigate the pleasure. The goal is not to get good at sex, the goal is to alter your consciousness so radically that embodied existence is no longer a limitation. This balancing act of engaging and allowing paradox is the meat of the practice.

In the Indian Tantric tradition, the earth and our bodies are seen as the feminine forces of the world, known as *mudra* and *lila*. They are the creative, receptive and random forces of reality, often likened to warm wax or soft mud: they are pliable. The complementary masculine forces are seen through the concept of *karma*, action and causality, and *dharma*, the structure or architecture of reality. Tantric scholar Douglas Brooks says that these opposing forces interact in a kind of dance that forms the interconnected fabric of our world. From a non-dual cosmological perspective, we as humans are seen as microcosms of one whole. When we engage these principles in our bodies we learn to change not only our internal state, but also the state of affairs beyond our bodies. All of nature, including humans, moves to a pulsing rhythm, and we are all weavers of reality.

We are no different from the nature that surrounds us. In this method of engaging our senses, we feel that we are walking *in* the earth rather than *on* the earth. James Hillman, in his *Introduction to Ecopsychology* echoes this concept from a psychological perspective. His essay, "A Psyche the Size of the Earth", explains the notion of internal realities mirroring external landscapes. He writes: *The "bad place" I am "in" may refer not only to a depressed mood or anxious state of mind; it may refer to a sealed-up office tower where I work, a set-apart suburban subdivision where I sleep, or the jammed freeway on which I commute between the two.*

He continues his inquiry, asking: *Is any suffering, grief or loss ever really personal? What if the sadness we feel were always collective, always shared?* The massive disappearance of the natural world—a healthy landscape that mirrors a full spectrum of being—has been replaced by limitations and masculine structures of metal, steel and tar. Where is the feminine: the softness, the *lila*, the *mudra*, the pliability and playfulness?

Man has created the world in his image, but it is time for women to step back to the forefront as creators, making a world in her image, one that is inclusive, cooperative, and circular. What if we try this philosophy on for size? Imagine every person you encounter is a reflection of yourself. Suddenly the rude jerk who cut you off in traffic becomes a frazzled mother with a crying baby in the back seat. And maybe the unsympathetic insurance agent on the phone is just a guy with a difficult job.

If we place ourselves back into the natural landscape and remove ourselves from unconscious projections on one another, we can regard one another with the same objective compassion with which we view the harmony of nature. I try to consider this in terms of the traditions of colonialism as well. Those people acting in violence are searching for some unmet need—they are searching for water in their own way—the kind of water that keeps them from feeling constant thirst. Jesus uses that metaphor too, that certain teachings lead us to a spiritual quenching. From the Book of John: *Whoever drinks of the water that I will give him will never be thirsty again. The water that I will give him will become in him a spring of water welling up to eternal life.*

Rediscovering the roots of Western mysticism brought me a new understanding of the stories of India. I no longer felt I was a visitor, I felt I was at home—an explorer who needed to study an intact tradition in order to help restore what my own family had lost. I no longer needed to escape and stay gone, I had somewhere to return home with a purpose. I recall the Vedic origins of the Goddess Danu and consider what seems separate is always connected if we look back far enough or down deep enough. Points on a linear surface that are far apart will end up next to one another if that line coils into a spiral. I had felt profound grief at the loss of Danu's story, of the Western sacred stories, but maybe she had not so much lost herself as expanded into a wider aspect of herself. Like a water droplet dissolving into the ocean, the individual is lost, and a new collective is gained.

Nature turns toward you the same face you turn toward her. This land, England, had merely mirrored my disgust with myself. I had seen myself clearly, and decided it was time to go home. Well, almost. I took one quick detour before the flight back to Florida.

County Cork, Ireland. September 2007.

I stocked up on Celtic myth, legends and fairy tales before the brief flight west, and by the time I landed I was practically checking under my seat for fairies. Ireland was a magical place my mother had idealized her entire life but never visited. I could hear the need to see this land in her voice when she sang *When Irish eyes are smiling*, taste the homesickness in her boiled cabbage on New Year's Eve and smell the sadness when she missed mass on Sunday.

I had already planned to fall in love with this magical place, and the stomach flu that was brewing in my lower intestines was not going to stop me. I had only three days, but I spent nearly every moment outdoors with my camera and my notepad. I bundled up against the cold and took countless pictures of sheep, pastures, stones, roses, moss, gray clouds and misty fields. This land was pregnant with secrets. I was enchanted. *This is where the O'Brien's are from. I am from somewhere*, I thought.

I felt intrigued and enchanted, though nothing happened externally. I found words from the Celtic mystic John O'Donohue and let them sink deep into my heart:

You have traveled too fast over false ground;
Now your soul has come to take you back.

Take refuge in your senses, open up
To all the small miracles you rushed through.

Become inclined to watch the way of rain
When it falls slow and free. [. . .]

Draw alongside the silence of stone
Until its calmness can claim you.

I walked on the soft soil and didn't even mind the permanent caked mud on my shoes. I chatted with others at the hostel and mostly zoned out—I just wanted to enjoy their lyrical accents. I had proved my internal experience was up to me. I could bring magic to the most mundane of situations, or I could resist every moment and make myself miserable.

I noticed it is easier to identify with the people who have been victimized; it feels safer in some ways. I wanted to be Irish, and not English. But I am both. It is incredibly painful to see the violent and selfish parts of myself, but it is entirely necessary. I learn to feel into the middle of the ouroboros, that strange circular devouring snake. I am the head and the tail, but I am neither at the same time—I am both extremes. My skin is white, and I cannot change that. I was born into relative privilege, and because of that gift it is my choice to use it wisely.

~~~

When I got back home to Florida, I went right to work. I took out my nose ring and cut off my hair and let it grow back in its natural color, a kind of brown-blond that reflects my mixed ancestry. It was time to dig deeper into my own traditions and find meaning and value in my unique situation. I had to trust that I was the color I was for a reason. Wherever I was, that was exactly where I needed to be. I began to feel the pull to move west like a river might notice the ground's incline shifting.

Those realizations during my time in England, the self-loathing, the desire to escape my skin, propelled a deeper inquiry into my roots. I had already begun to study the work of Carl Jung and gotten deeper into the understanding of myth and archetypes, and I took his admonition to heart about Westerners running to the Eastern traditions as a way of continuing to project an external savior where Jesus is replaced by Buddha or a guru.

Jung advised Westerners to return to their own traditions. So I tried. I took apart the symbols of Christianity and truly gave it a shot. I thought: how can I salvage this text, the Bible, with my deeper understanding of metaphor? Can I see how Christ was actually pointing toward a non-dual reality when he talks about the Kingdom of Heaven within? I kept up yoga as a way to integrate the essential body-based practices that Christianity left out, but something still felt off. I probably couldn't have even put my finger on it at the time, but I knew I needed a strong female image of the divine.

After some time, I eventually realized I was past reconciliation. Christianity wasn't fulfilling me, but I did find a healing with the tradition that was not present during my initial split. I then allowed myself to think back further into my Western roots. Christianity didn't spring up from nowhere like oil in Texas—it covered up older practices that came from the people who lived in balanced relationship to a land alive with spirits.

I pored through the European myths looking for a lady to inspire the kind of devotion I felt toward Kali, Durga, or Tara, and I found the Greek goddess, Artemis. I was especially drawn to her connection with all wild things, her love of moonlight, and her invisible but potent presence within the community. The thirsty part of my psyche demanded depth. Artemis helped me as an image that provided a container and a portal into unknown aspects of myself. Here, I found my connection back to the natural world I knew so well as a young girl. Here, finally, was a wild woman who lived by her own rules, was at home in the forest, and didn't care what anybody else thought of her. She was not servant to any man. She turned inward for answers.

I felt a softness about the depth of my pagan investigations, I knew I was moving with care and trying to expand my cultural understanding. The critic in my mind (quiet, obedient Mary) had helped me to challenge images that felt oppressive and had led me here, so I kept going. I had a less intense talk with my mother this time—she had always had such nostalgia when she talked about Ireland, so I think her own longing for her roots knew I was onto something.

I found a fullness of connection with my Celtic roots and symbols and stories that felt like home. In the pagan community back across the Atlantic, I found leaders and elders willing to be real with me and a community of shared leadership. The poetry, the invocations, the way of being in nature, it all clicked. I started with the stories, as always, and then began to watch my dreams change. I fully felt that my search for meaning and connection was a form of spiritual activism. I felt myself opening up to those around me, I got better at my work, became more creative, and started making enough money to survive. I returned to writing, not as a journalist, but as a poet.

I moved to California the following year and kept John O'Donohue's words in my pocket as I traveled toward the land of the setting sun in my perpetual search for darkness.

Your soul knows the geography of your destiny. Your soul alone has the map of your future, therefore you can trust this indirect, oblique side of yourself. If you do, it will take you where you need to go, but more important it will teach you a kindness of rhythm in your journey.

I had been uprooted again by the move, and California was competitive and unfamiliar. I used these words as a reminder, trying desperately to recapture a past experience of peace, but my internal critics were well trained in their ways of doubt. Some element of basic trust was needed to abate the deep feeling that something in me was broken beyond repair. I could not quite understand why I still felt lost. I felt the fragmentation of my culture and felt pulled to keep gathering pieces. The pagan community of California seemed to swim in the wounds and wear them as badges. I was putting together bits of memory and meaning but I still felt the sharp pain of absence and separation permeated my community.

I was working all the time, keeping myself busy as possible, not spending any time outside, and I felt my spirit wilting like a flower without sun or water. I recognized an all-too-familiar pattern: I was hiding in a tradition I thought I could escape through but I was not connecting to others. I wanted to feel at home already, but the answer I got once I showed up at the door was a stern finger pointing me back out into the confusion. I didn't quite understand, so I kept trying to make camp. China Galland writes that: *In recovery, the very wound that drains one's life is the greatest source of healing and transformation . . . the journey takes one from the depths to the heights.*

I know my gift has something to do with paradox and bridges, so I knew there would probably be much more of this confusion to come. I had enough understanding to trust the confusion, to stay with the discomfort, and to honor the other side of fear as power not yet transformed, but I was still trying to fly when I needed to land. I want to be as grounded as the serpent but also as free as the dove. I eventually decided I could not find all the answers from one source, and I reconsidered my abrupt discard of the Eastern practices.

In the Eastern texts, there are considered only three main lies we tell ourselves, and they manifest in the many convoluted pains we create as a result. They are called *malas* meaning the dust or dirt that keeps our light from shining. The mirror of our inner selves is always intact, but if it is covered with this dust, it cannot reflect our true selves. The three lies are:

One   That we are broken or imperfect in some way

Two   That we are lacking in energy or time

Three   That we are separate from others.

I believed all three and was trying to get clarity without cleaning the mirror. Maybe I was being too extreme by discarding all the Eastern practices once I reconnected to my roots. I am saddened to see that so much wisdom and beauty has been lost from my European ancestors, but I feel a new gratitude for the Indian texts that were closely guarded. All non-dual cosmologies embrace the widest ranges of diversity as essential parts in the totality, and again I learned to include both rather than compete with one or the other. No talent or quirk is discardable: every color on the spectrum is needed to create fullness.

A kaleidoscope depends on every tiny element to create one beautiful whole, and the tiniest shift then alters the entire image. As I learned from the river of traffic in India, it is important to invite all aspects of myself into my life. With this in mind, I allowed the kaleidoscope to turn—I returned to the Eastern traditions from a place grounded in the Western memories with a slight shift in perspective, and all the pieces are rearranged. My hands are open and the need to grasp or explain has softened. I believe this acceptance and self-love brought an inner lushness and fertility that opened my womb to the magic of conception, but I still needed to make peace between the Virgin Mary and Mary Magdalene within me.

RIO MAGDALENA

Spirals in an Infinite Eddy

A woman in harmony with her spirit is like a river flowing. She goes where she will without pretense and arrives at her destination prepared to be herself and only herself.

Maya Angelou

Colombia. April 2014.

I OFFER THREE PINK ROSES on the waning banks of the Rio Magdalena, who was called Yuma by the Muisca people before the Spaniards arrived. Roses are a symbol of the Queen's balanced energy—the soft petals alongside the protection of the thorns balance her receptivity with absolute sovereignty. The Yuma River has been overused, and her thorns cut off. I watch the petals spiral in the current and find their direction.

On this particular day just after the spring equinox the clouds are undecided—permitting sun and then shade at random intervals. I take off my poncho again as the sun heats my face. The rose petals float, and their pink darkens to almost red before the water carries them out of sight. She seems to have lost her life force—the water is frothy and flat, cracked mud and plastic soda bottles line her shores. A group of locals, Cantos del Agua, has taken to singing to her to try and revive her, bringing awareness and respect to some of her shores. But this river was sold to corporate greed a long time ago.

This river connects the inner highlands of Colombia to the Caribbean, which allowed for trade and markets to blossom along her banks. Her waters also carried human slaves from Africa to the farms and jungles across the country.

The Rio Magdalena is named for the only female disciple—and according to the gnostic gospels, the wife—of Jesus Christ. To conservative Christians, Mary Magdalene is a reformed prostitute who does not deserve much commentary. She is often depicted in art as a red-haired, sensual woman. The archetype that surrounds her is one of the loose women, the amazon, the flirt and sometimes a sorceress. In modern times, she might be seen in the conservative community as the unwed mother.

In Bogota, the number of single mothers is so great that there is an entire restaurant chain, Crepes and Waffles, that exclusively employs, as part of their policy, single mothers. Why do so many women raise children on their own? In a recent blog post on Mike's Bogota Blog, one Colombian spent May 9, Single Mother's Day, interviewing locals about why they thought there were so many single moms in their country. The most common response blamed the women, saying that they had children at too young an age. No one mentioned the lack of education or access to contraception.

Another common reply was that the men tend to run around and cheat or abuse the women, and the women choose to leave them. Men feel entitled to have a virgin-like wife as well as a wild lover because of the psychic split created by the image of Mary the virgin or Mary the prostitute in the predominantly Catholic society. The two women are limited in capacity and trapped into roles that rob them of their wholeness. There is also a cultural expectation that women should primarily be mothers, at the center of family life, like the Virgin Mary. Young women feel the need for purpose and meaning, and decide to have children in order to fill that feeling of emptiness that a lack of respect has left as a hole in the psyche.

And women aren't the only ones being treated poorly, the water in the capital city, Bogota, is widely mismanaged and abused. The Bogota River is a dried up creek, even though the city receives an average rainfall of almost forty inches—that's twice San Francisco's average. The streets flood, but the inhabitants of the city go without water. In a land of tropical rainforests, large populations of people smuggle water in the trunks of their cars to the coast. While some go without cooking water and daily showers, others have personal swimming pools and elaborate fountains. And this pattern of disparity is not unique to Colombians.

By 2025, almost two billion people on this planet will live in severely water scarce areas. Almost all of these people live in the geographic south. North Americans use an average of one hundred gallons—the amount of water it takes to fill two standard bathtubs to the top—of water per person, per day, while in the rest of the world the average is closer to five gallons—the amount we use in one flush down the toilet—per day. This is the steep canyon of disparity of access that few people try to scale, a gap which is growing wider each year. I want to try and trace the start of this divergence to the initial splitting moment.

Hundreds of years ago, foreign priests started building churches on Colombia's hillsides, and the indigenous people conformed to these new laws as a means to survive. The poetry in their languages was forbidden and then forgotten, and their shrines to native spirits were often covered over with images of Jesus and Mary. Their dark goddess became lighter, wore pale blue, and submitted to the name Mary.

The sacred, medicinal coca leaves used in a ritual context were farmed and refined for the profit of foreigners, and in turn, the medicine became a poison in the culture creating deep division between the indigenous people and the elite. The rebels and guerrillas of Colombia are only just now coming to peace talks in Cuba. The emotions of this land are boiling over, as they are being funneled through an increasingly small spectrum of acceptance. This searing rage has been literally poured out on women's heads: there have been a number of cases of men throwing burning acid on women to show anger after a fight or hate after being rejected. One friend of a friend was in critical condition in a hospital after such an attack during our visit. She was wrapped in a full-body cocoon and awaiting extensive skin-grafting surgery.

Women are in a metaphorical cast as well. The full rainbow of emotions the mother goddess once embraced is erased and replaced with a few monochromatic moods. Mary is dressed in blue and looks like an ocean goddess, and the root of her name in fact means sea, but Yemanja and Ursula were never so domesticated. Mary has been shrunk down into a model colonial woman: humble and obedient, the all-suffering mother. Women around the world have used the Virgin Mary as an impossibly pious role model to emulate.

~

Naples, Florida has some of the most beautiful natural beaches in the world, that is until the developers decided to improve them. The city added a pier and a hundred feet of fake white sand. Red tides were common after that, and my grandma and I couldn't find shells anymore. My grandmother always seemed to be in tune with the ocean. It felt as if it had become red with anger and was too sad to be generous. Last time I visited was only a month after the 2010 BP oil spill in the gulf. I soaked in the warm, turquoise water and cried when I considered the massive oil plume that was surely heading this way. But that day everything was picturesque, a true calm before the storm.

Grandma Florence had recurring bronchitis, every fall it came back and she would cough up red and brown phlegm. According to Chinese medicine the lung is where we hold our grief, and my grandmother seems to carry her share heavily. She used to get up before sunrise and paint the sunrise coming up over the water. Hers are some of the saddest and loneliest paintings I have ever seen. They are quiet and sweet, but also put me into an unrivaled state of melancholy.

She seems to prefer to paint on small, unobtrusive objects. I've received many tiny wooden spools hand painted with tender care, like minute tapestries. Her talent and care in small-scale details is impressive. It's as if she prefers to let her creativity out as a highly controlled, miniscule stream rather than a surge of waterfalls. She also has a knack for painting on hollowed out egg shells. She makes pinprick holes in the ends and patiently blows out the yolk, and then begins work on the delicate canvas. She doesn't mind if the eggshells break, I think part of her may even want her art to be fragile and impermanent. She has no studio, but sets up her paints and easel in the dining room or on the back porch when it's not too hot.

I have one of her paintings in my room over my water altar. It's hung politely in the center, above the floating shelf full of seashells and perfumes facing west toward the ocean. The canvas is about eight by ten inches, a petite window into her soul. She's outlined the canvas with a rough wooden frame my dad made for her. She won't keep gifts, but turns them back into further gifts. Modesty insists she never titles or signs her paintings and usually only makes them as gifts for the family or on request.

My eyes wander to the painting from time to time, but it often blends in with the familiar scenery of my studio. With her brushstrokes, she's created a group of sparse cedar trees hung with Spanish moss. Their roots extend into the murky water as the scene leads from a cozy cove out to the ocean. The edges are dark blue and black, while the distance shows a faint hope with light coral and purples. Their reflection reaches well past the center of the small canvas, making their shadows seem almost more real than their trunks.

A flock of birds flies in the distance, coming toward land or perhaps retreating out toward the sea? It is hard to say. They are an accessory just below the crescent moon which hangs centered in the clearing of sky. In the bottom right corner a gray heron steps through reeds and pauses with her long, skinny leg in the air. The heron stares into the water intently, piercing through the surface to find what she's hunting.

When her son, my father, stopped cutting his hair and moved into a tipi in the forest with his collie, my grandfather was furious. But Grandma Florence was tickled. She looked through the troubling social situation and saw her favorite son following his heart, and she put down what she saw in a painting. Not just any canvas would do, and so she used the panel of an old wooden bridge.

Home is a tipi that sits centered on the tall, 20 by 10-inch, wooden canvas. The body of the tent—this home—is tan and gray, and the surrounding forest an imposing kind of dark green that seems to be rolling in like fog. I've looked at this painting so often, I almost forget to notice that all the trees are bare in the foreground. Maybe it is winter, just around the tipi. The front flap is open, and the mouth into the tiny circular structure is dark. Only the viewer's imagination enters the space.

The sky is also a blue-green, and for years I thought maybe it would rain on this little structure. The tension and absence of warmth and life feels nostalgic for me. I hang this painting up first whenever I move, because it makes the new house feel like home. Home, in this sense then, means a kind of melancholy, the fullness before rain, the emptiness and mystery of a moment as captured in the water's reflection, in a bird's intent gaze, and in the dark round door leading into a tipi.

The story of love through Florence's eyes is told through the image of a castle she makes as one of her largest paintings at 22 inches by 28 inches. It was inspired by a photograph my father sent her while traveling in southern Germany. It's the Neuschwanstein Castle in Bavaria, as seen from above. The postcard is sharp and a little droll as a result, and my grandmother's seeing of it softens the edges and adds fog that lends the castle a mystical atmosphere. This forest in Bavaria is known as the Black Forest, which is where many of the Grimm's fairy tales take place. I can feel the rich darkness pulling me into the painting with a gravitational force. The fear of the place without light suggests something of the connection between fear and love. Maybe fear is that tightening, a hesitancy that comes just before a full opening, and surrender to love.

The blue and white tower is barely visible in the cloudy surroundings. Green predominates the canvas, as if one were in a melting forest of mirrors. I wonder if she had dreamed of a fairy tale wedding when she married her Navy man, whom she called her Sailor Boy, and set right away to having babies. This is when she began building her own internal dam, just as she was taught in church and school and in every conversation with her female friends. She closed off her body from her head at the neck, and reinforced the structure with scripture. From the Book of Ephesians 5:18: *For the husband is the head of the wife, even as Christ is the head of the church: and he is the saviour of the body. Therefore as the church is subject unto Christ, so let the wives be to their own husbands in everything.* And so she was.

I wonder who was sad first, or if my grandmother and the ocean were simply friends bound by their shared grief who found one another as the sun warmed their faces and lightened their heavy loads. Despite her sadness, Grandma Florence had a warmth and vulnerability to her that Grandma Clara did not. She was somehow more alive, more willing to be seen than most people I had encountered. Florence was a bigger, softer, rounder woman than Clara. It is as if she needs more space in her material form to hold all the emotions.

When I told her I was studying journalism, Grandma Florence said she would have liked to have done something like that if she could live her life over. She would have loved to write and travel. I would never have guessed this from the way she keeps herself busy in the kitchen and in the garden. She fusses over the neighbor's cat who is having kittens, but of course grandpa will never let her have a kitten. He hates cats.

Shortly after moving to California with my own little gray cat, I dreamed that there was a tsunami coming in and my Grandma Florence and I were in a large glass skyscraper on the shore. She was afraid and crouched behind a couch, but I rooted my feet down through twenty plus stories into the earth and held the entire building up as the water rushed over it. I've had fun interpreting that dream in different ways since then: first as a powerful statement of my own growth, then as an indication of some sort of ego inflation or savior complex, and now I think it may have been something more transpersonal between my grandma, water and myself. She is a woman who feels so much, but lacks a container big enough for expression.

As apparent as it is that she has a lot of heavy grief, I've never seen Grandma Florence cry. Why are rage and anger more acceptable in our culture than tears? Maybe it's because one cannot argue against the lack of reason in tears. Emotions are contagious, and cause a loss of composure, a surrender of power and control. The Western world has decided against all costs to keep emotions stuffed down, especially the vulnerability of tears. There is too much to risk in authenticity.

What scares my mother and grandmothers so much about losing control? Perhaps that external need for approval is so strong that the fear of losing one's standing in society is greater than the need to express a full range of oneself. The waters are held in under strict control and only surface in acceptable ways. She can only express herself through the details of her surroundings. She identifies with the objects around her—the animals, the weather, the new wooden carved chairs, the special china.

Grandma Florence and I used to write letters to one another, and hers were always full of stories about the birds coming and going in the birdhouses she made them; what the squirrels were up to; the snake she saw slip through the gate; the grapefruit tree that is almost ripe; how the neighbor's cat was sunning in a beautiful spot next to their hammock; and how she was worried that the flowers were too dry or freezing.

I always felt maybe she wanted to tell me something else, but she never did. She seemed to prefer to stay slightly behind her veil, carrying her burden quietly. I always picture her in blues and purples, kind of like a Madonna, full of grace and maternal energy. What would her life have been if she had modeled herself only a little more like Mary Magdalene? Maybe she would have traveled, or maybe not, but at least she might have valued her work, or allowed herself to have a cat. Maybe her paintings would have brought in reds and yellows, and maybe the figures would have interacted with one another in conversation or in dance.

Woman became tame in order to survive. Where the Virgin's image was accepted, the women became subdued. This submissiveness and martyred ability to endure is testament to women's strength, but does not wield that power with wisdom. Women all over the world allow men to cut and mutilate their bodies with various piercing devices, weapons of fear that teach women to recoil from their own instincts. Violence causes more death and disability worldwide amongst women aged fifteen to forty-four than war, cancer, malaria and traffic accidents combined.

Women agree to have their pleasure centers removed in the name of virtue. They give birth on man's metal table, for his convenience, anesthetized to their own strength. Just as water goes humbly when drastically re-routed to serve higher paying populations, the woman acquiesces to man's preference. The baby is born, and the woman becomes a mother. A flurry of medical staff in sterile white uniforms counts and measures and determines the baby's health. Then, after the numbers are recorded, maybe there is attention and time paid to the essential bond that helps the baby to feel welcome.

I was born in a giant red-brick hospital in West Palm Beach, Florida three miles from the Atlantic Ocean. I am a C-section baby. That means different things to different people, but to me it means I was ripped from the warmest sleep, dreaming an infinite ocean of pulsing, beaming stars and shoved into a sharp, metal reality with bright lights, cold hands and unfamiliar air, sounds and scents. The procedure can be used as a legitimate last resort in true emergencies, but in the United States more than thirty percent of babies are born in this way.

Cesarean sections were first introduced in the 1960s, and

at that time only about 5% of babies were born under this emergency procedure. But there's been a suspiciously steady increase in that rate since 1996 that cannot be indicative of the number of women who actually need surgery. The most likely reasons for this increase include: concerns about liability on the part of the hospital; pressure to get the baby out quickly; casual attitudes about major surgery; side effects of labor induction or epidural—lying down on a table and not being able to feel your legs is not the best posture to push out a baby; monetary incentives for the providers to deliver quickly; the common practice that a woman who has had one C-section is discouraged from trying to deliver her second child vaginally; and ignorance or inability to express rights on the part of the parents.

Labor is one of the first big decisions in a baby's life—the womb grows uncomfortable and so the baby emits mild stress hormones that initiate the contractions. The baby essentially decides it's time to venture into the unknown, she has outgrown this stage of co-dependency.

My mother was told her hips were too small for vaginal birth, so she never went into labor with me. The doctors scheduled the procedure on February 11 at 8am, as if to take care of *it*—that's me—first thing, Monday morning. I was not due for two weeks, but my mom remembers the doctor had planned a golf trip later that month. My life began with this re-routing, this acquiescence to serve the convenience of a male doctor and the prescriptions of science. Meandering and finding one's way through labor takes time and energy, and so the woman's body becomes a procedure that fits into a pre-determined shape.

My mother's unconscious body was pierced, her uterus was sliced open, her fluids were scattered, and when the drugs wore off she was the mother of the tiniest sleeping child she had ever seen. Mom said her first thought was that I seemed sleepy for the first few weeks of my life, as if I was not really there. My older sister, whom she had labored with for a few hours before the doctors hurried her to the operation room, had been chubby and bright with a full head of dark hair and large, open eyes.

Birth cannot help but be sacred. My mother called me her peach fuzz baby because of the soft blond buds sprouting from my scalp. She offered her body as my home all those months and then became my food. I can see now how she is living herself into an archetype she admires, and I cannot fault her for that choice. There is no greater gift than the one a mother offers to her children, no matter her inevitable imperfections.

Back on the banks of Rio Magdalena, I wonder about my mother. I always equated her with a Virgin Mary figure—I think she would have liked that. I also realized I had always seen her qualities of endurance and devotion as weakness. How different would the world be if women admired other strong women? How would mothers care for themselves and their children differently?

Symbols can be reclaimed and revived by those who need them. The emergence of the Black Madonna and the veneration of Mary Magdalene all across South America is an indication that the subversive power behind story and symbol is alive. As the Magdalene, Mary is no longer separated from her body as virginal; a passive character who speaks to God but is not herself divine; submissive to "the way things are"; and modesty is no longer her greatest virtue. She is embodied, celebrated, defiant, divine and proud.

Colombia. April 2014.

The eucalyptus trees sing in the gentle wind, and their scent opens my lungs after the tense flight and the long drive from the airport. These trees cover the hillsides of Subachoque, the small town my partner and I travel toward to meet his family.

Eucalyptus are majestic hardwoods, but they are not native here. They were planted by the Spaniards and other Europeans when they came. While the hardwood is useful for building houses, furniture, and boats, the tree itself drinks much more water than the smaller, native trees and is partly responsible for the dwindling groundwater supply in the area. But their leaves dance in the wind and make a gentle sound like the ocean as they release a soft, sweet, cool scent into my lungs. I am eager to wander around the hills to ground myself.

I say *hola* to his parents and wander around their patch of the hillside. His mother, Stella, is a painter and has a studio facing the mountains across the valley. The windows are wide and light enters on three sides. The beams are exposed, built by Sebastian's step-father, from some of the smaller, local trees of the area. I step inside tentatively, not sure if I am invited into the space.

The studio is a mess of colors and creative flow. Bizarre-shaped sculptures hang from the ceiling, reminiscent of Joan Miro's surrealist style, and giant canvases cover tables and easels around the room. The eyes on one canvas draw me in; it's an abstract face surrounded by reds and oranges and splashed through with purple. The movement and emotion on such a flat surface is startling, and pleasant. This woman, this artist, has either refused to build dams or has routinely torn them down when they interrupt her internal waters.

That evening we walk down toward the little orange and white colored houses of the town square. The church at the cobbled city center has a statue of Mary outside. And while she is draped in the traditional blue veil, the dress underneath is pink, and some of the local people have draped her with yellow flowers and lit different colored candles at her feet. This Colombian version of Mary is somewhere in between the most pious of rivers, full of litigation and dams and the most amazonian and wild of rivers. She is balanced and at home here.

The next morning my stomach is a system of knots and tangled vines writhing. I feel like a balloon dying to burst, but no one is able to offer me a pin. All I've eaten are arepas and cheese. Some tofu, some hot chocolate, queso and bread. No vegetables, no fruit. At least there is water. This morning during my yoga practice I got the funny feeling I shouldn't be twisting, even though the twists usually feel so good. My period is late, but maybe it's the food?

I confirm my suspicions three weeks later, back at home in Berkeley. The two blue lines on the stick form a cross: pregnant. I'm shocked—and happy. I've never been pregnant before and didn't know I could actually do it. I'm a real woman!

I never thought pregnancy would feel this way. I imagined motherhood as a point perpetually far off in the distance, and I had no direct intention of walking toward it. But here I am. I haven't finished a book, still have no idea what I want to be when I grow up, have a massive mountain of student loans from three Master's degrees I was planning to be able to work to pay off. And now I'll have a baby. I didn't think I was done with the "me" part of my life, but now it's over, ready or not.

My pregnant body fascinates me with constant changes. The ways I am learning to trust my body excite me. I've moved from a tiny creek of energy and flesh, to a full, wide river, unapologetic in my needs and desires. It's easier to listen internally because that still, silent voice within has now got a megaphone. My body dictates my food, my sleep, and all my other movements. It's relaxing to turn off my mind, as if I am floating downstream. I feel the dark sea of my womb expanding. This is how it feels to host an internal ocean, the constant churning and eddies of the river give way to a consistent direction downward and toward the ground rather than the circular currents I felt in my low belly before pregnancy. Some memory in my womb has brought out the ancient pattern of weaving, like a divinely influenced spider, and is craftily weaving spirit into matter. I am honored to take my place in the long line of mothers who cross this threshold into womanhood, like Oshun the river goddess reaching out to her big sister Yemanja, the Ocean and the waxing moon moving toward fullness.

I've only known Sebastian a couple years. I was in another relationship when we met, but he had steadily remained in touch with me for a year after we met at a full moon circle. Just saying hello, sharing dreams, building a connection. The night I first agreed to go to dinner with him I wore a beanie over my short hair so it wouldn't look like I was dressed for a date. I chose to meet at an unimpressive Thai place a block from my house, for convenience and the air of casual non-concern. But when I saw his big smile from out the window something in me stood still and paid attention. All my senses were alert. He opened the door and I smiled like a sunrise. He spoke and I dropped into myself another five layers. His voice transported me to a place of home deep inside myself.

And now here we are.

I place my hand on my growing belly and wonder where our baby will claim as his home. I'll tell the story of his conception in a eucalyptus grove on the hillside of Subachoque in the center of Colombia and ask if he remembers being starlight. Maybe he'll tell me how it felt to fall to the earth, and maybe he'll look at me as if I've lost my mind.

I don't know if he'll be a darker boy, like his father, or lighter like me. I don't know how white men might project their fears onto him and white women may project their desires. I cannot protect him from being an actor in this cosmic play. He'll have to learn to live with one foot in the north and one foot in the south. Perhaps in his teenage years he will choose to identify with one culture and then the other at alternating times. And when he struggles and he asks, "Which one?"

I will answer, "Both."

There is one story that comes to mind in light of my impending motherhood. While I had always looked to the river goddesses as a maiden, pregnancy has started to connect me to the ocean. I am preparing for a little death; my life is about to look and feel completely different than it has for my first thirty years. There is no way to prepare, but it helps to hear stories of characters who have made it to the other side of vast transformation. The story of Sedna is one of connection to core values, deep rebirth, satisfying partnership, and profound acceptance and courage in the face of fear.

The Story of Sedna, Skeleton Woman, from the Inuit

Once there lived a beautiful and wild princess who loved to walk on the ocean cliffs near her father's castle. She would go barefoot across the beach and feel the sand between her toes, the wind blew through her long dark hair, and the salty spray sprinkled her arms and chest. She felt the power of this place and knew she would not live if she left it.

Her father was a political man who, when the time came, chose to have her marry a prince from a kingdom far inland. Princess Sedna downright refuses to marry as her father decrees, even though disobeying the king means death. She is punished and tossed into the ocean she so dearly loves and drowns.

Sedna sinks to the very bottom of the ocean floor—her long hair in ribbons around her and her body eventually wrapped in sand. Over the course of hundreds of years fish gnaw at her flesh until she is only a tangled heap of bones, an aged skeleton.

While her bones rest, her untethered spirit haunts the cove, and the people of this bay remember her story and warn fisherman not to bring their boats to the cove. But one dreadful winter, a desperate fisherman decides to risk his luck. He enters the cove and throws down his nets. Almost instantly he feels a tug at his line and feels the rush of expectation. It's a big one! This could finally be the catch of a lifetime. He daydreams of the riches that will be his as he pulls in the line. But just as he's about to burst from suspense and delight, his net comes into view above the surface and he sees a human skull.

Frightened beyond words, he drops the net hastily and tries to make a quick getaway, without noticing the lines tangled about his ankles. He makes some distance before he gathers the courage to look back and nearly dies of shock when he sees the skeleton appears to be chasing him.

Faster he flies, running through the village toward his home. Each time he looks back he sees she still chases him.

Finally he dives into his igloo and secures the door shut behind him. It is dark now and he is trembling. After a few deep breaths he gathers the courage to light a fire to see that he's safe. No sooner does he move to get up than he hears a rattle of bones at his feet. He freezes, and then looks a little closer.

He notices the netting is tangled around her bones just as it is tangled around his ankle. Moved by some wordless compassion, he slowly begins to untangle the nets.

As he does this he sings gently to himself. Once the nets are removed he tenderly places her bones back into the shape of a woman. He lies her bones next to the fire and goes to sleep.

The fire warms the watery ghost of a woman and she begins to wake up. She looks around and examines the kind man as he sleeps. The tiniest tear drop rolls down his cheek and she catches it with her finger and drinks it.

As if by magic, this drop of water born of compassion brings her back to life. Her long dark hair returns and once again she feels dirt beneath her toes.

He wakes up and begins playing a drum that re-starts her heart and calls back her flesh and womanly curves. The two dance and embrace and from that day forth never separate.

～

The story of Sedna contains codes for living in joyous harmony with the masculine and feminine. It begins with a maiden's refusal to follow the law of patriarchy. Because of this rebellion, she undergoes a death-like initiation in the depths of the primordial mother, the ocean. She waits there until her inner masculine comes searching for something. He may not even know it, but he is looking for nourishment more than what the fish can provide. He takes a risk and travels into the cove of myth. There he faces elation, fear and confusion. He runs for his life until he remembers to find his center in stillness. He then clearly assesses the situation and is moved to compassion.

His patience and diligence are rewarded with a divine partner. Both have done their work as two parts of one soul that are now reunited. His challenge looks more active externally, but hers is no less profound for its bravery and depth. When the masculine and feminine dance in harmony with the ocean and the drums, a new life is created.

YUBA RIVER

Dissolves into the Sea

By the time it came to the edge of the forest the stream had grown up, so that it was almost a river, and, being grown-up, it did not run and jump and sparkle as it used to do when it was younger, but moved more slowly. For it knew where it was going, and it said to itself, 'There is no hurry. We shall get there someday.'

A.A. Milne

Berkeley. November 2014.

I SIT IN THE COMFORT of the villa and look out onto the waves. It's a clear, blue day and the sun reflects like glitter on the gentle ripples in the water. I am wearing a light, golden sundress and am surrounded by family. My little boy is by my side and we inhale a wide breadth of salty sea air and look down at the water together. The water is clear, and it is easy to see a group of large fish swimming together. Suddenly the fish scatter, and a massive shark comes into our view. This shark is about the size of a blue whale.

And there is not just one shark, there are nine. I realize these are not regular sharks, but spirit sharks asking to be fed. As I notice these great creatures, I feel some certainty in my low belly. It is time. I give my son a warm hug and kiss, and get my boat ready. I don't have a single second thought. I am one in a long line of sworn priestesses who have offered themselves to the spirits of the sea when the time came to restore balance. I take my boat far away from the island of Malta, and before I have time to hesitate I throw myself into the circle of sharks.

I consider using my skills as a priestess to escape my body and avoid the pain, but instead I accept the moment and decide to experience it with curiosity. I feel myself sink into the water, and then I feel a massive ripping of my limbs from my core. There is too much sensation for pain. The moment of fear and discomfort passes, and what is left of my spirit sinks to the ocean floor. Connected to profound beauty, I die.

I wake from this dream to the sound of a light rain falling steadily on the back porch. Maybe I am still dreaming? It's early, but I grab my robe and slippers and check the window. Water drops on the panes and against the inner screen—I can't believe it—it is finally raining! I start the tea kettle and open the kitchen door to breathe in the fresh, moist air—*ahhh*, the water enters my chest and causes the muscles of my lungs and the moisture of my spirit to soften and widen.

The sky is gray and cloudy as the sun diffuses itself through the falling water. Vibrant green plants are framed a brighter green against a backdrop of soil and sky, and the dust has been washed from their leaves. Even the faded red paint on the wooden boards of our back porch is bright and alive with the shine of the water. The wind chimes hanging from the bamboo plant next to the fence dance gently, and I feel myself sigh and rest somewhere near my toes. The anxiety and scarcity of the long drought has eased momentarily, and I turn my thoughts toward my dream over my cup of raspberry leaf tea. My left forefinger absent-mindedly traces the tiny crack in the side of the mug that's just over the red cherry blossoms on the side. This crack is what makes the mug lovely, and the death I experienced in my dream makes this day shine more brightly.

The block in my throat has softened. Something inside me has given itself over to devotion. I faced my fears of the waters and offered myself fully to it. I feel wider, more spacious with this courage. I've come some distance internally from my dream of the panther swimming in the dark in the spring of this year. There, I was afraid for my life and focused on self-preservation, but last night I willingly offered my life for something larger than myself.

Like Sedna, I experienced the death of my ego, and my spirit merged into the vast ocean. I feel a flash of life, as if I have found my internal shape, and no longer have to worry about the container around me. I am a liquid who knows how to maintain my essential structure between vessels. I am fluid, and so there is no need to try to be solid. The broken vase of lost cultures doesn't matter right now; wherever water goes, she is water. Something in the hibernating tumbleweed has woken up.

I begin my morning yoga routine with the taste of this dream still on my tongue. Coconut water and golden hues, like rose and dark chocolate. I sit still, cross-legged on the floor and open my central channel from the crown of my head down to my perineum. I used to experience this channel as a thin pathway about the width of two fingers, but even in my first trimester I already felt the channel turning from a creek into a full river, a highway rather than a pathway. Today I am aware that I am wider than my physical form and flowing like a waterfall.

I take hip stretches and stay close to the ground, lengthening my sides and relishing the air in my lungs. It is easier to ground in the last trimester of pregnancy, I have much more energy at my navel. There is a strong, steady stream of endorphins that flood through my system from even the most miniscule elongation. Some days I wake up feeling charmed.

It's impossible to stay small and constricted when there's so much beauty and life around me. My heart fills up like a teacup that is about to spill over the rim, and I worry it's too much. But then I remember to relax, to breathe. To let this moment come, touch me, and let it go. I stop trying to hold on to it, and then it flows through me like a soft shower of gratitude. My internal waters are fully awake and flowing; my inner ecosystem is lush and fertile with big warm leaves open like the banana trees in the jungle.

I drive five miles over the waters of the San Francisco Bay on the bridge from Berkeley to the city several days a week. I used to be afraid of bridges, but fear lessens with familiarity. The steady stream of traffic over this six-lane bridge forms a daily ritual in the morning and evening. The tide pulls us into the city for work with the sunrise, and pushes us back out at sunset. Luckily, it's a breathtaking view with the mountains to my right and the ever-changing waters of the bay to the north and south. The water of the sea reflects the sky, and the sky is painted elaborately different from day to day.

The fall is coming to an end and the earth begins to turn into herself as she empties into the deep exhale of winter. I feel myself slowing down too, growing larger, slower and turning inward. I don't know if it's because my body has become more fluid, the hormone surges or something else, but predictably every morning, right as I pass Treasure Island and see the fog over San Francisco's growing downtown skyline, I start to cry. It's as if there is an invisible veil between the East Bay and the city that is lifted, and the transition startles me every time. Maybe it's feeling so much water beneath me. Maybe it's having finally overcome that fear of bridges that was so prominent for me as a young girl. Or maybe it's the generations of grandmothers crying through me as I move toward motherhood, finally letting their waters flow in an act of healing.

I am a river that's crossed the entire North American continent and now rushes to her death in the sea. When Oshun meets her big sister Yemanja as the ocean, she disappears into something bigger. The crescent moon too gives up her dark space as she reaches fullness and the maiden makes way for the mother. Fresh water dissolves into the salt water and begins a new cycle. This death makes way for life to flow. The water of the ocean evaporates and returns to the sky to fall down again as rain or snow and continue the journey across land to the sea. It is a common miracle, but no less for its persistence.

Each drop of water is identical—and unique. Water always forms into a hexagram, but each snowflake organizes into this shape according to her own desire. Human tears are also unique in this way, they hold a particular feeling, a story in their expression as they roll down cheeks or are wiped away by tissues. The immensity and naturalness of the awareness of this little death I'm experiencing spontaneously pours from me in streams down my cheeks, and makes me feel grateful for the abundance of water in the bay and in my body.

Water is the only substance that expands when it freezes, just as a woman's body expands during the contractions of labor. Both women and water inherently hold this paradox as a gift, that ability to expand and contract in the same moment brings life and beauty to the world. Separate molecules of water form bonds so strong that they defy gravity to move up the stems of plants. This process is called cohesion; it can be likened to the bonds of sisterhood. Imagine how we could organize to have a greater effect on hierarchical structures if we spent less time pushing each other away or getting trapped in jealousy. Water knows better, and teaches us how to work with cooperation rather than competition.

A recent UCLA study shows that women's ability to gather and support one another allows them to live longer. In addition to the testosterone that is secreted during the fight or flight response in times of stress, oxytocin kicks in for women and they care, protect and gather. The study found that the length of time that women gather has a direct correlation with the length of their lives. We make life worth living when we support each other, and we help keep each other alive. Perhaps men live statistically shorter lives because they do not have the same connection to one another.

And yet, both men and women have access to the fluidity of water within their own bodies. But many men, as a result of cultural programming, believe they need to be solid and stable. This is, as we have seen, physiologically impossible. This damming up of emotions has historically caused them to burst in fits of violence and rage, like the wildfires burning across California. Women are often the targets of this rage, but we can no longer afford to see a one-way arrow from perpetrator to victim: it's a circle. Cycles of violence are broken through an understanding of the root cause, the longer arc of the story that feeds the pain. Men have to reclaim the stories that keep them trapped, and women have to reclaim our ability to make choices rather than playing the role of victim.

Women, in many ways, have an easier time confronting the healing before them, whereas men are compounded by a lack of socially acceptable body-based tools to unwind the centuries of tangled emotions, oppressions and acts of unthinkable violence they have been on both ends of throughout human history. What if we took the time to rediscover the stories that bring back our relatedness, to ourselves and to our resources on this planet?

As Sobonfu Somé writes, *competition is counter-productive in village life.* This was the lesson of the drums: if you can hear yourself drumming in a circle, you are doing it wrong. She writes: *Life is growth; life means helping, and being helped, by everyone around us; life is an eternal force that brings increasing insight and wisdom—things which are outside the realm of competition.* This is, of course, true on a vibrational and cellular level as well. The body would die without absolute cooperation and communication between organ systems. Cancer is essentially a lack of cooperation between a group of cells that choose to behave selfishly and eventually kill the entire system, including itself. This is true on the macro level as well: successful ecosystems are symbiotic and support one another.

The paradigm shift back toward the collective is paramount to feminist perspective. The concept of evolution by struggle, destruction, exploitation, and violence is an outdated point of view that has proven inaccurate and destructive. Humans have again projected their understandings onto nature and seen it as essentially violent and competitive rather than cooperative with a longer arc. The paradigm the majority of the world embraces is separation and scarcity, and so the opposite acts as antidote: symbiotic aid is essential for evolution. In order to survive on this planet, humans need to imitate nature. *Survival of the fittest* may need to upgrade *to survival of the most connected.*

The law of struggle and violence softens into one of grace and acceptance when the illusion of separation disappears. When we recognize a feeling of cooperation internally, we create more internal space that in turn resets our ability to circulate essential fluids and nutrients through the blood. As it says in the *Tao de Ching*: *Flowing water does not decay*. So the key is to keep moving with the new insights, trusting the invisible something that causes curiosity to guide the feet in a new direction.

My first few moments of metaphorically swimming in the dark—of allowing my feet to be held by water rather than planted on the land—were frightening. The dream of the panther guiding me to swim in the dark signaled to me that I had committed to a path of inquiry. I had no idea where this river would lead me.

I knew something was missing in my life, and so I went looking for what was lost. Part of my pain was a visceral longing for the primordial mother. In my trip to Ghana, I journeyed somewhere in my psyche that was very, very thirsty. The drums, the moonlight and at the ocean reminded me of the water I had been seeking, the mother I had not even allowed myself to miss.

Humans originated in Ethiopia and carried their stories across the globe from Africa. The land in West Africa held the memory of a connection to earth older than language. I remembered a place from deep in my DNA that knew how it felt to live in community, embedded in ritual, song and dance. The three goddesses (maiden, mother and crone) come from Africa, and all the stories that follow are a result of cultural overlays that came later. The way the pagans of Europe saw the natural world was based on an implicit memory from the original African stories. Like a geologist, we can trace the movement of stories like the layers of sediment in stone: reds on top of white and tan and yellow forming a marbled human history. I had followed one lone spiraling branch down the trunk to the taproot, and I stood in front of the source herself when I returned to Africa. I opened here because I escaped the stories of my modern village long enough to re-wire my circuits.

One of the best things about the earth is that she is round. We have direct access to the source at her warm center no matter where we travel. It's the depth and darkness that nourish the mystery and magic within each of us.

I feel there is an underlying—Carl Jung might call it archetypal—longing for darkness. It's as important as sleep. All we can see in the world is light or the way that light reflects off objects. Vision is inherently an externalized thing, but feeling is of course internal, and we are all being starved away from this basic human need by our light-obsessed culture and frenetic pace. It feels natural for us, as humans born from wombs, to search for a home or understanding that is based on feeling and connection rather than sight. John O'Donohue writes: *The world rests in the night. Trees, mountains, fields, and faces are released from the prison of shape and the burden of exposure. Each thing creeps back into its own nature within the shelter of the dark. Darkness is the ancient womb. Night time is womb-time. Our souls come out to play. The darkness absolves everything; the struggle for identity and impression falls away.*

Slowing down and noticing what's behind the obvious, material structures helps me to drop back into the parasympathetic nervous system and realize the home and dark waters I carry with me.

California. November 2014.

Just the other day, Sebastian and I were walking with our dog on Mt. Tam. The entire landscape is crisp and golden, having been worked on by the sun relentlessly. A few rare trees provide an oasis of shade, and the water stored from the little bit of dew sustains a fragile ecosystem that lives on a reflection of the sun. There is a creek that springs magically out of the side of one of the hills, and the three of us walk toward it, panting and walking slowly in order to breathe the burning air.

The internal ocean I am carrying makes me extra sensitive to temperature changes. Being seven months pregnant is like placing a soccer ball sized water balloon under your skin, right up against your most sensitive internal organs. When it's cold out, that water holds the cold. When it's hot, the heat is captured.

I lift my feet that have become heavier from the additional flow of blood through my arteries. Pregnancy is preparation and initiation into super-human powers. My senses are sharper—sounds and smells are either ten times more pleasant or ten times less tolerable. I stop for a moment to expand my breath and swipe a strawberry from Sebastian's backpack. The sour-sweet liquid revives me as I bite into the soft red flesh of the fruit. All the juices in my mouth are active, and the sugars invigorate my blood. I am ready to walk on. I don't hear water, but I see a change in the plants up ahead.

There is a precise trail of greenery parting the sea of golden grass that runs along a gentle crevasse. I see a white peace lily, a flower that always reminds me of my mom because of the way it folds into itself, and we step over a little spot of mud. Sebastian bends down to cup a handful, but the trickle is too small to gather without getting the dirt. A blue dragonfly lands next to the stream and drinks. I spy a crumb-sized black spider in the center of her web between two blades of grass. A few drops of water rest on the threads she's weaving. I am moved by the delicate gift of this small oasis.

I can feel the water flowing underneath our feet, and that invisible force is enough to keep the rabbits, reptiles and insects alive that in turn support the larger cycle. There is plenty for all of us if we use it well. Taking the time to protect what needs to be secret, what needs to be underground or invisible requires a wisdom that is not based on instant gratification or rampant consumerism.

The sun sets early these days as winter approaches, the earth exhales and rests before she gives birth again. Darkness, like the seeds in the ground, provides a place for change and growth. It gives us a break from the outer world and allows us to look within for guidance. The darker shades of the spectrum have a profound effect on us that is not better or worse but is very different from a popping yellow or bright pink. It is this dance of the opposites that drives life forward. As bell hooks says: *Conversion means not only turning away from one's past, but entrusting oneself to the unexpected, uncharted way into the incalculable future . . .*

I continue my practice of taking time at home. I slow down my breath and feel both of my feet on the wood floor, even and balanced. I take an inhale and allow my exhale to lengthen. The next moment rises in sync with my breath, peaks like a wave on the shore, and dissolves back into the ocean of moments. As soon as that moment, that breath, is gone, another one rises and the emergence continues. I remember to put down the weight of the world and float on the rhythm that surrounds me. I have learned this before, but it is so easy to forget.

Yuba River, California. Summer 2012.

In the middle of the summer, in the middle of the worst drought in California's history, we go camping. A group of friends is miraculously free on the same weekend to celebrate Sarah's thirtieth birthday, and we drive a few hours northeast from the city up to the Yuba River just outside of Grass Valley. We arrive on a warm, pleasant night to the sound of crickets. We set up camp, build a modest fire in the metal fire-pit and sing until we sleep. I lay face up in my sleeping bag and look up at the stars. Several shooting stars hurry past, and I drift into dreams.

In the morning, we put on our bathing suits and head for the water. The Yuba River is alive and well, racing over rocks and bounding around the bend. We walk along her banks up to see the rapids. This section of the rapids is classified as Class Five, the most severe in the human classification system. We enjoy a picnic in the sand and then climb up the rocks to have a look.

We disperse ourselves evenly as humans do in larger groups. I walk alone and find a perch where two stones hold me. I look down at the raw, raging power of the turbulent water and listen to the rushing river. I am being washed. I lean over a little closer and feel real fear, wondering how my body would respond under so much external pressure. I back away to a more respectful distance. Almost instantly I feel an electric current of white-hot fear move up my spine. A scream.

I look upstream and see Justin standing by the river's side. Where's Anna? A few of us rush over to him. He's got his eyes glued to a spot in the river, and he's gesturing wildly like those inflatable hand waving tube men that car dealerships put outside to lure customers. Then we see her: a tiny spec surprisingly far downstream, clinging on to a large rock near the opposite bank. He's waving and screaming at her, and I just stand there. She manages to scramble over to the other bank and drags herself up toward the road. She waves, and we are silent.

How did she do that? We hug and hold her and then walk her back to camp, and then we interrogate her. What happened? *How are you alive?* Anna is surprisingly calm about the entire ordeal. She says she just slipped, and once she realized she was in the water she went limp, like an antelope in the jaws of a lion. She didn't do anything; she let the water have her.

That turned out to be the best possible choice. The water knew where it was going, and she ended up coming out the other side of the rapids. Had she flailed and tried to right herself, she would have locked into a struggle against the current and been pulled deeper under.

That night, we were all a bit more solemn after having been reminded the power of the river. We go to bed earlier, a little shaken, but full of gratitude.

The next morning we walk down the other side of the river, to the swimming spot. A beautiful, shallow oasis that seems like a different river entirely. The current is smooth, and the depth is shallow enough to find your footing at most places. The banks are sandy, and we set up a hammock under a few trees to lounge. The water is inviting and refreshing—like bathing in liquid light. I lie on my back and let the river rock me here and there. I trust the force beneath me, and let go.

In order to thrive in this life, you must trust the raging waters of your heart and let go of control. Prepare for death and allow re-birth. I have learned that I can rest at any point and realize the elements surrounding me are carrying me, or I can choose to live my life as a struggle against the way things are. If I choose to deny impermanence and search for something lasting everywhere I go, I will be disappointed.

And so, finally, my psyche can relax—I know that I have no idea what happens next or where to go from here. I am the sankofa bird again, and in the middle of this wild, unmeasurable ocean I have found a perch. I can rest inside.

As humans we grapple with a feeling of being torn between form and formlessness. We are solid flesh, but we are also invisible, ineffable feelings. As flesh, we need tangible symbols we can interact with in order to make our inner experiences feel real.

Like flying out over the ocean with no idea when or where we might land and rest—the psyche needs a reliable perch. Symbols and stories allow us to play with the sometimes unbearable tension of being spirit in human form. The Black Madonna, the Virgin Mary, the Spider, the Snake, the Panther, Oshun, all of these are powerful symbols that provide a perch or a tether for us as we delve into the depths and darkness of our inner sensations.

The meaning behind these symbols comes partly from culture, but also from us: we have the power to switch them around, and in effect, change our worlds. There is an Amy Grant song that comes from an African proverb:

The same sun that melts the wax can harden clay
And the same rain that drowns the rat will grow the hay
And the mighty wind that knocks us down
If we lean into it
Will drive our fears away.

I see that this facing of my fears, again and again, has brought me further down the spiraling root toward my own ground of awareness and knowing. Like descending a spiral staircase, the center looks different from many points along the way, but my feet have carried me persistently home.

With the perspective of my first thirty years behind me, I write the first third of my life in my own words: my own story.

California. December 2014.

I am a woman who has chosen to reside in-between the worlds. I've always been drawn to the edges, and my only constant is motion. I am blessed to see that my family constellation taught me the wisdom of pulsing paradox from the start. I was born to be wide-eyed and curious—with one ear to the ground—and nature has been my greatest teacher.

I wake early to hear the dawn breeze whispering poetry as the sun paints the day. I see divinity in the memory of purple clouds that hang low over the central Florida sky and feel presence in the silver moonlight shining through green leaves.

I am the perpetual maiden who spends timeless hours under the shady row of sunflowers in our garden. I nurse countless puppies, sheep, calves and birds back to health with all-night songs. I am home in the smells of the earth, the sounds of the ocean, the warmth of campfires and the ease of wind in the trees. I love to swim, dance, play drums and weave. I am always hungry for stories, and each time I hear a new myth something in me stirs, and my entire being says yes!

I've found refuge and inspiration in words since I could hold a pen, and now I've found the courage to value that craft.

My heart has always pulled me toward the deepest mysteries. My mother read us the Bible from start to finish, year after year, and while I ultimately did not find a personal practice in Christianity, it paved the way for understanding metaphor and symbols that still shapes me strongly today. I became curious about Eastern texts and yogic practice, and I decided to weave together the different colors of my experiences into one tapestry of acceptance.

In college I studied anthropology, religion and journalism—looking for truth, beauty and adventure. My inner seeking brought me to Tibetan Buddhist temples in the mountains of California, yoga ashrams in India, and Native American tipis in the deserts of New Mexico. I traveled as much as I could, falling in love with the jungle in Thailand, dancing under the full moon in Ghana, sinking into revelatory peace in Montemartre, fasting in the Mojave, making tobacco offerings with the Q'ero Elders, and fiercely protecting the impermanent sand paintings of my father. I have searched wide and worked to reconnect many broken fragments of my family's story. I mourn and long for my village. I dance, I do yoga, I listen, I write. I recharge myself in the natural world and in my own internal wildness.

Frustration has come time and again when I follow the law of others, when I measure myself by their standards of perfection. I have battled myself to be free of the internal tension and restlessness for too long. I want so badly to understand. I want a clear, straight path—lined with stone. I want to truly know one thing. I want to arrive home and stay there. But the most profound beauty I have found so far is based in paradox, in living between the worlds, in embracing the messy mystery of opposing forces and unseen realities.

Water does not move in straight lines, but meanders according to the patterns within and beneath her. I am learning to surrender to the currents, with open palms and an open heart. This heart churning has helped me to ground into a radical compassion with the understanding of the play between individuation and interconnection that brings peace at last.

This peaceful point balanced on the very tip of opposing forces speaks to the flavor of the original allure of the river goddess, the maiden. She is the little sister, the fresh water bursting from the ground. The source of life. The radiance of Oshun, the innocence of Reina, the wildness of the seal-woman, the patience of Isis, and the raw power of Ganga, are all inherited by the one who has the courage to swim in the dark and the memory to re-weave the broken web of connection.

The maiden river goddess eagerly rushes toward Mother Ocean, even though it is her death. It is her fate, and she learns to move backwards and forwards in time—pulsing like the tide—as she gets closer to that threshold. She resists and allows the new shape to take her. She weaves the currents of grace and memory, playfulness and youth into her wider form that is grounded and certain. She chooses not to become one or the other, but to remain both maiden and mother.

The birth dream, January 2015

My hips bulge, my belly protrudes. A trickle becomes a surge, the waters feel their way down my leg in streams and make their way across the ground, finding the grooves of memory in the dirt. They form into branches and tributaries, emptying from inside me. I am the source.

The grandmothers remember how this is done, and they wake up the frozen memories in my blood with the drum of my heart beating. I channel Florence's blue threads of tenderness, Clara's yellow and pink clarity, Maria's dark red freedom, the amber and jade words of my grandmother who braids my hair in dreams, Grandma Afrika's orange and indigo patience, and my mother's violet devotion, and they flow through me in luminous darkness, rising like a mist over my right shoulder. The colors weave from separate streams, they form a transparent river that widens to include each one's uniqueness. As they weave together, I expand further than I know how.

It's time. I call the women; they gather the waters, the flowers, the herbs. They call the men, they make the fire, build the lodge, prepare the drum. The bulge of my belly is mediated at my throat. From here the floodplains of my emotional past rest and widen across my chest.

I breathe the heavy grief of my ancestors, and when I move to release it the mass of it sticks in my throat. Something big and strong is moving down, and all my seven gates open. Something big and strong is moving up, and my vocal cords vibrate.

I lower myself into the water, to finally land here, not a shining starbeam but a woman, round and full. I taste unconditional freedom and let down the cosmic armor, a human among humans. I soften as I loosen the stories, lounge in the water and let my starlit eyes adjust to the dark. I anchor beneath the sea, under whales' full bellies, even lower than starfish—I dive in and embrace the experience. I plant my feet on the earth and bend my knees into a squat, the shape of Kali-Durga. I open and close. Expand, contract. I smell lavender and jasmine, I hear the drums.

I let out the sound of my voice that I've stifled like thirteen dammed rivers revolting at once. This river dissolves into the ocean. I turn into the full moon and give birth to a son.

BIBLIOGRAPHY

Alarcon, Jessica M. 2008. *Re-Writing Oshun*. Miami, FL: Torkwase Press.

Andersen, H. C., Isabelle Brent, and Neil Philip. *Fairy Tales of Hans Christian Andersen*. New York: Viking, 1995.

Anzaldúa, Gloria. *Borderlands/ La Frontera: the new Mestiza*. San Francisco: Aunt Lute, 1999.

Burke, Sandra. *Up from the Sea: A Jungian Interpretation of The Little Mermaid*. Carpinteria, CA: Pacifica Graduate Institute, 2006.

Campbell, Joseph, and Bill D. Moyers. *The Power of Myth*. New York: Doubleday, 1988.

Canan, Janine. *She Rises like the Sun: Invocations of the Goddess by Contemporary American Women Poets*. Freedom, CA: Crossing, 1989.

D'Este, Sorita, and David Rankine. *Visions of the Cailleach: Exploring the Myths, Folklore and Legends of the Pre-eminent Celtic Hag Goddess*. London: Avalonia, 2009.

Didion, J. "Some Dreamers of the Golden Dream" in *Slouching Towards Bethlehem*. New York: Farrar, Straus, and Giroux, 1968.

Downing, Christine. *The Goddess: Mythological Images of the Feminine*. New York: Crossroad, 1981.

Fernandes, Leela. *Transnational Feminism in the United States: Knowledge, Ethics, and Power*. New York: New York UP, 2013.

Freeman, Mara. *Grail Alchemy: Initiation in the Celtic Mystery Tradition.*

Galland, China. *Longing for Darkness: Tara and the Black Madonna: A Ten-year Journey.* New York, NY, U.S.A.: Viking, 1990.

Gilbert, Jack. *Refusing Heaven: Poems.* New York: Knopf, 2005.

Hạnh, Thich Nhat. *Cultivating the Mind of Love.* Berkeley, CA: Parallax, 2008.

Jackson-Opoku, Sandra. 1998. *The River Where Blood is Born.* New York, NY: One World.

Jones, M. (2006, January 15). "Shutting Themselves In," *The New York Times.*

Leary, Joy DeGruy. *Post Traumatic Slave Syndrome: America's Legacy of Enduring Injury and Healing.* Milwaukie, OR: Uptone, 2005.

Levine, Peter A. *Waking the Tiger: Healing Trauma: The Innate Capacity to Transform Overwhelming Experiences.* Berkeley, CA: North Atlantic, 1997.

Lorde, Audre. *Sister Outsider: Essays and Speeches.* Trumansburg, NY: Crossing, 1984.

Matthews, Caitlin, and John Matthews. *Ladies of the Lake.* London: Aquarian, 1992.

Murdock, Maureen. *The Heroine's Journey.* Boston, MA: Shambhala, 1990.

Murphy, Joseph and Mei-Mei Sanford, ed. 2001. *Osun Across Waters.* Bloomington, IN: Indiana University Press.

O'Donohue, John. *Anam Cara: A Book of Celtic Wisdom.* New York: Cliff Street, 1997.

Prechtel, Martín. *The Disobedience of the Daughter of the Sun: Ecstasy and Time.* Cambridge, MA: Yellow Moon, 2001.

Rich, Adrienne. *The Dream of a Common Language: Poems, 1974-1977.* New York: Norton, 1978.

Roszak, Theodore, Mary E. Gomes, and Allen D. Kanner. *Ecopsychology: Restoring the Earth, Healing the Mind.* San Francisco: Sierra Club, 1995.

Shiva, Vandana. *Water Wars: Privatization, Pollution and Profit.* Cambridge, MA: South End, 2002.

Starhawk. *Dreaming the Dark: Magic, Sex, & Politics.* Boston: Beacon, 1982.

Steinbeck, John. *East of Eden.* New York: Penguin, 2002.

Somé, Malidoma Patrice. *The Healing Wisdom of Africa: Finding Life Purpose through Nature, Ritual, and Community.* New York: Jeremy P. Tarcher/Putnam, 1998.

Somé, Sobonfu. *Falling out of Grace.* Berkeley, CA: Berkeley Hills, 2001.

Taylor, S. E., Klein, L.C., Lewis, B. P., Gruenewald, T. L., Gurung, R. A. R., & Updegraff, J. A. "Behavioral Responses to Stress: Tend and Befriend, Not Fight or Flight". *Psychology Review*, 107(3):41-429.

"Water: Our Thirsty World." *National Geographic*, April 2010.

ABOUT THE AUTHOR

EILA KUNDRIE CARRICO grew up in rural central Florida. Her curiosity led her down a meandering path of discovery from a young age. She was inspired by her studies in journalism, anthropology and religion to travel around the world and teach in Paris, Ghana, Thailand and India. She studied yoga and embodied archetypes for nine years before completing a master's degree in Engaged World Psychology and then an MFA in Creative Writing and Consciousness in San Francisco.

Eila delights in the mystery and magic of landscapes and memory. Her first book, **The Other Side of the River**, was completed in early 2015. Eila lives in Berkeley with her partner and their baby boy where she teaches yoga and weaves stories.

www.EilaCarrico.com

ABOUT THE ARTIST

L EAH MARIE DORION, who created the artwork used for the cover of *The Other Side of the River*, is an interdisciplinary Metis artist raised in Prince Albert, Saskatchewan.

A teacher, painter, filmmaker and published writer, Leah views her Metis heritage as providing her with a unique bridge for knowledge between all people. Leah holds a Bachelor of Education, Bachelor of Arts, and Master of Arts degree. She has numerous creative projects to her credit, including academic papers for the Royal Commission of Aboriginal Peoples, books for children, gallery showings of her art works, and numerous video documentaries that showcase Metis culture and history.

Leah's paintings honor the spiritual strength of Aboriginal women and the sacred feminine. Leah believes that women play a key role in passing on vital knowledge for all of humanity which is deeply reflected in her artistic practice. She believes women are the first teachers to the next generation.

www.leahdorion.ca

Womancraft
PUBLISHING

Life-changing, paradigm-shifting books
by women, for women

Visit us at www.womancraftpublishing.com
where you can sign up to the mailing list and receive samples
of our forthcoming titles before anyone else.

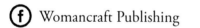 Womancraft Publishing 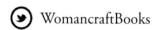 WomancraftBooks

If you have enjoyed this book, please leave a review
on Amazon or Goodreads.

Lightning Source UK Ltd.
Milton Keynes UK
UKOW01f1314190816

281073UK00003B/65/P